From Selma to Sorrow

The Life and Death of Viola Liuzzo

From Selma

to Sorrow

Published by the University of Georgia Press
Athens, Georgia 30602
© 1998 by Mary Stanton
All rights reserved
Designed by Erin Kirk New
Set in 10 on 14 Sabon by BookMatters
Printed and bound by Maple-Vail Book Manufacturing Group

The paper in this book meets the guidelines for permanence and
durability of the Committee on Production Guidelines for Book
Longevity of the Council on Library Resources.

Printed in the United States of America

02 01 00 99 98 c 5 4 3 2 1

Library of Congress Cataloging in Publication Data
Stanton, Mary, 1946–
    From Selma to sorrow : the life and death of Viola Liuzzo / Mary Stanton
        p.   cm.
    Includes bibiographical references (p.   ) and index.
    ISBN 0-8203-2045-5 (alk. paper)
    1. Liuzzo, Viola, 1925–1965.   2. Women civil rights workers—United States—
Biography.   3. Civil rights workers—United States—Biography.   4. Murder—
Alabama—Lowndes County—History—20th century.   5. Selma—Montgomery
Rights March, 1965.   6. Afro-Americans—Civil rights—Alabama—History—
20th century.   7. Alabama—Race relations.   8. Civil rights movements—
Alabama—History—20th century.   I. Title.
E185.98.L58S83   1998
364.1'523'09761465—dc21   98-779

British Library Cataloging in Publication Data available

For my sister, Kathleen McSherry

and my parents

Joseph Francis McSherry

and Mary Lemmon McSherry

We shall not cease from exploration

And the end of all our exploring

Will be to arrive where we started

And know the place for the first time

—T. S. Eliot

Contents

Preface

This is a true story. It all happened. The people I searched for, whether they welcomed me warmly or refused to speak with me, are presented as I found them.

All the incidents that are recounted here—the march, the trials, the reactions to Viola Liuzzo's murder—have been carefully researched and reconstructed through newspaper accounts, television coverage, and the reports of eyewitnesses. When I speculate about the motives of Mrs. Liuzzo's assassins and present an alternative scenario of the events of the night she was murdered, I do so on the basis of the testimony of witnesses who were never interviewed by the FBI and evidence that was ignored, misplaced, or buried. When I enter Mrs. Liuzzo's consciousness, I do so drawing from a profile that her three daughters, her best friend of twenty years, and those who went out of their way to comment on her character—clergy, classmates, teachers, and neighbors—sketched. Important people like Jim Liuzzo, who died before I began my research, have been reconstructed through the comments they made to journalists and through the recollections of family and friends who knew them well.

This is not a work of the imagination. Who could make something like this up?

Acknowledgments

The writer Graham Greene observed that "All writing is therapy. To some extent all writers seek their craft to heal a wound in themselves." This is certainly true of the writing of *From Selma to Sorrow*. I undertook this project when I felt lost, and it opened doors to new worlds that absorbed my imagination and kept my hands busy for four years. My personal demons took me to a place I probably would not have gone except for them, and for that I feel a paradoxical sense of gratitude.

This work could not have been completed without the help of many others. I want to thank my friends Donna Perry and Carolyn Jackson for reading the manuscript through many drafts and offering expert editorial assistance and constant encouragement; Martha Hughes, who told me to dump the idea of a traditional biography and write the story of the story; my sister, Kathleen, for traveling with me, sitting in on many of the interviews, offering invaluable insights and suggestions for revision, putting up with my ugly moods, and never doubting that the book would be published; and my mother for passing along her love of history.

Thank you to those who gave so generously of their time and shared their memories, especially Mrs. Sarah Evans, Tyrone Green, Penny Liuzzo Herrington, Mary Liuzzo Ashley, and Sally Liuzzo Prado. Thanks also to Virginia Durr; Joanne Bland of the National Voting Rights Museum and Institute; Morris Dees of the Southern Poverty Law Center; Sara Bullard and Gale Hill of the center's Teaching Tolerance Program; Rev. Hosea Williams of Feed the Hungry, Atlanta; Mrs. Janice Sayers and Mark Sayers; Rev. Jonathan Sams, rector of St. Stephen's Church, Troy, Michigan; Rev. Meryl Ruoss; Father Timothy Deasy of Christ the King Parish, Daphne, Alabama; Beatrice Siegel, author of *Murder on the*

Highway; Pat Bartkowski, assistant university archivist at Wayne State University; and Stan Modjesky owner of The Book Miser in Baltimore, who can find any book, on any topic, anywhere. Thanks also to "Lynda" and "Bob" of Selma, who gave me a sense of what it was like to witness the historic march and its aftermath, and to "Alice," who wouldn't talk to me and so made me even more curious. Thanks to Jamie Wallace of the Selma Chamber of Commerce and Andy Britton of the Montgomery Area Chamber of Commerce.

Thanks, too, to the staffs of the institutions where I did my research: the Schomburg Center for Research in Black Culture in the New York Public Library; the Museum of Television and Radio in New York; the Ecumenical Library at the Interchurch Center, New York; the Montgomery Public Library; the Alabama Department of Archives and History; the World Heritage Museum, Montgomery; the Alabama State College Library, Montgomery; the Dexter Avenue King Memorial Baptist Church, Montgomery; the National Voting Rights Museum and Institute, Selma; the Selma Public Library; Wayne State University Archives, Detroit; the Detroit Public Library; the Library of Congress; and the Martin Luther King Jr. Center for Non-Violent Social Change, Atlanta.

And finally, thanks to Malcolm Call, senior editor at the University of Georgia Press, whose enthusiasm for the Viola Liuzzo story nearly equaled my own and whose good advice I was smart enough to follow, and to Kristine Blakeslee for her superb and thoughtful editing of the manuscript.

From Selma to Sorrow

Prologue

On March 26, 1965, I was eighteen years old, just out of high school, and working as junior secretary to the director of a brokerage firm in the City. If you lived in the borough of Queens, Manhattan was "the City." It was another world—exciting, electrifying, sometimes frightening. When you "rode over to the City" you left predictability behind.

My job at the brokerage house was to make and serve the boss's coffee, water his plants, relieve the switchboard operator for lunch, and endlessly type orders, make journal entries, and generate receipts.

The senior secretary at the firm, Ethel, typed letters, handled the boss's calendar, and supervised me. Ethel was a lady I truly despised. All my frustrations were focused on that poor woman, who actually *liked* being Rockwell Schaefer's senior secretary. It especially irritated me that Ethel considered her work important. I didn't know exactly what I wanted to do with my life, but I was certain I wasn't grooming myself for Ethel's seat!

In those days a kind of twilight existed between high school and the rest of a young woman's life. We believed, in 1965, that after high school we had only five or six years to "do something." That something might be college, or a job, or travel, but it was time-limited—a last adventure before marriage—unless of course one chose to be an old maid, which no one ever did (at least no one I knew). Singleness was imposed, not sought. After five years, a young woman was expected to settle down and raise a family. Not having your future nailed down by the age of twenty-five was cause for panic.

My father held two jobs to keep food on our table and make the mortgage payments, so college wasn't an option for me. I went to work. My girlfriends were getting engaged with the rapidity of machine-gun fire, but I wasn't ready for marriage. The guy I had been seeing was studying at the police academy. He couldn't wait to graduate and get settled—get *us* settled—and buy a house on Long Island. Every time he talked about it my chest constricted. Were my only options Rockwell Schaefer's office or a split-level ranch? I shuddered at the thought.

At seven o'clock on March 26, 1965, the television was tuned to the *Evening News with Douglas Edwards*, as it had been every night for as long as I could remember. I hadn't been paying much attention to the voting rights march in Alabama that week. I was far more interested in the escalating action in Vietnam and the growing anti-war movement. In February, President Johnson had announced the first bombings of North Vietnam, and early in March he sent 3,500 marines to Da Nang.

The national news in those years was Johnson, the war, and the protesters—and Martin Luther King, Bull Connor, and the Freedom Riders. In Queens, at least in my white, working-class neighborhood, all protesters and demonstrators were lumped together as likely communists. This was America, after all: love it or leave it.

While I quietly supported the anti-war movement because most of the guys I knew were terrified of being drafted, something completely outside my experience was happening in the South. Though Queens was connected by the 59th Street Bridge to the biggest, most sophisticated city in the world, I'd never spoken with a black person until 1960, when I entered high school. Many blacks were in honor classes with me, but I accepted the neighborhood notion that southern blacks were lazy and stupid. "The coloreds down South *like* the way things are," my uncle assured me. "They wouldn't bother going to the polls even if they *could* vote. These marchers don't care about them. They just want to stir up trouble." It never occurred to me to ask: trouble for whom?

I wasn't a political animal in those days. One afternoon when I bought a Joan Baez record (a 33 LP) on my lunch hour Ethel asked if I didn't think Joan was "a little pink." I smiled noncommittally, not wanting to give Ethel the satisfaction of knowing I had no idea what she was talking about.

All through high school I'd followed the civil rights movement on television. I had some sympathy but no real social conscience. The lunch counter sit-ins and the freedom rides of 1961 and 1962 caught my attention but not my conservative imagination. In 1963, when I was a junior, I'd watched black teens in Birmingham get hit with the spray of fire hoses and bitten by police dogs as my father asked, "How much more freedom do these people want?"

"What's happening to this country?" my mother sighed as the station wagon belonging to three missing civil rights workers was dragged from Bogue Chitto Swamp in Mississippi the summer I graduated from high school—Freedom Summer, 1964. That same summer Harlem exploded in riots. As reports of looting and violence filled the seven o'clock news, from Flushing to Howard Beach, Corona to Bayside, the white working-class citizens of Queens felt justified in their long-held belief that "the Negroes were going too far."

Douglas Edwards opened his *Evening News* with the report that Viola Gregg Liuzzo, a housewife and mother of five from Detroit, Michigan, had been murdered near Montgomery a few hours after the voting rights march ended. Mrs. Liuzzo was thirty-nine years old. She was one of twenty-five thousand demonstrators who traveled from Selma to Montgomery to deliver a petition to Governor George Wallace demanding protection for blacks as they tried to register to vote. A sniper's bullet killed her on the highway as she and a young black male volunteer drove to Montgomery to pick up marchers waiting to return to Selma. "Mrs. Liuzzo's death follows by just two weeks the Alabama state troopers' beating and tear gassing of voting rights demonstrators on the Edmund Pettus Bridge in Selma," Edwards reported. I dried my hands and hurried into the living room to hear the rest.

The cameras cut to a grim-faced President Johnson. "Mrs. Liuzzo went to Alabama to serve the struggle for justice. She was murdered by the enemies of justice who for decades have used the rope and the gun, the tar and the feathers to terrorize their neighbors." Suddenly a picture of Mrs. Liuzzo flashed across the screen. She looked younger than thirty-nine— pretty, with light, curly, shoulder-length hair and intense eyes. "They struck at night as they generally do, for their purposes cannot stand the light of day," the president continued, and he directed the FBI to work around the clock to find her murderers.

Reactions in my house were heated. What was she doing down there, a woman like that, old enough to know better? Why would a woman with five children go to Selma? Was she crazy? Where was her husband? Couldn't he stop her?

Soon the entire nation was buzzing. Viola Liuzzo would become the most controversial of the civil rights martyrs.

I was glued to the television set for the next few evenings, following her story. I bought the *Herald Tribune* every morning on my way to work and the *New York Post* every afternoon on the way home. Who was this woman? Where did she get the courage to go to Alabama alone? I didn't know *any* women who would do that. Mrs. Liuzzo's independence impressed me far more than her civil rights commitment. On one hand, I was mesmerized by her courage, on the other, horrified by what the press and almost everybody around me was saying about her. She was accused of abandoning her family, of having an affair with a black teenager, and of using drugs.

The media took only days to completely transform Viola Liuzzo from a murder victim to an outside agitator and a symbol of reckless female defiance. The hatred with which people attacked her—white people, especially white women—frightened me. Their anger at her seemed out of proportion to what she had done. And what had she done, really? She had gone on a freedom march. Thousands of other people—lawyers, students, clergymen, nuns, and social workers—were doing that all the time. And she had gotten herself killed. Why was everybody so angry?

I remembered when the bodies of the three civil rights workers murdered in Mississippi—Andrew Goodman, James Chaney, and Michael Schwerner—were found the summer before. I had heard some grousing about their having no business going to Mississippi, but that criticism paled next to the hatred hurled at Mrs. Liuzzo. A year later those young men were heroes. It was already apparent that this was not going to be Mrs. Liuzzo's fate.

Life-changing events aren't always big ones. That newscast in 1965 began what I look back on as a subtle shift in my thinking. A window opened. At eighteen it felt to me as if my life was already winding down, and I didn't know what to do about it. I knew I didn't want to be a secretary or a wife, but there were few female role models to show me there was anything more. Yet that night I heard about a woman who had thrown off middle-class constraints for something she believed in—a white woman, middle-aged, from Detroit, from a neighborhood like mine, a woman with five kids, like Mrs. McDermott next door, or Mrs. Esposito, or Mrs. Cleary across the street. Mrs. Liuzzo was only a few years younger than my own mother.

For the next thirty years, as American society underwent a series of radical changes, I would find myself remembering this woman, thinking about the ambivalent culture that produced and then condemned her, and about the courage it must have taken for her to simply get in her car and go. It was her sense of personal freedom I continued to admire, not her commitment to social justice. That would come later. In 1965 Mrs. Liuzzo gave me hope that a woman could hold on to a personal identity. That husband and children did not have to absorb a woman's life totally. That she could keep something for herself.

In the fall of 1966 I registered for night classes at Queens College. Four years and forty-eight credits later I met my husband there. He was also a night student and in the process of transferring to Union College in the heart of Appalachian Kentucky. Tom was going to finish his degree in philosophy at the small Methodist school in the mountains, and he wanted me to go with him. I was in love and convinced that Tom and I could create a marriage that would allow each of us room to grow. I had never seen such a union, but I had a vision of what it might be like. Two hours after the minister pronounced us man and wife we headed south. I was twenty-four and had never been away from the borough of Queens overnight. An electrifying culture shock awaited me.

I thought southeastern Kentucky was the wildest, most wonderful place on earth. Rich green hills rolled gently over the landscape, and the trees, at the height of their September foliage, looked like explosions of colored popcorn. We moved into a trailer camp on Walker Park Road, just out-

side Barbourville, where Union College was located. From our back door
I could see the Cumberland River flowing less than half a mile away.

We were in Knox County, one of the poorest counties in the nation. An
outpost in the War on Poverty, Knox was a mecca for social workers and
students of social work in 1970. It also attracted hordes of Office of
Economic Opportunity workers and Vista Volunteers. All were sure they
held at least part of the solution to the puzzle of Appalachian poverty.

Barbourville is the county seat of Knox. In 1970, downtown Barbourville was four square blocks that looked like the set of *Gunsmoke*. The
stores had wooden front porches with wooden awnings held up by long
posts. Whatever you needed could be found on the Court Square—in
Begley's Drugs, Hobbs Variety, Knox County Supply, or the J & B Cafeteria. For special occasions Hampton and Nau carried Botany 500 suits
and Arrow shirts, and Miller Yancey could order you the latest in living
room or bedroom furniture. If it wasn't on Court Square, you simply
didn't need it.

Knox County was a patchwork of dusty rutted roads dotted with small
homes with sagging porches and rusted washing machines in the front
yards. Occasionally a large wooden frame house with a wraparound
porch and long narrow windows would appear. Wooden churches were
nestled in the hills and signs along Highway 25E reminded you to START
YOUR DAY WITH JESUS.

In the food stores—the IGA and Piggly Wiggly—pads of blank checks
from the First National Bank of Barbourville and the Union National
Bank sat on the counter. After your order was rung up you simply ripped
off a check and filled it out. The cashier trusted that residents and students alike would have enough cash in their accounts to cover the checks.

I spent my first year soaking up the atmosphere, absorbing what for
me was high adventure. I read the *Mountain Eagle*, our local paper, faith-
fully, learned to eat grilled honey buns for breakfast, and visited exotic
places like Cumberland Falls, Stinkin' Creek, Lend-a-Hand, Flat Lick,
Cumberland Gap, and a town called Versailles (pronounced Ver-Sales)
where you could get a big plate of biscuits and grease for fifty cents.

In the spring, when Barbourville flooded, I stood on the flood wall
snapping pictures, and I wrote long letters home describing this strange

and wonderful place. Each morning we woke to the *Hopper Funeral Home Hour*. Walter C. Hopper Jr. provided a list of who he was laying out that day—what their accomplishments had been and who they were leaving behind. Mr. Hopper would pause reverently between epitaphs to play an appropriate musical selection or a favorite hymn.

Knox was a dry county, so our parties had the extra edge of being illicit. Although there were only four county police officers, they were well able to control fifteen hundred college kids—mostly northerners—who tried to skirt the liquor laws. Ably supervised by Chief Dogtail Lawson, a middle-aged man with one eye, a sunken chest, and a bad limp, they let few of us escape. I spent one night in jail with a student from Cincinnati who cried for twenty-four hours because she was convinced we would be raped before morning. When morning came, our honor intact, we found ourselves standing before Mayor Samson Knuckles to negotiate bail.

The community was far more interesting than the college. On campus, the girls' dorm, Pfeiffer Hall, had been christened Heifer Stall by the male student body. Women avoided it after their freshman year and moved into town. Union College offered a disappointing array of distractions including sororities and fraternities; academic, sports, and arts organizations; the Campus Crusade for Christ; the United Methodist Student Movement; and the notorious PhT (putting hubby through). It was pretty tame for 1970.

By contrast, the town of Barbourville was full of surprises: food was cheap, housing was cheap, and we made our own entertainment. The Magic Theatre, our only movie house, shared its projector with Messer's Drive-In. October to April we sat inside, and in the spring and summer we drove in—rain or shine. *Thunder Road*, the granddaddy of car-chase films, seemed to be all they ever featured. *Thunder Road* starred Elvis-eyed Robert Mitchum as Lucas Doolan, tough guy extraordinaire, who left an assortment of revenue agents, troopers, and snarling bad guys in his hundred-mile-per-hour dust along the two-lane blacktop of Harlan County. We had to travel up to Corbin if we wanted to see a real movie, and all the way to Jellico, Tennessee, if we wanted a "sit-down" drink. It was a goof, a hoot—all in all, a great time for a kid from Queens.

By my second year, however, the novelty of living in "hillbilly heaven" began to wear thin. By then I knew many of the townspeople. We had moved to an apartment in town, and I shopped in the stores with them, used the same laundromat, and stood in the same line at the Tastee Freeze. They were no longer cartoon characters but real people whose living conditions weren't very funny. I drove into the hills—the "hollers"—with some of the social work students and saw teenagers who had never been to school, old men crippled by black lung from years of working in poorly ventilated coal mines, children who were hungry and tired, and mothers who looked fifty but hadn't passed their twenty-fifth birthday.

I learned that what little the mountain people could extract from their land had been taken from them through "long form deeds." These were documents signed by their parents or grandparents selling off the mineral rights to their land for fifty cents an acre. Strip mining was in its heyday. Coal companies bought up these mineral rights, then brought in heavy equipment and literally removed the land in strips, layer by layer, to get to the coal. Once the land was stripped, it was useless for any other purpose.

To strip mine it is necessary to remove the earth from around a coal seam with a bulldozer, follow the seam to its end, and scoop up the coal, which leaves a big gash in the mountain. Then augers—huge rotating drill bits up to seven feet in diameter—bore into what is left of the mountain to bring out the remainder of the coal. In the process, sulfur—a by-product of coal—is released. When sulfur runs down a mountain into the streams it creates a solution of sulfuric acid that kills fish and anything else living in the water. In 1971 twelve thousand acres were strip mined in Kentucky.

Strip mining also eliminates the need for coal miners. Strip mining operations use machines to do their work, not men. As a result, unemployment, debt, and depression grew in epidemic proportions in Appalachia. I had never seen such wrenching poverty. Walls of listing shacks were held together with newspaper; homemade jam and biscuits was a meal; and there was no indoor plumbing.

While there was nothing romantic about the life these Kentuckians lived, there were so many things that were admirable about them. Trapped in a depressed land with little hope of economic relief, they seldom gave in to despair. There was an acceptance, beyond fatalism, especially among the elderly, that even limited life is sweet. Each newborn child was celebrated as a gift in lives that had few other causes for celebration. They loved the Kentucky mountains and many refused to leave even when government workers offered to relocate them. Their grown sons who left to get jobs to support their families often migrated only as far as Cincinnati or Dayton and returned home nearly every weekend.

"Resilient," one of the social workers told me, "that's what these folks are." I nodded, knowing it would take a whole lot less to make me fold.

Kentucky, birthplace of both Abraham Lincoln and Jefferson Davis, was where my social consciousness surfaced. It would have been impossible not to react to the wealth of the land and the poverty of its people. "The coal companies took our land, our trees, and our health," an elderly man told me. I began volunteering—answering phones, stuffing envelopes, typing letters for an organization called Mountain People's Rights, an information clearinghouse for state and federal entitlement programs.

Our efforts were not appreciated by the local power structure—legislators, lawyers, coal, lumber, and construction company executives—and even some of Union College's faculty. The fact that so many northern students were involved in the Vista and Appalachian Volunteer programs, as well as Mountain People's Rights, led to a cynical notion among these men that "this too shall pass."

"It was the blacks just a few years ago," they would snicker. "And now that the militants have kicked the whites out of their organizations, these kids are just looking to the Appalachian mountains for their next adventure."

After we graduated in 1973 Tom and I moved to the Pacific Northwest. I had landed a teaching fellowship in the English department at the University of Idaho at Moscow. Student housing was tight in Moscow, but we found a huge, cheap apartment in Pullman, Washington, seven miles across the border. The apartment complex was built on a steep hill overlooking Pullman. We couldn't believe our good fortune—until it snowed. Snowflakes began on Halloween night and fell steadily until Easter morning. We needed mountain climbing skills to get to and from our apartment every day and became intimate with the terms *black ice* and *snowblind*. The upside was that Washington allowed students to apply for food stamps, while Idaho didn't.

A year in the arctic circle was my limit, so I applied to Queens College's English department to finish my graduate degree, and we headed back east. We settled in New Jersey, where I became a commuter student and taught freshman English for a few years before working my way into a long career in personnel and labor relations. By then the South seemed far behind me.

From time to time over the years, however, my thoughts drifted back to the illusive Mrs. Liuzzo, whose death had had such a profound effect on me. I wondered why her name was never mentioned in the 1970s as the feminist movement grew stronger and more organized. When Christa McAuliffe, the teacher in space, was killed in the *Challenger* disaster of 1986 and rumblings began about a mother's right to leave her children to undertake a dangerous mission, I remembered Mrs. Liuzzo. Criticism of McAuliffe was mild compared to the hatred that had been hurled at Mrs. Liuzzo, but the old issue was clearly still around.

I asked Tom if he remembered the Liuzzo murder in 1965—he would have been in his late teens too.

"Well, I remember the march—vaguely," he replied.

"But the murder, don't you remember the murder—it happened the last night?"

"No," he said. "I honestly don't."

"But everybody talked about it for weeks, *everybody* was saying how she was crazy for going down there."

"Mary, I just don't remember."

Slowly we built careers. We worked hard, played hard, and waited for the right time to have children. But there was always another trip to make, always another degree to work on, an interest to follow, or one more adventure before we settled down. The right time never seemed to come; then we had less time for each other and separated in 1993.

I was single again after being married longer than I had been alive before my wedding day. We sold our house, Tom went to Florida, and I moved into the City. I was working as vice president for human resources at one of the largest social services agencies in the country, a job I'd had for nearly ten years. Within six months of my separation, however, I bumped up against the glass ceiling at the agency, then predictably plateaued. I was nothing if not trendy—moving at warp speed in the fast lane of marital and career disasters.

My work began to lose its zip (or I began to lose mine), and as I found myself dreaming about a mid-life career change I realized that what I really wanted to do was carve out time to write—an old dream from my school days.

For my forty-seventh birthday—two months after my marriage broke up—my best friend, Carol, gave me a biography of Beryl Markham, the first female pilot to cross the Atlantic from east to west. Carol's gift was intentionally symbolic. It was her attempt to inspire me out of my misery. But I wasn't budging. My life seemed stretched out before me like some great ocean, and there were days when just getting out of bed and traveling to work felt like a trans-Atlantic flight in bad weather. Neither of us could have anticipated how life-changing that gift would actually be.

Days later, laying across my just-delivered couch in my otherwise bare studio apartment, feeling very self-righteous and sorry for myself, I opened Mary Lovell's *Straight on Till Morning*. In the prologue Lovell recounts learning about Beryl Markham when her director husband made a reference to her on the movie set of *Out of Africa* in the mid-1980s. Markham had been a friend of Karen Blixen (Isak Dinesen) and Denys Finch Hadden.

After some quick-and-dirty research Lovell became fascinated with Markham. "I was well into work on another book when this happened," Lovell wrote, "and so my agent was surprised when I called and told him I was abandoning it to write a biography of Beryl Markham. 'Who is Beryl Markham?' he asked. I replied defensively, not yet ready to share Beryl with anyone else. 'I don't know yet. But I just know I've got to write about her.'"

Suddenly I knew what, or rather who, I was going to write about! I was ready for my own adventure. In April of 1994 I told my boss I was taking two weeks' vacation. I would spend the first week researching newspaper accounts of the Liuzzo murder to get the background I would need for a trip to Montgomery, Alabama, where it all began. I wanted to understand just what my long connection to Mrs. Liuzzo was all about—why I never forgot her. My job was clearly winding down, and I knew I would soon become just one more downsized worker of the 1990s. My twenty-three-year marriage was history, and I was looking fifty right in the irises. How much longer was I going to wait? For some reason this woman's spirit had traveled with me for thirty years, surfacing periodically through young adulthood, college, career, marriage, and divorce, and now into middle age. Why? What was she to me? I booked a flight to Montgomery and started on my journey to find Viola Liuzzo.

1 The Black Belt

The past is a foreign country.
They do things differently there.
—L. P. Hartley

As the tiny twin-engine commuter plane approaches Dannelly Field, Montgomery's sleepy airport, I wonder for the first of many times if maybe I'm going crazy. As the plane dips, shudders, and rattles its way from Raleigh-Durham, I have both the time and the inclination to consider the state of my sanity. *Who does this? Who takes off on a cold trail more than thirty years old?*

There's precious little information available about Viola Liuzzo's life, and no biography has ever been written for an adult audience. That generally means there isn't a story. And yet. . . .

When I tell my friend Carol I'm going south she is horrified. "Are you *crazy?* Do you think the Klan wouldn't kill you too? Why do you want to go messing around down there? Come with me to Acapulco."

Instead, I fill a suitcase with copied newspaper clippings, three legal pads of notes, and a change of clothes, and with only one solid lead I call the Delta ticket agent. My lead is Sara Bullard of Montgomery's Southern Poverty Law Center, the organization that sponsored construction of the Civil Rights Memorial. I wrote to Sara asking for help locating the surviving members of the Liuzzo family.

As the Alabama landscape rises to meet me, I marvel at my nerve. *What makes me think the Liuzzos are going be glad to hear from somebody who wants to write about their mother? What right do I have to invade their privacy? Will they tell me to get lost?*

The aerial view of the Montgomery countryside is breathtaking. The land is lush, with soft velvet hills carved out by the lazy curve of the Alabama River. As we approach the airfield, the sun shines brilliantly, peacefully. It is hard to imagine anything horrible happening here.

Twenty minutes later I am checking into the Madison, a sprawling, comfortable, downtown hotel with every one of its rooms either over-looking or opening onto a large atrium/cocktail lounge. From my window facing the street I can see a big bronze statue of Hank Williams in a small garden. Hank is frozen in time—a little man holding a too-big guitar, wearing a too-big hat, singing for the hometown folk who adore him.

The Madison sits between a busy business district and a state government office complex that slams up tight after six every evening and shuts down completely on weekends. When I ask for information about places to go for dinner I get directions to a strip of McDonald's, Domino's Pizza, KFC, and Shoney's Big Boy. I learn to eat big lunches.

For three of my five days in Montgomery I share the Madison with a contingent of Future Homemakers of America attending their annual convention at the civic center. I didn't think girls joined organizations like that anymore. I wonder if Future Homemaking is enjoying some kind of a revival.

Montgomery is hot even in April. I am told it is hot all the time. But then, the city has always generated heat—it is the birthplace of both the Confederacy and the civil rights movement.

Jefferson Davis took his presidential oath on the very spot where the Alabama state capitol stands today. You can tour the White House of the Confederacy on Washington Avenue, two blocks away. A block past the capitol, in the opposite direction, is the Dexter Avenue King Memorial Baptist Church, an old red-brick building with a white wooden "welcoming arms" staircase leading to the sanctuary. Martin Luther King Jr. was pastor there from 1954 to 1960, and it was from the Dexter Avenue pulpit that he raised the spirits of Montgomery's black community during their year-long bus boycott.

On December 5, 1955, Mrs. Rosa Parks, a tailor's assistant at a Montgomery department store, boarded the Cleveland Avenue bus at Court Square on her way home. When the white section of the bus filled, the driver asked Mrs. Parks, a black woman, to get up so a white man could sit down. Mrs. Parks had been waiting for such an opportunity. She had agreed to serve as a test case for the NAACP's legal division, who wanted to appeal the constitutionality of the city's bus segregation ordinance in federal court. She refused to give up her seat. When the bus driver threatened to call the police, she told him to go ahead. Mrs. Parks was booked for violating the bus ordinance and jailed until the NAACP could arrange bail.

Montgomery's black leadership met in the basement of the Dexter Church and drafted a plan for a boycott of the city busses. The image of Mrs. Parks, a hard-working, middle-aged woman humiliated by the segregation ordinance, galvanized a movement virtually overnight. The new pastor, twenty-six-year-old Martin Luther King Jr., was elected president of the Montgomery Improvement Association, and he directed the boycott from the office of his church.

Dr. King told his congregation at the first mass meeting, "We are here this evening to say to those who have mistreated us so long that we are tired—tired of being segregated and humiliated: tired of being kicked about by the brutal feet of oppression. For many years we have shown amazing patience. . . . But we come here tonight to be saved from that patience that makes us patient with anything less than freedom and justice."[1]

Mrs. Parks's case was heard by federal judge Frank Johnson, who declared the city bus ordinance unconstitutional. That decision was later upheld by the U.S. Supreme Court.

In the basement of the King Memorial Church an entire wall is covered in mural, part of a restoration project begun in 1979. One panel depicts scenes from Dr. King's journey from Montgomery to his assassination in Memphis. A second panel bears a likeness of Jimmy Lee Jackson, killed during a 1965 voter registration demonstration in Marion, Alabama, beside the portraits of Addie Mae Collins, Carol Robertson, Cynthia Wesley, and Denise McNair—four black children killed Sunday, September 15, 1963, when the Sixteenth Street Baptist Church in Birmingham was bombed. Denise, twelve, played the piano; Addie Mae, fourteen, wrote poetry. Both were members of the youth choir, and both wanted to be teachers. Cynthia and Carol, both eighth graders, were excited about attending Birmingham's first integrated high school in the fall. They served on the Youth Usher Board and were getting ready to take part in the Youth Day service. All had just completed a Sunday school lesson, and their text, Matthew 5:43–44, was still written on the chalkboard: "You have heard that it hath been said, Thou shalt love thy neighbor, and hate thine enemy. But I say unto you, love your enemies, bless them that curse you, do good to them that hate you, and pray for them which despitefully use you and persecute you." Beside the girls are James Chaney, Michael Schwerner, and Andrew Goodman, murdered during the 1964 Freedom Summer in Philadelphia, Mississippi. Out of the center of these eight figures an artist's rendering of the pale face of Viola Liuzzo stares hauntingly.

One block west and another south, at the corner of Washington Avenue and Hull Street, the Civil Rights Memorial stands. Dedicated in 1989, it commemorates forty lives lost during the movement. On a circular black granite table the forty names are braided in gold block letters through a time line beginning with the Supreme Court's 1954 *Brown vs. Board of Education* decision declaring segregation of public schools unconstitutional and ending with the death of Dr. Martin Luther King Jr. The names are of thirty-five males—twenty-eight black, seven white—and five females. The names of the four teens killed in the church bombing cluster together near the name of the only white woman: Viola Gregg Liuzzo. Between the first and last entry, space has been left to symbolize the names that have been forgotten. Water flows from the center of the table, running continuously over the time line. It has a soothing effect. Once the water is touched, however, a dramatic ripple begins. One touch, one action, one life, changes everything.

Architect Maya Lin, who also designed the Vietnam Veterans' Memorial in Washington, said that she chose the images of a circle, which heals, and water, which soothes, to remember the civil rights movement. "This is not a monument to suffering," she says. "It is a memorial to hope." Behind the water table, engraved in a curved black granite wall is a verse of scripture from the Book of Amos that Dr. King often quoted: "We will not be satisfied . . . until justice rolls down like water and righteousness like a mighty stream."

My eyes fill as I touch the names and see my face reflected back in the wet granite. Anger surges through me as I read, "killed in a dispute over whites only rest room . . . slain by nightriders . . . beaten in his jail cell and lynched . . . killed in the bombing of a car, a home, a church . . . shot by police . . . shot by a state legislator . . . shot by a deputy sheriff. . . ."

On the day the memorial was dedicated, several Georgia Klansmen tried unsuccessfully to get a permit to stage a protest demonstration across the street. Alabama's own governor, Guy Hunt, declined an invitation to attend the opening ceremonies. When asked why, he said it was important that he be in church that Sunday morning.[2]

Thomas Moore, brother of honoree Charles Eddie Moore, who had been murdered by the Klan along with his friend, Henry Dee, did attend. Thomas Moore was sure that his brother had been forgotten, but both Charles's name and the name of Henry Hezekiah Dee are carved into the memorial. "It was a dead issue," Thomas Moore said. "We were poor people. We didn't have a dream like this. And now, it's a reality. . . . Finally, after twenty-five years he's somebody out there with Medgar Evers and Martin Luther King. He's just as big as they are."

"When I first saw the memorial it took my breath away," said Karen Reeb, daughter of the Reverend James Reeb, who was beaten to death in Selma two weeks before Viola Liuzzo was murdered. Her sister, Ann Reeb, nodded. "It just eases the emptiness in my heart."[3]

I ran my fingers over Viola Liuzzo's name. She would be sixty-nine years old. She has a dozen grandchildren she never saw.

The Civil Rights Memorial is built on the plaza of the Southern Poverty Law Center, founded in 1971 by lawyer-activist Morris Dees. Dees petitioned to sponsor the memorial in 1987 after his center made a whopping $750,000 profit on the sale of a tract of land in downtown Montgomery. As a very young man, Dees had served as part-time pastor for a Baptist congregation in rural Alabama. When the Sixteenth Street Baptist Church was bombed he asked his congregation to pray for the families of the murdered children and to donate money to help rebuild their church. Most of the members walked out. At that point Dees left the ministry to study law. At the dedication of the Civil Rights Memorial he said, "Each name here is a history lesson, and we are saying don't just think of the deaths, but think of a movement of ordinary people who just got tired of injustice."[4]

Since its founding, the Southern Poverty Law Center has brought lawsuits that forced the Alabama Department of Public Safety to hire black state troopers, compelled the reapportionment of the state legislature along one-person-one-vote lines, stopped the involuntary sterilization of young black females by a prominent white Montgomery physician, and accessed governmental services for many poor black families in rural Alabama.

The center also serves as headquarters for Klanwatch, a subsidiary that has been monitoring the activities of the United Klans of America and other hate groups since 1979. The center's headquarters was firebombed in 1983 by Klansmen who tried to destroy the evidence Klanwatch had accumulated against them in support of a murder indictment.

On just three square blocks of downtown Montgomery, landmarks commemorating 150 years of southern history—good and bad—bake together in the blazing sun.

I enter the center and ask to see Sara Bullard, historian, writer, and director of the Teaching Tolerance program. I have spoken with Sara several times by phone. She has the addresses of the Liuzzo family members and friends who came to the dedication of the Civil Rights Memorial, and she agreed to forward letters to them for me.

Sara is an energetic young woman—shy, but intense. "There's not much in the history books about Viola Liuzzo," she agrees. "A line here, a paragraph there, but nothing substantial." Sara has written *Free at Last*, a book that provides background material on each person honored at the memorial. Viola Liuzzo's story takes up two pages in her book. *Free at Last* and Beatrice Siegel's *Murder on the Highway*, published in 1993 and written for young-adult readers, are the only works that have treated Mrs. Liuzzo's life in any detail since the publication of Jack Mendelsohn's *The Martyrs* in 1966.

I give Sara ten copies of the two-page letter I have agonized over for weeks. I am still not sure it says all I want it to, but I can't think about editing it one more time.

"Have you spoken with Virginia Durr?" Sara asks.

"No. Who is she?"

"Someone you should talk to—Cliff Durr's widow. Ever hear of him?"

I shake my head.

"The Durrs were white civil rights activists here in Montgomery when it was *really* risky—back in the fifties. Cliff was one of the lawyers on the Rosa Parks case. He put up her bond when she got arrested."

"Where can I find her?"

"In the phone book," Sara smiles. "Oh, and be sure to drive out and see the Liuzzo Marker, too."

"There's a marker? Here in Montgomery?"

"No," she laughs. "Only Jeff Davis and Hank Williams have markers *here*. It's out on the highway—right at the site of the murder."

"Really?"

She nods. "As you drive towards Selma it's about twenty miles in—you can only see it heading west, and there aren't any signs. But you'll spot it on the hill before you come to it—it looks like a big gravestone. Take the first turn-around after you see it and walk up the hill."

"Who built it?" I ask.

"The women of the SCLC—the Southern Christian Leadership Conference. Their third try, I believe. The markers keep getting knocked over. The first one was smashed up with a sledge hammer."

I shake my head. "I'll look for it. Thanks."

"Good luck. Come back and see us again," she says.

"I will."

Virginia Durr—Mrs. Clifford Durr—is not only in the phone book, she answers her own phone. She says she is delighted that I am writing a book about Viola Liuzzo. Yes, certainly she remembers the murder on Highway 80, but she never met Mrs. Liuzzo. My heart sinks. Can I come to see her? Why yes, yes of course. "Tomorrow afternoon," she tells me. "I'm always out on my porch between two and four, and I'd be glad to have a talk with you. Have you read my book?" she asks.

"No." I admit I haven't.

"Well, it's called *Outside the Magic Circle* and I've written all about my life and Cliff's. Back in the forties I worked with a group that was trying to get the poll tax abolished, you know. This was while Cliff was FCC commissioner in Franklin Roosevelt's administration. Well, it's a long story," she laughs, "everybody down here was sure we were communists. Anyway, I'll look out for you tomorrow."

I hunt up a bookstore and locate a copy of *Outside the Magic Circle*. Back at the hotel I find a quiet table in the atrium, order a pot of coffee, and quickly thumb through the index. It's there! *Liuzzo, Viola, p. 326.* "All these people were at our house the night Mrs. Viola Liuzzo was killed," I read. "John Brandon got a call from someone on the *San Francisco Chronicle* who told him a white woman had been killed over near Lowndesboro. . . . She had been ferrying back some of the marchers, and she was coming to get another load when she was killed. A carload of people pulled up beside the car she was driving and fired into the car and shot her."

That's it? Seven lines? And it doesn't say anything! Did I really expect Mrs. Durr would have known her? I suppose I did. I read on: "I used to think it was funny that my husband Cliff and I were later accused of trying to overthrow the government by force and violence just because we were trying to get voting rights for people.[5] Here was my grandfather, who spent four years trying to overthrow the government by force, who fought in the Confederate cavalry, and yet he was elected to Congress and became a very honored man and was head of the Shiloh Cemetery. I've often thought how strange it was that those who actually did try to overthrow the government by force and violence became great honored figures in the South, whereas we, their grandchildren, were reviled because we were trying to get the vote. The South is a peculiar place."

At two o'clock the following afternoon Mrs. Durr is sitting on the front porch of a rambling old house on Cloverdale Road, ten minutes from downtown Montgomery. All the houses on the cool, shaded street are huge, and most have porches wrapped around at least two sides. Cloverdale Road is quiet and empty. It could be 1944 or 1964 just as easily as today. There is a kind of musty elegance in this steamy, well-kempt neighborhood. When she tells me Zelda Fitzgerald lived just a few blocks away, I have no problem visualizing Zelda on a porch just like the Durrs' in a gauzy dress and sexy hat, torturing poor Scott.

Mrs. Durr walks to the edge of her porch. She is tall and elegant with long, snow-white hair pulled up and back into a cross between a French knot and a bun. As I come up the path she calls, "Welcome, welcome." We shake hands and she tells me to "pull up a chair, make yourself comfortable."[6]

Mrs. Durr is dressed as if she might be going to a meeting, or a card party—casual but classy. She is wearing an expensive-looking yellow cotton shirtwaist dress and a single strand of pearls. She has large, strong features, big teeth, and a warm, winning smile that spreads across her face easily and often. Her speech is clear, firm, and energetic, and her voice has the lilt of a much younger woman's. Only her eyes give her away. They have that watery opaque look of advancing age.

Who is it she reminds me of? As we make small talk about the heat, my trip, how I like Montgomery, and if I want some lemonade, I find myself staring at her. Have we met before?

I start to ask her questions from my notes, but Mrs. Durr knows exactly what she wants to tell me, so I sit back and wait my turn. She says she spent many years doing volunteer work in Washington. In 1938 she represented the Women's Division of the Democratic National Committee at the first meeting of the Southern Conference for Human Welfare in Birmingham. There she met Mary McLeod Bethune, founder of the National Council of Negro Women. Mrs. Bethune traveled to the Birmingham conference as part of Eleanor Roosevelt's entourage.

"The conference was a gathering of labor people, New Dealers, and social activists," Mrs. Durr tells me. "We were putting together a coalition to fight for the abolishment of the poll tax. That tax kept blacks, poor whites, and women from voting. We were also advocates of a livable wage, and so the unions were natural allies. Of course we all got labeled communists. Bull Connor was the sheriff of Birmingham even back then. He wanted to shut our conference down because we were integrated. The only reason he didn't was because he knew he couldn't get away with arresting the First Lady." Her eyes dance as she remembers.

When she takes a breath I ask what she recalls about the voting rights march in 1965, and she shakes her head. "People in Montgomery acted as if we were being invaded by a foreign power."

"And Mrs. Liuzzo?"

"Well, the talk was that Mrs. Liuzzo should have stayed home. And of course the gossip was terrible. People I respected—professional people—acted very badly. They said she should have known better than to drive around with a black man in the front seat of her car—that she was just asking for trouble. Families were split apart over civil rights in those days. You were either for or against the Southern Way. It was very hard to be a native and fight tradition. Cliff and I were called traitors. People like Mrs. Liuzzo could help, but she could always go home; we had to live with our decisions." She waves her hand as if to dismiss a thought and I'm struck by the familiarity of that gesture. *Who is it* that she looks like, sounds like?

I ask if she knew that Mrs. Liuzzo was raised in the South.

"No," she says, "I didn't know that. That's actually very interesting—"

Suddenly a car pulls into the driveway. Four people get out with bags and boxes and big smiles. "Oh, it's the Mayfairs," she tells me.

The Mayfairs sprawl onto the porch, everybody talking at once. A teenage boy and girl take the boxes and bags inside, while their parents drop onto the rocker and porch swing. From what I can gather they are on their way to North Carolina for a week's vacation. Dr. Mayfair teaches at a local university.

"We just brought over a few things we thought you might need while we're gone. Lord, my refrigerator was full up! I don't know what I was thinking stocking like that when we were going away, so I just had Terry clear it out and haul it over here. That's all right, isn't it Virginia?" Mrs. Mayfair asks without taking a breath.

"Much appreciated," Mrs. Durr smiles. "Since I stopped driving I can't keep mine filled. I'm much obliged."

They chat about their neighbors, the news, the heat, and they draw me into the conversation as if I had known them and the people they are talking about all my life. Mrs. Durr tells Dr. Mayfair about my book.

"Liuzzo? Oh, yes. I remember. Didn't her boy come back—in '82 or

'83 when they were campaigning to renew the Voting Rights Act—didn't he come back for the march, Virginia?"

"That's right!" she says, her eyes flashing. "There was a memorial march from Selma about ten years ago, and the Liuzzo boy led it along with Joe Lowery of the SCLC."

The professor chuckles. "Remember how those damn fools went down Dexter Avenue the night before and put dynamite in all the manholes?"

"Yes," she nods. "They were the same bunch that burned Morris Dees's office."

"Anybody get hurt?" I ask.

"No. One of them got cold feet and called the police—nice to know conscience wills out sometimes—and all the dynamite got collected before the marchers got to Montgomery."

The professor slaps his knee. "Well Virginia, wish us well, we've got to get on the road." They all give her a kiss, climb into the car, and wave as they back down the driveway.

I'm desperate to pull her back to my subject. "Mrs. Durr, you said that people like Mrs. Liuzzo and other people who came south could help. *How* did they help?"

"Well, they gave us the strength of numbers. They showed us we weren't alone, but you know, some of them were very naive and awfully arrogant."

"In what way?"

"Look, if you want to write about the South you need to appreciate how conflicted we were thirty years ago—some still are. I don't think many of us accepted—on a conscious level, anyway—our ambivalence about this way of life we were always defending. I mean, I grew up with a black mammy. I sat on her lap and cried out all my troubles to her, but I wouldn't sit next to her children on a bus, or in a restaurant, or even in church. What sense did that make?

"My father was a Presbyterian minister, and I was taught to accept things as they were—and they were *exactly* as they were supposed to be. I didn't start questioning anything about southern life until I was a grown woman."

"What happened?" I ask.

"I went up north to Wellesley College for a year when I was eighteen. Students got table assignments for breakfast and dinner in those days. When a black girl was assigned to my table I went straight to my adviser to get my assignment changed. She refused to do it. She told me that was my table for the rest of the term, and if I didn't like it I could just go home. I told her my father would be very angry if he knew I was eating with a Negro, and she said that wasn't her problem. When she asked why I felt it was such a terrible thing, I couldn't answer. I didn't *have* an answer. I said it's something we just *didn't do,* and she looked at me like I'd gone crazy."

I laugh, and she smiles back.

"That was the very first time my attitudes had ever been considered foolish by somebody, and it got me thinking. I realized that it wasn't *eating* with blacks I was afraid of, but my father's reaction if he knew I'd done it. See, I was raised to believe I was pretty hot stuff—that I was just the kind of white southern woman that the men of the Confederacy had died for. Anyway, that adviser started me thinking that it was probably time I figured things out for myself. So I went back to my table."

I sip my lemonade and watch her, completely absorbed in her story. Could she, I wonder, have understood somebody like Mrs. Liuzzo, who was a working mother, a member of both the PTA and the NAACP, a college student at thirty-nine?

Mrs. Liuzzo's faith was in action and Mrs. Durr's was in politics. Would they have trusted, even *liked,* each other? Would their considerable class, educational, and temperamental differences have gotten in the way? Probably. Most likely they would meet and move to opposite ends of the room. In the 1950s Mrs. Durr was dismissed as a communist, in the 1960s Mrs. Liuzzo was dismissed by the same angry segregationists as a whore. . . . Suddenly my rocker squeaks, and Mrs. Durr shakes her head.

"Now, what was it we were saying?"

"Um, that people like Mrs. Liuzzo were outsiders."

"Oh yes: outside *agitators.* And they were *hated down here*—especially the clergy, all those preachers who came down to march with Dr. King. They were hated worst of all."

"Why?" I ask.

"Remember I said how precarious it all was, how we held our way of life together by not examining it too closely?"

I nod.

"Well, white clergy marching alongside black people and singing "Jesus Loves Me" just about drove the segregationists mad. Just suppose it was true—what all those nuns and priests and rabbis were saying— that God loves *all* his children, *black and white.* If that was so, then segregation—and especially segregated *churches*—were not only wrong, they were evil. It meant God wasn't on the side of the Southern Way of Life at all. That, I will tell you, went to the very heart of the matter."

"I see."

"If God wasn't on the side of segregation, it meant everything we'd been taught and everything we'd fought for was all wrong. And if God was just, it meant we'd have to pay good and proper for treating the black people the way we did. That was terrifying—more than most could stand. That's why it was easier to believe that the outside clergy were frauds—that they were communists made up to look like clergy men and women and not ordained people of God."

"You mean they thought people actually *dressed up as clergy?*"

"That's exactly what I mean. Look, we struggled about so many issues, sometimes it got pretty silly. We had our share of nasty, horrible folks, and others just lived their lives scared, but some were essentially good people who were afraid to make a gesture or do what they knew in their hearts was right because they didn't want to be out of step—didn't want to be ostracized."

"Like you and your husband."

"Yes, like Cliff and me. You know, I'd been raised like all southern girls—to want everybody to love and admire me—so it was hard to take the ostracism."

Suddenly she looks very sad. It still hurts her to remember it! She still thinks she missed something.

"But once you made up your mind what was right and you made the break there was no turning back," she continues. "I was like a broken record about the poll tax because I believed in my heart that if you didn't have the right to vote then you were totally helpless."

"And now?"

"Now? Now, I don't know," she shifts in her chair and leans forward. "Seems like things started getting better—the poll tax was eliminated, the Voting Rights Bill got passed. Blacks, poor whites, and women all got to vote. But who did they vote for?" She flashes her big teeth at me.

I look at her dumbly and she slaps the arm of her chair with an open palm. "They put George Wallace right back in office! What sense did that make?" There it is! Suddenly I know who she reminds me of! Eleanor Roosevelt—actually Jane Alexander *playing* Eleanor Roosevelt. The long neck, the quick laugh, the big teeth. . . .

"What happened to all the idealism?" she sighs, sinking back in her chair. Her disappointment hangs heavily in the air. Once upon a time she was a young, gutsy woman who stood up to segregation when segregation was the law, and now she's an old woman sitting on her porch telling some stranger how she watched things come full circle. Had all her private pain been worth it? It's hard to tell what she's thinking.

Suddenly she laughs. "Well, if you live long enough, it's true what they say, you get to see *everything!* I guess freedom isn't freedom if you insist on making people do with it what you want them to."

We finish our lemonade and I tell her I should go. It is after four. I feel a vague sense of disappointment, but I thank her and she tells me she enjoyed our talk. She asks me to send her a copy of my book when it's published, and I ask her to autograph my copy of hers. "To Mary Stanton, from New York City," she writes. "I am delighted that you are interested in women in the Civil Rights Movement, Virginia Foster Durr."

I wave to her as I pull away. She is remarkable. Still on fire. She and her husband were the movers and shakers of Montgomery's white "resistance" and she wanted me to know that—that was clearly her agenda. Mrs. Liuzzo's story didn't interest her much. "Five minutes in Montgomery in those days and you knew a white woman did not ride around with a black man in her car at night," she told me. In her polite, gracious way Mrs. Durr dismissed Mrs. Liuzzo as being either foolish or provocative. That disturbed me. Was it true? Was Viola Liuzzo's death the result of simple carelessness? Had she underestimated the segregationists? Was she trying to provoke them? Did she think she was immortal? Did I come all this way to discover I was on the trail of someone who was simply self-destructive? Or was it a class thing, I wondered. Had Mrs. Liuzzo's spontaneous approach to life been interpreted as crude, aggressive, perhaps even ignorant by people like Mrs. Durr? How could I find out?

Mrs. Durr gave me an inside look at southern white society, but she hadn't led me any closer to Viola Liuzzo. She shook my faith in my mission, and that made me angry—not at her so much as at myself. My need to admire Mrs. Liuzzo was struggling with my need to know the truth. Whatever else I did this trip I would have to resolve that. Perhaps somebody would be waiting to help me in Selma.

Selma

We have no problems in Selma. If outside agitators would all get out and stay out we'd work things out here in our own way.
—Mayor Chris B. Heinz, 1965

The next day I head west for Selma. The drive takes me through Bloody Lowndes, which straddles the Jefferson Davis Highway (Highway 80), a fifty-five-mile road connecting Montgomery and Selma. Thirty years ago Lowndes County had a reputation like Birmingham, Tuscaloosa, or Philadelphia, Mississippi, because of the high visibility of its Klansmen, many of whom were sheriffs' deputies. Lowndes was a white police state where no jury had ever convicted a white man for murdering a black— mean country, where extremes of wealth and poverty co-existed uneasily. Wealth was centered in the white enclave of Lowndesboro, north of Highway 80. Fewer than ninety families owned 90 percent of the land. It was those families author Charles Eagles referred to when he wrote: "In 1960 whites controlled Lowndes County as completely as they had in 1860."[7]

Poor whites also called Lowndes home. Few had telephones, most had no indoor plumbing, and fewer than half owned cars. There were no hospitals, theaters, restaurants, or libraries in the county. While the rich whites of Lowndesboro had the means to access the social, health, and cultural facilities of Montgomery and Birmingham, poor whites were isolated and backward. Some had never traveled as far as Montgomery, and they tended to approach life with the same views their grandparents and great-grandparents had held—especially with regard to segregation and white supremacy.

Lowndes is the heart of Black Belt Alabama—that section of the South named for its large black population and its rich black soil. It was one of the wealthiest cotton producing regions in the United States before the Civil War. Where cotton grew, slave labor was in demand. By 1860 the black slave population in Lowndes had grown to 19,340, almost three times the white population of 8,362.

One hundred years later more than half the black population of Lowndes was still living in poverty in shotgun shacks—four-post shanties with wide front rooms that narrowed dramatically toward the back. (The name refers to the likelihood that a shotgun blast could go right through the house without disturbing any part of the structure.) In 1965 few black homes, like few poor white homes, had running water, and only twenty-five families had steam heat. Black men worked as sharecroppers and tenant farmers, and black women served as domestics in Lowndesboro and Montgomery. By 1965 the county was home to twelve thousand blacks and three thousand whites. Although not a single black person was registered to vote, Lowndes had two hundred more white voters on its rolls than it had white citizens of voting age. A black minister from Selma described Lowndes as a place worse than hell.

Driving toward Selma, I am overwhelmed by the beauty of the countryside. Gum trees and palmettos grow along the highway, many draped with Spanish moss. The land is rich velvet green. It rises and dips in lazy rolling hills. Farm country. Stands of pine trees rim the pastures. In the distance the farms still look like plantations. Along the side of the road every once in a while I pass a four-foot-high cement cross with GET RIGHT WITH GOD painted on it.

Halfway between Montgomery and Selma I spot the Liuzzo marker, sitting on top of a hill like a giant tombstone. Sara was right—you have to know what you are looking for. There are no historical marker signs. I take the first turn-around, pull off the highway, and walk up the hill. Nearly four feet high and cemented into a bed of gravel, the marker looms over the Jefferson Davis Highway: "In memory of our sister Viola

Liuzzo who gave her life in the struggle for the right to vote, March 25, 1965. Presented by SCLC Women, 1991."

A staff member at the Southern Poverty Law Center told me that in August 1979 the Ku Klux Klan held a fifty-mile "motorcade march" from Selma to Montgomery in support of "white rights," mimicking the 1965 voting rights march. They paused at the site of Mrs. Liuzzo's murder and spat on the ground.

A plastic wreath is lying beside her marker, the grass is a bit over-grown, and there is a barbed wire fence behind the stone, separating it from the neighboring farm. Nothing else is around. Nothing for as far as I can see. The old swamps have been drained, and Highway 80 is four lanes wide all the way now. It is hard to imagine the narrow winding swamp road of 1965. Once there were five bridges crossing Big Swamp. On the last bridge going toward Montgomery, a blind curve fed into a steep hill and led to a second blind curve. The shoulders were no more than six feet wide at any point. That is what I'm looking at—straightened now, a safe road, nothing like it was when Viola Liuzzo died there.

The more I learn about Lowndes, the more questions I have about the randomness of the Liuzzo murder. In *Outside Agitator,* Eagles noted that "In the early 1960s Lowndes was widely known among Alabamians and civil rights workers alike as a bastion of white racial prejudice in which whites would readily resort to violence to protect their segregated way of life. Lowndes seemed to symbolize Black Belt resistance to racial change. . . . In the spring of 1965 the leaders of the march from Selma to Montgomery worried most about what might happen when the march passed through northern Lowndes County on Highway 80. If violence against the marchers occurred, they believed it would happen in Bloody Lowndes."[8]

In 1965, Lowndes County State Representative Bill Edwards report-edly told Governor Wallace that if the marchers made it to his county they would probably be greeted with dynamite and snipers. But they made it through safely—all except Mrs. Liuzzo. What clearer message could be sent to "outside agitators" and "race mixers" than the execution of a northern white woman with a black man in her car in Bloody Lowndes? What stronger reassurance could be given to the Alabama segregationists that the South would protect their interests, even if the federal government refused to.

A shiver runs through me. Highway 80 is desolate. I feel sad but strangely unafraid. There isn't a car going east or west, or a person anywhere in sight at one o'clock on a weekday afternoon. How terrifying it must have been more than thirty years ago for a thirty-nine-year-old woman and a teenager at 8:30 on a March night to be chased by a speeding car on a winding, foggy swamp road with no shoulders, with no way of turning back or turning off—with only the hope of moving forward fast enough to get to safety.

A different kind of shiver passes through me as I cross the Edmund Pettus Bridge and enter Selma. Sometimes reality is underwhelming compared with our expectations, but the Pettus Bridge lives up to mine. It is a long, high bridge with heavy steel arches reaching over the Alabama River like strong arms.

Although Selma is a city, it feels rural. Its wide straight streets give the impression of openness, expansiveness. This is a modern feeling. Selma was a slave market before the Civil War and ultimately became a supply depot for the Confederacy. On April 2, 1865, a week before the Civil War ended, Selma was leveled by Union troops.

By the late 1800s, Selma had a reputation for being a lynching town. Some believe it was payback for its election of a black congressman during Reconstruction.

Birmingham sheriff Bull Connor was born here, and it was in Selma that Alabama's first White Citizens' Council—the "country club Klan" (sometimes called the "reading and writing Klan")—was organized.[9] Six months before the Montgomery Bus Boycott, attorney Alston Keith led a Citizens' Council membership drive that culminated in a white supremacy rally in downtown Selma. "We are going to make it difficult, if not impossible for any Negro who advocates desegregation to find and hold a job, get credit, or renew a mortgage," Keith told the crowd. Selma's chapter became the most active White Citizens' Council in Alabama.[10]

Citizens' councils were a middle-class phenomenon, composed mostly of bankers and businessmen organized to resist the Supreme Court's

1954 order to desegregate the public schools. With that decision, the court placed limitations on individual states' rights in matters of civil rights. Citizens' council members believed that once classrooms were integrated, intermarriage between the races was inevitable. Senator Walter Givhan of Mississippi charged that "the real purpose of the Supreme Court's decision against school desegregation is to open the bedroom doors of our white women to Negro men!"[11]

The councils were considered respectable alternatives to the lower-class Klan, but like the Klan they supported the preservation of strict segregation of the races and retention of power by white, Anglo-Saxon, Christian men. They engaged in economic lynching of blacks and those whites who supported integration. Georgia Governor Herman Talmadge addressing the White Citizens' Council in 1955 advised that "anyone who sells the South down the river, don't let him eat at your table, don't let him trade at your filling station, and don't let him trade at your store."

Selma's White Citizens' Council controlled municipal politics and used every tactic it could muster to stonewall integration. Anyone who stood up to the White Citizens' Council suffered. In 1962, Rev. George Hrbek, a white Lutheran pastor, publicly objected to a Montgomery Baptist minister's biblical defense of segregation. The citizens' council censured him so publicly that a faction of the Selma Ministers' Union proposed adopting a resolution to support freedom of speech by clergy members regardless of their position on race. That proposal was resoundingly defeated. The dissenting ministers argued that it would only create controversy and serve no useful purpose. Rev. Hrbek left Selma shortly after the vote.[12]

In 1955 twenty-nine black parents petitioned the Selma School Board to integrate the public elementary schools. More than half the signers of the petition lost their jobs and were refused credit by Selma's stores and banks.

When Ernest Doyle, a local NAACP leader who earned his living as a handyman, refused to withdraw his name from the petition the citizens' council sent a black man over to tell Doyle to remove it or else. He refused, and for the next twenty years no white in Selma would hire Doyle.

In 1965 blacks were a majority of the twenty-nine thousand inhabitants of Selma yet only 3 percent of the voting rolls. Black Belt whites clearly understood the implications of a repressed majority going to the polls and electing its own representatives.

As a result of passage of the Thirteenth, Fourteenth, and Fifteenth amendments to the U.S. Constitution (1865–1870) and the Civil Rights Act of 1875, blacks were in theory free and equal citizens. The Civil Rights Act guaranteed that all persons within the jurisdiction of the United States were entitled to full and equal enjoyment of inns, public conveyances, theaters, and other places of public amusement. When they were refused admission to hotel dining rooms and smoking cars on passenger trains, blacks began to bring their grievances to the courts. In 1883, however, the Supreme Court ruled that acts of *social* discrimination by individuals could not be legislated by the federal government and declared the Civil Rights Act of 1875 unconstitutional. Southern states then began passing state constitutional amendments upholding public segregation and limiting black voting rights. These were the Jim Crow laws that ushered in the era of "separate but equal" accommodations.

Mississippi denied the vote to any person who had not paid his poll tax or who was unable to read any section of the Constitution or understand it when it was read to him. In 1895 South Carolina followed suit. Louisiana created the notorious grandfather clause in 1898. Grandfather clauses excluded from disenfranchisement all descendants of men who had voted before the Civil War, thus exempting all white men who were illiterate or without property. In 1901 Alabama rewrote its state constitution to deny the vote to anyone who could not pass a literacy test or could not pay a poll tax.

By the 1960s the issue of free access to voting rights was still not settled. An additional piece of federal legislation was needed to enforce voting rights for blacks under the Fifteenth Amendment because the Civil Rights Act of 1964 had been a compromise. In 1964 its voting rights provisions were negotiated away in order to accumulate enough votes to break a Senate filibuster and get the core provisions of the act passed.

In 1965 Dr. Martin Luther King Jr., writing for the Op-Ed page of the *New York Times,* noted that "Selma has succeeded in limiting Negro registration to a snail's pace of about 145 persons a year. At this rate it would take 103 years to register the 15,000 eligible Negro voters of Dallas County."[13]

Selma was, therefore, the ideal place to focus America's attention on the struggle for voting rights.

After crossing the Pettus Bridge, I make a sharp left turn onto Water Avenue and pull up in front of the National Voting Rights Museum and Institute. Like most of Selma's buildings, this one has been carefully restored. It is a renovated brick storefront—once the headquarters of Selma's White Citizens' Council—that opened as a museum in 1991.

Inside, yellowed signs are exhibited declaring WHITE ONLY, WE SERVE COLORED CARRY OUT ONLY, and COLORED SEATED IN REAR. There is a Women's Suffrage Room, a Freedom's Children Room, a Mississippi Room honoring the work of Fannie Lou Hamer and the Mississippi Freedom Democratic Party, and Nelson Mandela and Martin Luther King Jr. walls.

What grabs my attention right away, however, is the "I Was There" living history exhibit—a wall of mirror etched with the image of the Pettus Bridge and covered with index cards carrying the names and comments of people who were on the bridge on Bloody Sunday, March 7, 1965. That was the first attempt to march to Montgomery, and it resulted in a brutal attack on the demonstrators by mounted Alabama state troopers using clubs and tear gas. "Charles Bonner. I was eighteen years old. I walked all the way. Now 47 and living in California. . . . Roy Collins. I was thirteen years old. I'm a social worker in Chicago. . . . Annie McQueen. I was thirty-nine, I'm still in Selma. . . . Effie Johnson. I was a thirty-seven-year-old housewife. I came over from Marion. Now I'm retired."

I'm taking notes furiously when a tall, stocky black woman with a broad smile and round face asks if she can help. "I'm Joanne," she says, "tour director for the museum." I tell her I am doing research for a biography of Viola Liuzzo and trying to find people who might remember her.

"Well, of course!" she laughs. "*Everybody* remembers Viola Liuzzo! She stayed with Willie Lee Jackson, over to the Carver Homes. I was just a kid then—nine or ten, but even *I* remember." I look at her, dumbfounded. *She's younger than I am.*[14]

"You *remember* her?"

"Sure do." She shakes her head. "I lived right next door to the Jacksons. Me and one of the Jackson girls went through her purse. We were

bad kids. We took her money and stole her birth control pills! Don't look
so shocked," she laughs, "we didn't like her. She was bossy. She was helping Mrs. Jackson with the kids and acting like a mother hen, and we
didn't like that. I didn't want to be told anything by a white woman. I'd
already heard too much from white people."

I nod, trying to get down every word. When I finally look up I can't tell
if she really wants to help me or if I am annoying her. The expression on
her face hasn't changed. "See, I was on the bridge on Bloody Sunday, too.
I got so scared I fainted. I saw what white people were capable of doing,
so I wasn't interested that some white lady came down from Detroit to
help me. What was she going to do?"

"What did you think she was going to do?"

"I had no idea. I was too busy looking at all those young ministers Dr.
King brought with him from Atlanta. Everybody was in love with
Bernard Lafayette in those days. What a beautiful boy he was!" The office telephone rings and she runs to get it. I trail after her and wait
through an endless conversation. Joanne has all the time in the world. As
I shift uncomfortably she winks and motions for me to wait—or maybe
for me to sit down, maybe both. Finally, she hangs up.

"What else do you remember?" I ask.

"Viola Liuzzo, yes . . ." she sits behind her desk. "Well, that she
smoked a lot, and, well, I guess I'd have to say she was a man's woman,
you know?"

"I don't understand."

"A talker. Sit down, be comfortable." I pull up a chair. "Mrs. Liuzzo
was always talking—with the men *and* the women. Some of the black
women felt she was a threat to them—because she was white. But I guess
even if she was a black woman from the north they would have seen her
as a threat. She had a lot of opinions, and she always wanted to talk
about them with somebody."

"What about the rumors?" I ask.

"The rumors. I *knew* we'd get to them. Rumors always get going about
women comfortable with men, don't you think? People are quicker to
pass on the bad stuff than the good stuff anyway. Some people down here
will tell you she was a great lady. Others call her nothing but a white

whore. Me? I don't know. I guess I didn't like her just because she was white."

My head flies up involuntarily. Joanne is sitting back, smiling. "Well, you want the truth don't you?"

I grin back. "Yeah, but don't try so hard to spare my feelings." She lets go a roar of laughter and slaps the desk. "I *knew* there was something I liked about you, girl. What else you want to know?"

"What about Leroy Moton, the guy who was with her that night?"

She shakes her head. "Leroy was all broke up. People here gave him a real hard time. Most everybody thought *he* should have known better even if *she* didn't. Some people told him that he was the one killed that woman. He left after the trials, and they say he never came back. But I heard he did come back once, in the middle of the night, to see his mother. Last anybody knew he was up in Connecticut someplace."

"Is Mrs. Jackson, the one Mrs. Liuzzo stayed with, is she still in Selma?"

"No. She moved to Florida years ago. But there are others out at the Carver Homes who remember. I'll give you some names, but I want to show you something first."

We walk back to the living history exhibit, and she points to a photo of a large, moon-faced black woman with sad eyes. "That's Miz Cooper," she says, "Annie Cooper. She passed recently. She was our local hero."

"What did she do?" I ask.

Joanne smiles. "This little lady here slapped the shit out of Sheriff Jim Clark."

I start to laugh.

"She did, truly. She was marching to the courthouse to register to vote and she felt this big paw grab her in back of her neck. She just spun around and slapped as hard as she could, and the man jumped three feet in the air before she realized it was old Jim Clark. Miz Cooper took four civil rights workers into her home during the march and lost her job on account of it. The only work she could get after that was housekeeping on the night shift at the Torch Motel. She used to talk about how Dr. King and Bernard Lee and Andrew Young and Hosea Williams all knew her because they stayed at the Torch when they came to Selma. She would have been a good person for you to talk to. It was the feisty ones like Annie Cooper who kept everybody going."

Feisty. Feisty women were valued in the black community. In white society they were trouble. In 1965 black women didn't wait for black men to give their lives direction, to protect or support them. They did their own fighting. I wondered if Mrs. Liuzzo might have bumped into Mrs. Cooper during her stay in Selma. Stranger things happen. They would have had plenty to talk about.

"I'm sorry I missed her," I tell Joanne.

"Well, there's others. I'll give you the address of the lady Jonathan Daniels stayed with. Do you know about him?"

I shook my head.

"He was one of the white ministers. He came down during the march and came back afterwards. Alice can tell you all about him." She goes back to her desk and writes some names and numbers on a piece of paper. "Good luck," she grins as she hands it to me, "and let me know what happens."

"Thanks. I will."

The George Washington Carver Homes is a brick federal housing project with long rows of two-story apartments. It opened in 1952 and has landmark status now because of its role as headquarters for the Selma Voting Rights Campaign. It is well maintained, probably looking much like it did the day it opened. GWC faces Brown Chapel, a maroon-and-white brick church with two white rounded steeples that make it look more like a mosque.

Brown Chapel, built in 1906, was the focal point of the voting rights march. Outside a six-foot white granite monument with a bust of Dr. Martin Luther King stands with the words "I Had a Dream" etched on it. "The demonstration that led to the most important advance in civil rights for millions of black Americans began here, March 21, 1965. . . . This is a tribute to those who planned, encouraged, marched, were jailed, beaten and died to change Black Americans from second class citizens to first class citizens."

A second, slimmer stone rests right up against this one. "They gave their lives," it reads, "to overcome injustice and secure the right to vote for all Americans,

James J. Reeb, Boston
Viola Gregg Liuzzo, Detroit
Jimmy Lee Jackson, Marion, Alabama
Dedicated August 11, 1979."

Joanne gave me Lynda's name and address, so I walk up and down the paths inside the project searching for her apartment. People look at me curiously, but if they are wondering what a white woman is doing roaming around GWC they don't ask. It occurs to me that this is something I would never do back home. Wandering through a project in Harlem or Bed-Stuy—even if I were guaranteed the Pulitzer Prize—wouldn't tempt me. I push the thought out of my head. If I think about it long enough maybe I *will* get scared. Finally I spot Lynda's apartment.

"Oh yes, *sure* I remember," Lynda tells me, "there were hundreds of people staying with families around here all that week. A lot of the civil rights workers slept out on the grass at night, and people opened up their apartments to let them sleep on their floors." Lynda says that her husband worked with the SCLC's transportation service along with Mrs. Liuzzo and Leroy Moton. Things got hectic near the end, she remembers, more people came than even Dr. King expected, and there was a shortage of cars and drivers. "My husband was supposed to work with Mrs. Liuzzo that night, but in the afternoon another car was freed up, and they asked him to take it out, so Leroy went with Mrs. Liuzzo. I don't actually remember her myself, I just remember somebody coming down to pick up her clothes."

I go to the next name on my list: Alice. Alice tells me to come back, she's taking care of her grandkids just now. When I ask when, she says "two hours." Exactly two hours later I am back, and her apartment is shut up tight. Nobody answers my knock, although I hear somebody moving inside. I sit on a lawn chair and wait another hour. People pass on their way home or on their way out—they glare, they smile, they just keep going. Finally, a tall teenager walks up to the front door and pulls out a key. "What you want?" he asks.

"I'm waiting for Alice," I tell him.

"My grandmother?"

"Yes."

"Why?"

"I'm writing a book. I want to ask her some questions."

He gives me an impatient look and heads inside. Almost immediately he calls out, through the screen door. "She ain't here. I don't know when she's comin' back." I write a quick note, including the phone number of the Madison Hotel, and leave it in the mailbox. I come back the next day, but Alice still isn't home.

Alice and her husband made room for ten marchers in 1965 in addition to their own eleven children. They fed them, provided sleeping space, and made them feel welcome in a hostile environment. Alice opened her apartment to the young ministers of the Southern Christian Leadership Conference and to the Student Non-Violent Coordinating Committee—men like John Lewis, James Orange, and Stokely Carmichael, who strategized at her kitchen table and ate pigs' ears and tails, hot links, cornbread, and grits with her family.

Frank Seroca, a white SNCC worker from California who roomed with Alice's family, rescued her young daughter Rachel on Bloody Sunday when the seven-year-old girl was nearly trampled by Sheriff Clark's posse as she attempted to march across the Pettus Bridge. Seroca scooped Rachel up and ran back to the Carver Homes with her in his arms. He was chased into the complex by white men on horseback who were shouting, "Kill him! Kill him!"[15]

Jon Daniels, the white seminarian Joanne mentioned, lived with Alice's family for almost six months. He came to Selma to take part in the voting rights march and returned to work with the Lowndes voter registration project. On August 20, 1965, five months after the Liuzzo murder, Daniels was shot to death by a white Lowndes County deputy sheriff. The shooting happened less than an hour after Daniels was released from jail in Hayneville. Alice obviously didn't want to talk about those days anymore, at least not to me.

Bob was also hesitant. He was a SNCC worker in 1965. Joanne had his phone number but no address. I called him. "Look," Bob said, "in those days a lot of white women ferried black and white marchers back and forth to Montgomery. Even before 1965 there were white women who would ignore the convention and ride in cars with black people—male and female. The bigots made a big thing about it, but I'm telling you there were people in those days who really believed in the dignity of human beings. The segregationists had a hard time accepting that. They said she came here for a sex orgy, and a lot of folks wanted to believe that. They said she was having an affair with a nineteen-year-old boy. But I believe she was genuine. Look, you sound like a nice lady, but I'm through talking. I've talked to enough people for a lifetime. Good luck with your book."

I hold the receiver until the dial tone buzzes, then slowly place it back in its cradle. I'm disappointed, trying not to get discouraged. I spend the next two days in the Selma and Montgomery libraries, in newspaper offices, and in the Alabama State College archives. Things are getting so complicated that I hardly remember what it was I was originally looking for.

Why were so few people willing talk to me? Did they feel used by white journalists who considered the movement's stories more interesting than its goals? Were they just sick of talking, like they said? Was there something that had I been a better interviewer I could have teased out? Were they *still* afraid? I had driven to Selma with the foolish notion that the civil rights movement had changed everything.

While the movement ended some discrimination and oppression, it didn't achieve its vision of a better world—at least not for the blacks of Selma. Selma is still a segregated city. In 1990 there were still two Elks clubs, two American Legion posts, and two First Baptist churches—one for each race.

And Selma's schools remain segregated. When blacks were finally admitted to the public schools in the 1960s, white parents pulled their children out and registered them in private academies. Blacks were left with the deteriorating school buildings. In March 1990 when people gathered in Selma to celebrate the twenty-fifth anniversary of the voting rights march, they found the city bristling with new sit-ins, protest marches, and demonstrations. Black activists were protesting the white-majority school board's decision not to renew Superintendent Norwood Russell's contract. Russell was the district's first black superintendent.

Selma attorney Rosa Sanders said the demonstrations were to ensure that black children wouldn't continue to be segregated through a curriculum tracking system—a system Russell was trying to dismantle. "Blacks and whites go in the same school door," Sanders said, "but once inside they go to separate and unequal classes."[16]

While Selma's racial violence is over, it has been replaced by new problems: serious drug dependency among black teens and a high rate of black-on-black crime. In the summer of 1994 the *New York Times* ran a four-part series on life in southern Black Belt communities. Southern Bureau Chief Peter Applebome, who covered Selma, observed that the median family income was still only $18,349—half the national average. "In Selma," Applebome wrote, "everything and nothing has changed."[17]

I went south in all my naivete expecting that blacks would remember Mrs. Liuzzo fondly, expecting to hear how the voting rights march and all it represented weakened the Klan's grasp on the Black Belt. I heard nothing like that. In fact, I never heard the word Klan used outside the Southern Poverty Law Center. Whites referred to supremacists or segregationists and blacks to bigots or crackers, but nobody I spoke with used "Klan."

I thought by tracing Mrs. Liuzzo's footsteps I would begin to understand who she was and why she went. Was she afraid? Was she careless? Had she been the Klan's intended victim all along? Was she disappointed, exhilarated, or disgusted when the march ended? Would she have come back?

Mrs. Durr gave me a good sense of what the segregationists were all about and why they hated Mrs. Liuzzo so much, but my picture of the woman from Detroit was still fuzzy.

For the next three and a half years my search for Mrs. Liuzzo would take me to Michigan: through the decimated neighborhoods of central Detroit, the posh suburbs of Troy and Birmingham, the middle-class neighborhoods of Royal Oak and Southfield, and the college town of Ann Arbor. I would communicate by letter and phone with people in Bakersfield, Sacramento, and San Francisco, California; Selma, Birmingham,

Montgomery, and Daphne, Alabama; Washington, D.C.; and back in Detroit. The staff at Detroit's Central Library on Woodward Avenue and at the Wayne State University Archives began to know me by name. But it wasn't until I located the FBI investigative file of the Liuzzo murder that the story began to take shape. After reading that file I suddenly understood what questions needed asking, and I began to make sense of the hesitant, cryptic responses I sometimes received from those I knew knew more than they were willing to tell me. If there had been no Freedom of Information Act, I'm not sure this book would ever have been completed.

In the spring of 1994 I began my search in the public libraries of Selma and Montgomery. Through the eyes of reporters for the *Montgomery Advertiser*, *Alabama Journal*, *Birmingham News*, and *Selma Times Journal* I pieced together the events of the last few days of Viola Liuzzo's life. I recreated, day by day, the week of March 21, 1965, which culminated in her murder on the Jefferson Davis Highway. It was a start.

2 The Story

The past isn't dead. It isn't even past.
—William Faulkner

Six hours after Viola Liuzzo's murder, Gary Thomas (Tommy) Rowe called the FBI regional office in Birmingham, Alabama, to report that he knew who her killers were. He claimed to have been in the car from which the fatal shots were fired. Early the next morning Rowe, thirty-one, and three other white men—Collie Leroy Wilkins Jr., twenty-one, William Orville Eaton, forty-one, and Eugene Thomas, forty-three—were arrested. All were charged with conspiracy to injure and intimidate persons in the exercise of their rights under the United States Constitution, a federal offense.

When President Johnson learned that all were members of the Ku Klux Klan he denounced the KKK as a "a dirty band of bigots" and vowed that through the Justice Department he would wage all-out war against it.[1] Johnson soon received a telegram from Robert Shelton of Tuscaloosa, imperial wizard of the United Klans of America, and Calvin Craig, grand dragon of Georgia, requesting a face-to-face meeting. Charging that the president was partial to "left wingers," their wire read: "Representing the true feelings of millions of Americans we desire personally to confer with you concerning your statement about the Ku Klux Klan, selection of Supreme Court judges, rising crime rates, obscene literature flooding America, sex perverts and communist agents within our government."

The arrest of four suspects eight hours after the Liuzzo murder stunned law enforcement officials and Klansmen alike, but Matt Murphy, defense counsel for the Klansmen, assured the press that "these four boys will be exonerated." Collie Leroy Wilkins's mother wrote to President Johnson asking why he had branded her son guilty on national television. "I would like for you to explain to me," she wrote, "why this was done before my son was even interrogated or given any kind of hearing or trial by jury. I feel like my son and these three other men will not have a fair trial because they were branded guilty before the nation by the President of the United States." Mrs. Wilkins's letter was picked up by the national press on April 4. When President Johnson failed to respond to her or to the imperial wizard, Robert Shelton told a Klan rally in South Carolina, "We are not going to accept the mandate, or heed it, of Lyndon Johnson who says we must accept the unacceptable. If he continues with his yakking, he will be one of the greatest organizers the Klan ever had."[2]

Defense attorney Matt Murphy told the press that the president's remarks would make it impossible for his clients to get a fair trial and that he would seek dismissal of all charges. The United Klans of America posted $150,000 for bail, since all the men were members of UKA chapters located in and around Birmingham, Alabama.

An Alabama federal grand jury indicted the Klansmen on April 6, but rumors of betrayal began to circulate when Tommy Rowe was brought to court three hours after the others, accompanied by three FBI agents. Then, on April 15, the charges against Rowe were dropped.

On April 21, under heavy guard and wearing his own gun, Rowe testified before a state grand jury for over two hours on behalf of the prosecution. The following day, Wilkins, Eaton, and Thomas were charged with first-degree murder. The *Washington Post* broke the story that Tommy Rowe had been granted immunity from prosecution in the Liuzzo murder because he was a paid FBI informant. Once the men were indicted, Rowe disappeared.

Nobody, including Matt Murphy, could believe the strange turn of events. For more than two weeks Rowe had lied to his defense counsel about the events of March 25. None of his co-defendants could believe that such a zealous segregationist would work undercover for the FBI. Rowe had been a high-ranking member of the Eastview Klavern 13, the group alleged to have bombed the Sixteenth Street Baptist Church in Birmingham in 1963 and to have conspired in the death of Lieutenant

Colonel Lemuel Penn, a black army officer who was shot on his way home from reserve training in Ft. Benning, Georgia. Penn was murdered just one week after Goodman, Chaney, and Schwerner disappeared in Mississippi. Lieutenant Colonel Penn fell victim to the same kind of night-rider assassination as Viola Liuzzo.

But on the morning of March 26, 1965, all anyone knew was that the FBI had made four speedy arrests. President Johnson called a press conference and, with Attorney General Nicholas Katzenbach and FBI Director J. Edgar Hoover flanking him, told the nation that its "honored public servant, Mr. Hoover," had come through for them. "I cannot express myself too strongly in praising Mr. Hoover and the men of the FBI," the president said, "for their prompt and expeditious performance in handling this investigation." The FBI's glory was short-lived, however. As Mrs. Liuzzo's body was being flown back to Detroit, all hell broke loose inside the agency.

An Eyewitness

The days that are still to come are the wisest witnesses.
—Pindar

Tommy Rowe's account of the Liuzzo murder began on Thursday, March 25, the last day of the voting rights march. He claimed to have been assigned by Grand Dragon Robert Creel to rendezvous with Wilkins, Eaton, and Thomas, members of the Eastview Klavern 13's "klokan," or militant-action group, handpicked for "missionary squad" duty. Klan missionaries were terrorists. For weeks, Klan rallies had been held throughout central Alabama to discuss "The March." Imperial Wizard Shelton encouraged Birmingham Klansmen to "if necessary, you know, do what you have to do."[3] The missionaries were scouting out weak links in the layers of protection that surrounded the marchers. President Johnson had sent 2,000 army troops to Alabama (including a military police battalion specializing in riot control), 100 federal marshals, and 100 FBI agents. He had also federalized 1,800 Alabama national guardsmen, many of whom were from Selma.

Dr. King's speech at the state capitol earlier that day had infuriated

Klansmen all over Alabama. "They told us we wouldn't get here," King had said. "And there were those who said that we would get here only over their dead bodies, but all the world today knows that we are here and that we are standing before the forces of power in the state of Alabama saying, 'We ain't goin' let nobody turn us around.'"[4]

The missionaries considered both the demonstrators and the federal troops foreign invaders. They were especially anxious to harass northern agitators who had come to march. But they could not create an opportunity, Rowe claimed, because the armed forces were still on duty Thursday afternoon.

Disgruntled, the four men piled into Gene Thomas's red-and-white Impala and headed toward Selma. On the way, they stopped at Jack's Grill for a few beers. They drank for about an hour while Thomas arranged to have everyone bonded—"just in case they got picked up." Shortly after leaving Jack's, they were issued a warning ticket for speeding by Officer James Haygood on Highway 80 at Tyler's Crossing. It was 6:20 P.M. That ticket placed them on the highway approximately two hours before the Liuzzo murder.

The men drove on to Selma's whites-only Silver Moon Cafe, complete with swinging doors and tin spittoons. Behind the bar, shelves were stacked with bottles of whiskey, aspirin, Alka-Seltzer, cans of soup, and boxes of corn flakes. At the Silver Moon you could order anything from oatmeal to bourbon. Inside, Rowe recalled, Thomas spotted brother Klansman, Elmer Cook, drinking with three men. Thomas led Eaton, Wilkins, and Rowe to Cook's table and introduced Cook and his friends as the boys "out on bond for the beating." They were William Hoggle, thirty-six, and Hoggle's brother O'Neal and R. B. Kelly, both thirty. All were suspects in the beating of Rev. James Reeb, thirty-eight, a white Unitarian minister from Boston, that had occurred right outside the Silver Moon two weeks before. Reeb and two other ministers had taken a wrong turn after eating dinner in Walker's Cafe, a gathering place for out-of-town marchers in the black section of Selma. Taking what they thought was a shortcut, they got lost on Washington Street in Selma's tough white section. Cook, Kelly, and the Hoggles allegedly accosted the ministers, screaming, "You want to know what it's like to be a real nigger?" and one of them fractured Reeb's skull with a baseball bat.[5] Reeb died two days later. Although Cook had been arrested twenty-six times for assault and battery between 1948 and 1965 he was out on bail, drinking heavily with the Hoggles and Kelly, on the night the voting march ended.

A month later at the grand jury hearing for the Reeb case, Judge James A. Hare would begin his charge to the all-white, all-male jury by sharing with them his theory about the cause of Selma's troubles. "Many self-anointed saints took it upon themselves to come here and help us solve our problems," he said. "But integration will solve no social problem. . . . These bleeding hearts who dash down here—all they've done is read the Declaration of Independence and think they can solve these problems." Judge Hare believed that Selma's difficulties stemmed from the fact that Selma's "Nigras" were ancestors of the "Ebo" and "Angol" tribes of Africa. He assured the jury that Ebos and Angols were incapable of achieving IQs of more than sixty-five. They were comparable in intelligence to "white riff-raff and river rats."[6]

Despite Judge Hare's forty-minute lecture, the grand jury returned murder indictments against Elmer Cook, William and O'Neal Hoggle, and J. B. Kelly. Yet, on December 10, 1965, an all-white, all-male jury would take only ninety minutes to acquit them of second-degree murder and first- and second-degree manslaughter. Their defense attorney argued that the blow Rev. Reeb received was not fatal and that civil rights leaders had "knowingly and deliberately allowed the minister to die to provide a martyr for their cause."

Respectable white residents of Selma never went near the Silver Moon Cafe after dark. Some believed that Reeb and the other ministers had "asked for it" by going there. Although the *Selma Times Journal* encouraged local churches to hold memorial services for Rev. Reeb, few white pastors were willing to participate. There was little sympathy from the white clergy for the northern ministers, priests, and rabbis who were coming to Selma. A black Baptist minister was refused entrance to the First Baptist Church, and Selma's white Catholic church not only turned away all blacks who attempted to attend Mass but all priests and nuns who had come to the city for the march. Rev. William Sloane Coffin, chaplain of Yale, observed that "To the majority of Southern white min-

isters segregation was a matter of politics, and religion was above politics. It was an illusion of course: their Christianity simply upheld the status quo."

Wilkins, Thomas, Rowe, and Eaton spent forty-five minutes in the
Silver Moon Cafe with Cook, Kelly, and the Hoggles on the night of
March 25. Finally, Elmer Cook leaned across the greasy table and grinned
at them. "You boys go do your job," he said. "I already done mine."[7]

"We intend to," Thomas told him. "It's going to be a big day for us."
They spent the next twenty minutes, according to Rowe, driving through
Selma, half drunk and very frustrated. Selma, like Montgomery, was still
filled with federal troops.

In April 1985, Morris Dees, prosecuting the Eastview Klavern 13 in a
civil suit for the lynching death of black college student Michael Donald,
deposed the then fifty-one-year-old Tommy Rowe. During his deposition
Rowe recalled the Liuzzo murder:

> We all . . . got in the automobile and . . . started cruising the
> streets [of Selma]. I wasn't sure what the hell was happening at that
> point. The first place I recognized was a black church [Brown
> Chapel]. There must have been two hundred blacks and whites min-
> gled standing out around this church.
>
> About that time Wilkins says, "Hey, look, lets get them two son-
> of-a-bitches right there." It was a very attractive-looking white
> woman and kind of an older black guy, probably in his thirties. And
> the woman wasn't no more than nineteen or twenty, in a pair of
> short shorts. Looked real good. The black man had his arm around
> her waist and they was standing there and Wilkins said, "That's it."
>
> Gene started heading the car toward them and I said, "Holy
> shit!" Just off to the side was a military jeep with three MPs stand-
> ing by it, mounted with a .30-caliber machine gun on the back. I
> said, "Goddamn, Wilk, look over there. Let's get the shit out of here.
> They've got fucking troops over there with goddamn machine guns,
> fool, let's get the hell out of here before we get in trouble."[8]

Deciding to return to Montgomery, they turned down Water Avenue
and spotted a white woman with a black man in a car stopped at a traffic

light waiting to cross the Pettus Bridge. It was Viola Liuzzo and nineteen-year-old Leroy Moton, another SCLC volunteer who had worked with Mrs. Liuzzo providing transportation for the marchers. They had just left Brown Chapel and were heading back to Montgomery to drop off a set of car keys for the Transportation Committee and to pick up a group of marchers waiting to return to Selma.

Wilkins turned to Rowe, "Lookie there, Baby Brother," he said, "I'll be damned." Thomas nodded. "Will you look at that. They're going to park someplace together," Wilkins said disgustedly. "I'll be a son of a bitch, let's take them."[9]

According to Rowe, they followed Liuzzo's car along Highway 80 for the next twenty miles. Rowe said Liuzzo accelerated to almost ninety miles an hour when she realized she was being tailed. But the Impala kept up with her. Rowe maintained that they tried to pull up alongside Liuzzo's 1963 green Oldsmobile four times. Each time they were forced to drop back—first by a jeep load of National Guardsmen, next by a highway patrol unit, then by a crowd of black marchers trying to cross the highway, and finally by a truck in the oncoming lane.

> The lady just hauled ass. I mean she put the gas to it. As we went across a bridge and some curves I remember seeing a Jet Drive-In Restaurant on my right-hand side. I seen the brakes to the car just flash one time and I thought she was going to stop there. She didn't stop there, she in fact gave it more gas. . . .
>
> We kept pursuing them further and as we went around a curve the woman—she was just erratic. She began to drive fast and at that point I seen a sign that said Craig Air Force Base. . . . The lady started to turn the car in, you could just tell the way she swerved her car, and for some unknown reason she swerved it back out and stomped the gas and got up to eighty, ninety, ninety-five miles an hour. She passed that.[10]

If there were guardsmen and highway patrol officers on the road why didn't Liuzzo stop? Why wouldn't she try to get their attention? Why didn't she pull into the drive-in or the Air Force base? Perhaps she believed that no Alabama official could be trusted. Or maybe she felt she could make it back to Montgomery—to the safety of federal troops, newsmen, and television cameras. But even if *she* didn't stop, why didn't the troopers stop *her*? If Rowe can be believed, both his car and Liuzzo's were doing well over eighty miles an hour. Why didn't the police give chase, especially since the Impala had been pulled over and given a warning ticket for speeding on its way into Selma two hours before? What *really* happened?

Rowe asserted that halfway between Selma and Montgomery on the desolate strip through Big Swamp the Impala pulled alongside Liuzzo's car. "We got pretty much even with the car and the lady just turned her head solid all the way around and looked at us," Rowe said. "I will never forget it in my lifetime, and her mouth flew open like she—in my heart I've always said she was saying, 'Oh God,' or something like that. . . . You could tell she was startled. At that point Wilkins fired a shot. . . . He fired three or four more shots. . . . Her car kept rolling along the road and I said I don't think you hit them. Wilkins slapped me on the right leg and said, Baby Brother, don't worry about it. That bitch and that bastard are dead and in hell. I don't miss."[11]

Liuzzo was killed instantly, and the Oldsmobile skidded into a ditch. Leroy Moton, covered with her blood, escaped by pretending to be dead when the murderers came back.

When the Klansmen returned to Bessemer, Eugene Thomas insisted that they stop at Lorene's Cafe. Thomas was a regular customer and was sure he could trust the owner, Lorene Frederick, to provide them with an alibi. Eaton, Rowe, and Wilkins waited at a table while Thomas spoke with Lorene at the counter. When he came back, he told the men, "I got us an alibi."

Then Thomas, still elated according to Rowe, drove them all to Grand Dragon Creel's house to brag about what had happened. Creel's lights were out, however, so they left without waking him. Rowe claims that at 11:15 P.M. he called his FBI control agent, Neil Shanahan, from a telephone booth and asked to meet him in the parking lot of a Birmingham hospital.

A Cover-Up

██████████ False face must hide what false heart doth know.
—Shakespeare

Why, reporters asked, if an FBI informant was in the car, had the murder happened? Why had Rowe gone along with it? Why didn't he notify the FBI of the missionary squad's plans to terrorize the marchers?

Nationally syndicated columnist Inez Robb wrote in the May 17, 1965, issue of the *Washington Daily News,* "What troubles me is the moral aspect of Rowe's presence in the car when an innocent woman was gunned down. Under what kind of secret orders did Rowe work? Was the infiltration of the Ku Klux Klan more important than the saving of an innocent woman? . . . the FBI owes the nation an explanation of its actions in the Liuzzo case." Robb's column appeared in 132 daily newspapers across the country. In response to her disturbing questions, her background was thoroughly investigated by the FBI.[12]

Gary Thomas Rowe had been the bureau's chief informant inside the KKK since 1960. During a Senate hearing in 1975, Rowe would testify that he participated in numerous acts of violence while working for the government. The bureau had full knowledge of his brutal attacks on blacks, civil rights workers, and journalists. Days after the Liuzzo murder, as information began to surface about Rowe's volatility, FBI chief J. Edgar Hoover panicked. He realized the bureau had to deflect attention from the Birmingham field office's glaring incompetence in permitting Rowe, despite his violent history, to go to Montgomery without backup and without FBI surveillance. It was also imperative to bury the fact that Rowe *had* telephoned his FBI control agent on the day of the Liuzzo murder to report that he was going to Montgomery with other Klansmen and that violence was planned. While Rowe claimed not to have known exactly what the plans were, he said that Grand Dragon Robert Creel told him personally, "Tommy, this here is probably going to be one of the greatest days of Klan history. Probably be one of the days you will always remember until the day you die."[13] This remark led to some speculation, never substantiated, that the Klan missionaries were scouting for an opportunity to kill a much more prominent figure—possibly Martin Luther King Jr. Rowe, however, has repeatedly denied such claims.

Rowe's FBI contact instructed him to go to Montgomery and observe. The bureau obviously accepted Rowe's participation in violence as the price for getting information about the Klan.

Special Agent Spencer Robb offered his services to "the Chief" to cover the Birmingham office's gaffe by circulating an internal FBI memo declaring that Mrs. Liuzzo "had puncture marks in her arms indicating recent use of a hypodermic needle." The memo was leaked to the press. This deliberate attempt to shift the focus from Rowe to Liuzzo failed miserably when her autopsy report showed no signs of either needle marks or drugs. The memo was kept classified for nearly twenty years.

Jim Clark, sheriff of Selma, charged that Mrs. Liuzzo's murder could have been prevented if FBI agents had worked more closely with his deputies. He insisted that the bureau had Gene Thomas's Impala under surveillance the whole week of the march. If this seems a strange charge for Clark to make, the bureau's response was even more curious. An FBI spokesman called Clark a "malicious liar" and said his accusation was "typical of his weakness in handling his responsibilities."

But Sheriff Clark stubbornly maintained that the Klansmen's car *had* been under FBI scrutiny. In retrospect it seems safe to assume that Clark learned of Rowe's status as an FBI informer shortly after the arrests and realized that the bureau would be looking for scapegoats. Clark was going to make certain that he wasn't among them. Sheriff Clark welcomed the resources of the FBI, the State Police, and the Klan in his efforts to maintain a segregated Selma, but he wasn't going to get caught in their crossfire.

Clark told the *Detroit News* that Gene Thomas's Impala had been stopped by state troopers for speeding on the afternoon of the murder. "The FBI agents have always worked closely with us in the past," he said, "but this time for some reason they didn't. If we had known about it, we would have tried to keep that car under surveillance. The shooting didn't happen in my county. I regret that it happened, but I've been getting telegrams from all over the country blaming me for it. We had a march today on the courthouse [in Selma] and the demonstrators indicated that I was to blame for what happened. If they want to blame anybody, they ought to march on the federal building."

While he had the reporter's attention, Clark couldn't resist taking a swipe at Viola Liuzzo. "I have five children too," he said. "But the night this happened my wife was at home with the children where she belongs."[14]

The FBI was also adamant. Bureau spokesmen angrily maintained not only that the Impala had *never* been under surveillance but that Tommy Rowe was actually a hero. Although powerless to prevent the murder, Rowe had broken the case and shown moral courage by agreeing to testify against the other Klansmen. Rowe, they insisted, came within minutes of saving Liuzzo's life. It was a lie, but Hoover was desperate.[15]

The FBI chief bristled at any criticism. On March 30, the *Los Angeles Times* reported, "[Hoover] said his agency is doing everything possible to investigate violations of civil rights laws, but he stressed that its role is that of an investigator—not an accuser, prosecutor, jury or judge. 'I refuse to let the FBI be forced into practices which smack of police state actions, regardless of the circumstances,' [Hoover] said. 'To my mind the freedom and rights of our nation can be implemented as well as preserved without resorting to totalitarian tactics.'"

At a private meeting with President Johnson, the agitated FBI director reported that Jim Liuzzo, the murdered woman's husband, was a Teamster organizer with "a shady background" and that Viola Liuzzo had been sitting "very very close to the Negro" in the car. It seemed to Hoover that the situation had "all the appearances of a necking party." When Johnson ignored his innuendoes, Hoover instructed FBI staff to leak his speculations to Klan informants, who then leaked them to the press. The resources of the FBI were employed in a feverish hunt for derogatory information about the Liuzzos, their friends and associates, and any organizations they belonged to. FBI agents spent considerable time tracking an unfounded rumor that Jim Liuzzo was arrested during the 1940s for handing out communist literature in Port Arthur, Texas. It wasn't true. Rumors of Mrs. Liuzzo's adultery, instability, and criminal activity began to circulate. In *The Fiery Cross* author Wyn Craig Wade notes that "In less than a month the national topic changed from the willful murder of Mrs. Liuzzo to her moral character."

Reflecting in the *Washington Post* on the seventeenth anniversary of Viola Liuzzo's death, columnist Jack Anderson observed, "Evidently aware of the embarrassment the FBI would suffer from the presence of its undercover informer in the murderer's car, J. Edgar Hoover marshaled the Bureau's resources to blacken the dead woman's reputation. This came at a time when the Bureau was also trying to smear [Martin Luther] King and find links between the SCLC and the Communist Party."[16]

Hoover's disdain for civil rights activists tended to dignify Imperial Wizard Shelton's declaration that Liuzzo was being "set up to become a martyr and another rallying point for the Civil Rights Movement. If this woman was at home with the children where she belonged," Shelton said, "she wouldn't have been in jeopardy."[17]

As the FBI continued to feed the press misleading and distorted information about Mrs. Liuzzo, many Americans began to believe that the imperial wizard had a point. Reporters were seduced by juicy rumors, especially when they came from such knowledgeable sources. Scandal sells papers, and America's impression of Viola Liuzzo became twisted beyond recognition.

Shelton claimed to have uncovered confidential information about Viola Liuzzo's "police record" and her "liberated relationship" with her husband. Klansmen fueled rumors of week-long orgies in Selma and claimed there were eyewitnesses willing to testify that they saw Liuzzo behaving like a whore. None ever came forward, but nothing in Viola Liuzzo's past would be sacred from this point on. A victim of a capital crime, she was investigated by the United States Federal Bureau of Investigation as if she had been a criminal herself.

3 Unlocking the Past

Errors, like straws, upon the surface flow;
He who would search for pearls must dive below.
—John Dryden

Back home in New York City I find it impossible to concentrate. My thoughts won't leave Alabama. Will any of the Liuzzos answer my letter? Was I clear? Was I credible? Should I write another one?

Two weeks later a package arrives from Gale Hill, secretary of the Teaching Tolerance Program at the Southern Poverty Law Center. "Dear Mary," she writes, "enclosed are the copies of your letters and self-addressed stamped envelopes that were returned to us. I tried to follow up on each one, but it appears that the people are either deceased or moved and did not leave a forwarding address. Good luck with your book on Viola Liuzzo."

Six letters returned! Only four were delivered! Where did everybody go? The Civil Rights Memorial was dedicated in 1989—only five years ago—how could six people in four different states disappear so fast?

With my determination fueled by rising frustration, I keep at the detective work, hoping to unearth more names—other names. In Manhattan's Museum of Radio and Television I run and re-run the television coverage of the 1965 voting rights march. NBC, CBS, ABC. Some commentators are frankly sympathetic to the marchers, some are disdainful. The march happened before the era of political correctness, in a time when even the most liberal of anchormen—there were no anchorwomen—refer to blacks as "them."

In the Central Research Library on 42nd Street I compare coverage of the Liuzzo murder in the big-city dailies. What some editors leave out is often more interesting than what others include. The *New York Times, Los Angeles Times, Montgomery Advertiser,* and *Detroit Free Press* all run a picture of Viola Liuzzo as a young, pretty woman—a photo taken when she was no more than twenty or twenty-one years old. The *New York Daily News, Atlanta Journal, Detroit News,* and *New York Post* run a later image. Mrs. Liuzzo is holding her daughter Sally, who is about three years old, on a rocking horse. She is trying to balance the child and look up at the camera at the same time. Her concentration distorts her expression, making her look distracted, anxious, high strung.

The *Chicago Tribune* runs a picture of her parents, the only one I ever found. They have just arrived from Georgia, a couple in their sixties, numbed by grief. Mrs. Gregg is slim with dark brown hair and glasses, an ordinary-looking woman, with a dazed expression, who probably set her hair in pin curls and carried pictures of her grandchildren in her pocketbook. Her husband is lighter in complexion; his hair is thinning, yet he is strikingly good-looking with strong features softened by the openness the camera catches in his expression.

My evenings are spent scanning thirty-year-old newspapers, making notes, charts, and time lines. Stacks of photocopies fill my studio apartment. I list names and track them through news accounts, magazine articles, and old broadcasts. I construct theories about what was reported, what was ignored, distorted, or suppressed, and who stood to gain by turning public sympathy against the Liuzzos. I make, remake, and discard theories on a weekly basis.

It's like putting together a jigsaw puzzle, like opening an attic trunk. I am obsessed with finding more, making connections, searching for the woman behind the spiraling events of the week of March 21, 1965. When I began my research I was afraid I wouldn't have enough material. Now I am overwhelmed by the sheer volume and complexity of the public record. Why hasn't anyone tackled this? Why do I seem to be the only one who finds it riveting?

I discover that on April 1, 1965, two days after Viola Liuzzo's funeral, a cross was burned in the backyard of her home. Her husband Jim was suddenly inundated by obscene phone calls and hate mail. Detroit's population was more than 60 percent white in 1965; it was a city of single-family homes, and many white Detroit property owners were not pleased by the activism of their neighbor on Marlowe Street. Didn't Vi realize that blacks, who made up less than a third of the city's population, constituted almost 80 percent of its relief rolls? What was she thinking about?

In the *Detroit Free Press* I find a picture of Jim Liuzzo sitting in his living room looking bewildered. He is a burly man, with a dark complexion, rugged features, and sad eyes. The call that changed his life came in the middle of the night on March 25, 1965. One of the first names I traced was that of Rev. Meryl Ruoss, a Presbyterian minister who assisted Hosea Williams, the SCLC's logistics director for the 1965 march. (Hosea Williams had co-led the March 7 Selma demonstration with John Lewis of SNCC that had ended with both being beaten, trampled, and gassed on the Pettus Bridge.) Rev. Ruoss placed that fateful call from the Dexter Avenue Church in Montgomery. He informed Jim that his wife had been in an accident.

"Is it serious?" Jim asked.

"Yes, I'm afraid she's dead."

Jim threw down the phone and began screaming. Ruoss held the line for ten minutes, but no one picked up again. In desperation Ruoss called his friend, the Reverend C. Kilmer Myers, Episcopal bishop of Detroit, and asked him to drive to the Liuzzo home as quickly as possible. But Jim Liuzzo refused to accept help or comfort from Bishop Myers. "I'm a Catholic," he insisted, "and I want a priest." He believed the Protestant clergy had been instrumental in getting his wife involved with this cause that killed her.

By midnight the Liuzzo house was filled with family, neighbors, and reporters. "I tried to discourage her," a distraught Jim Liuzzo told the press, "but she told me four or five of her friends were going, and I couldn't stop her. . . . She was the biggest hearted woman you ever saw in your life. Her big heart was her downfall."

For the rest of the night Jim called every official he could rouse in Selma and Montgomery. He was repeatedly told he had contacted the wrong jurisdiction. In desperation, he finally called the White House. Jim Liuzzo had no way of knowing that J. Edgar Hoover was counseling President Johnson not to accept his call. Hoover insisted he was trying to protect the president because Liuzzo had a background that "wasn't too good."

Within days the *Detroit Free Press* reported that Jim's sons Tommy and Tony were being called "nigger lovers" at school and that six-year-old Sally had rocks thrown at her on her way home from first grade. Garbage was strewn across the Liuzzo lawn, and shots were fired at the house. Jim finally hired armed guards to protect his family.

Perhaps most despicable was the anonymous letter sent to Jim with a clipping enclosed from the *Birmingham News* classified section. I read it in disbelief: "Do you need a crowd drawer? I have the 1963 Oldsmobile 2-door that Viola Liuzzo was killed in. Bullet holes and everything still intact. Ideal to bring in a crowd. $3,500."

Jim hadn't even finished paying for his wife's car. When it was impounded as evidence, he stopped making payments and it was repossessed. After the police released it to the finance company, it was resold to a private citizen in Birmingham.

For weeks after Mrs. Liuzzo's murder, journalists and cameramen filled the house at 19375 Marlowe Street interviewing every member of the stunned family. Reporter Jean Sharley summed up her discussions with the Liuzzos on March 26: "What [Viola] taught her children, was to take their lumps, to live intensely, treat all people as equals, and to keep their promises."

Sharley walked through the Liuzzo home, from the living room, where pictures of the children were arranged in steps on either side of the wall clock that hung behind the couch, to the den, where one wall was filled with Mrs. Liuzzo's books. Then she peered into the master bedroom and simply listed the things that were left behind on Mrs. Liuzzo's bureau: "a single strand of pearls, a picture of her mother, a bottle of holy water, a hair dryer, a book about chess, Anna Freud's *Psychoanalytic Treatment of Children*, a clown's face drawn by her daughter Sally, and a newspaper story about Selma."[1]

Marlowe Street

▆▆▆▆▆▆ I did not wait and ponder what I should do. That would not have
been me.
—Dr. Elisabeth Kubler-Ross

The Liuzzos always lived on Marlowe Street but not always above Seven
Mile Road in the spacious two-story brick corner house at 19375. For
more than ten years they had lived at 18491 Marlowe Street, near
Dearborn. The move to northwest Detroit in 1963 was the result of Jim
Liuzzo's success as a business agent for the Teamsters. He had steadily
moved up the ranks and was finally able to afford a bigger home in a better neighborhood, two cars, a small summer cabin in Grayling, and
household help. He encouraged his wife to stop working and concentrate
on finishing her degree at Wayne State University. In 1963 things seemed
to be looking up for the Liuzzos.

Eighteen months later, Jim Liuzzo's wife was dead. When he was asked
about her involvement with civil rights he said, "Nothing could stop Vi
from doing what she thought was right. I couldn't, the children couldn't,
nobody could."

After her murder, as reporters began releasing disturbing rumors about
Viola Liuzzo, Jim's grief turned to rage. Stories started circulating about
her abandoning the family, being emotionally disturbed, and having a police record. Jim tried to untangle the cruel distortions, to explain his wife's
reasons for participating in the march, but every attempt he made to defend her seemed to backfire. He told Walter Rugaber of the *Detroit Free
Press*, "My wife was a good woman. She's never done anything to be
ashamed of."[2]

Yes, Jim acknowledged, it was *technically* true that Vi had a police
record. But she had been arrested for social activism. In 1964 Vi had challenged the Detroit Board of Education. She took issue with a recently
passed Michigan state statute that reduced the age at which a student
could drop out of high school without permission from eighteen to sixteen. Vi believed children should be required to stay in school until they
were eighteen. She thought this would protect them in the way that child
labor laws had once protected children from being exploited. Vi was

sorry she had quit school at fourteen and believed such a law might have kept her from being so cavalier about her education.

Vi met with representatives of the Detroit Board of Education to plead her case. They told her that while they agreed with her, there was nothing they could do. But she refused to let the matter rest. Ultimately, she decided to take action to call wider attention to it.

She took her sons Tommy, thirteen, and Tony, ten, and her daughter Mary, sixteen, an honor student, out of school in protest. For more than a month she tutored them at home. After the children were absent forty days, Vi was cited by the school board for violating the State School Compulsory Age Law. She was arrested at home on June 16, 1964. This was the arrest Imperial Wizard Robert Shelton called a matter of public record.

At Vi's court appearance in June, Judge Joseph Gillis adjourned the matter until September, expressing hope that Vi and the school board could work things out. Shortly thereafter Judge Gillis received a letter from the board saying that they did not desire to prosecute Mrs. Liuzzo. But Vi insisted on being tried.

Less than a year later, a reporter for the *New York Daily News* would comment, "Viola Liuzzo lived a life that combined the care of her family and her home with a concern for the world around her. This involvement with her times was not always understood by her friends, nor was it appreciated by others around her."

When I read this, I slid forward in my chair in the library to refocus the microfilm. I didn't like this story. It was unnerving. *NO! Don't do it!* I heard myself mumbling. *Don't pull those kids out of school! Can't you see it won't accomplish anything? Without support, even the board's admission that the law is short-sighted means nothing. They told you they were powerless to act! This isn't the way to do it*, I wanted to scream. *This isn't going to change anything!*

I was wrong. Mary bitterly resented her mother's decision to disrupt her education. The dropout age issue held no interest for Mary, who enjoyed school. She railed against the self-sacrifice her mother expected. How would ruining her grade-point average benefit anybody else? Vi's zeal for the cause blinded her to the consequences she was bringing on herself and on her daughter. At midterm Mary had been on the honor roll, but after losing forty days of school she wasn't able to recoup. Mary began acting out, openly challenging Vi, running up her mother's charge accounts, and finally running away from home. When she was returned, the officer in charge of the case noted, "essentially the problem is that the mother allows the girl to do certain things, and then insists that the girl is disobeying her. The father just wants peace and quiet."[3]

In July 1964, Mary went to stay with Vi's parents, who had moved to Fort Oglethorpe, Georgia. Vi's oldest daughter, Penny, who had also spent her senior year in high school living with her grandparents, was then staying with Vi's sister Mary in Ypsilanti. Twenty-seven-year-old Mary Gregg, who had always been close to her sister Vi and her two teenage nieces, was planning a September wedding. Only ten years older than Penny, Mary had played big sister to the girls, taking them ice skating and to the movies and teaching them the latest dances. Vi had watched over Mary after their parents moved back to the South, and the sisters remained close until the Liuzzos moved to northwest Detroit—the time everyone seems to agree was the beginning of the end for the Liuzzo family.

With Penny and Mary out of the house, tensions eased somewhat, but Vi missed her daughters terribly. She had worked hard to make all the children feel they were part of one family. Had she pushed too much? Wanted too much? Demanded the impossible?

The Selma to Montgomery march appealed to Vi Liuzzo for a variety of reasons. Its stated purpose was to call the country's attention to the fact that black American citizens were being denied their constitutional right to vote—to shame "those in charge" into doing the right thing. This was the very thing that Vi had attempted with her school board protest two years before. By 1965, however, she had given up independent crusading. Hard experience had shown her that you can't change laws or attitudes all by yourself. Her one-woman protests had left her feeling defeated, frustrated, and guilty over family disruptions. Gradually, her understanding of social change broadened, and she became involved in campus activism at Wayne State University.

Viola Liuzzo's last one-woman protest was recorded in the Wayne State

University campus newspaper, the *Daily Collegian*, two weeks before her death. Protesting the paper's policy that all letters to the editor be typewritten, she wrote neatly on lined paper in blue ink:

> To the editor:
> The letter that cannot be read. . . . Obviously, George Orwell's imaginary predictions for the year 1984, in his book, *1984,* are much closer to realization than Orwell predicted. I speak with the authority of the silence forced upon me by the mechanistic "typespeak." Hence, I need write no more, since the art of legible longhand is banished from our culture. Although I still identify myself as Viola Liuzzo (Mrs. A. Liuzzo), I will willingly conform to progress and sign myself,
> Sincerely,
> I.D. #283009

While her letter was dismissed as the work of a crank, less than two years later students nationwide would be protesting their increasingly depersonalized campuses and carrying signs which told the world I AM A HUMAN BEING. DO NOT FOLD, SPINDLE, OR MUTILATE.

Within a few days of her murder, however, Viola Liuzzo's involvement with social justice was a nonissue. The question of her fitness as a mother became paramount. This was nothing new. In 1960, Marjorie Swann, a peace activist and mother of four, had been jailed for civil disobedience during a demonstration at an ICBM missile installation outside Omaha. The judge who sentenced Mrs. Swann called her "an irresponsible, irrational, stubborn, foolish woman, and a bad mother."[4] Mrs. Swann replied, "I love my children dearly. . . . I know that if there is another war—a nuclear, global war—they will die. So will millions of other children all over the world. . . . The children must know that we care." The judge was not impressed.

Five years after Mrs. Swann's trial, criticism of Viola Liuzzo for leaving her husband and five children to go to Selma grew so vicious that Rev. James J. Sheehan, a veteran of the Selma march himself and chairman of the Detroit diocese's Human Relations Committee, addressed it directly as he delivered her eulogy: "Many Detroiters have criticized Viola Liuzzo for leaving her children to make the trip," the priest said. "People travel all over the world for business and pleasure and nobody criticizes them. But Vi's death touched consciences. . . . Today America hurts. All of us who have pride in what our country stands for are in anguish over the death of Viola Liuzzo. . . . The great work was in Selma, and that's where she belonged. Now that she is dead, all over the United States people are picking up the torch that she dropped, people who feel guilt for their brothers."[5]

Mary Liuzzo, interviewed seventeen years later as the Voting Rights Act came due for renewal, told journalist Ken Fireman, "We were always taught a respect for life, so it was no surprise when my mother got involved in the struggle for civil rights—for *human* rights."

A neighbor who knew Vi for more than ten years told reporter Anthony Ripley, "There's been a lot of remarks that this woman should have been home with the children and not off in Alabama on a freedom march. But nobody talks about the fact that they had help at home. She never left them alone and uncared-for. If this murder had happened to someone else she would have been the first one to that house to see what she could do."[6]

Everything I read about Vi Liuzzo makes me hungry to know more. Complex, unpredictable—I am drawn to her directness, her sense of outrage. She desperately wanted her life to mean something. Ambitious, generous, sometimes fixated, sometimes insensitive—she was all these things. Issues that were important to her all seemed to carry the same weight.

I keep digging and find that in 1961, four years before Selma, when her youngest daughter, Sally, was three, Vi decided to return to work. She had been a cashier and a waitress before her marriage to Jim, but now she wanted more substantial work. She was thirty-five years old and had been a full-time mother for ten years.

On March 19, 1961, she began night classes at the Carnegie Institute, a training school for medical assistants, where she enrolled in a one-year certificate program. Vi threw her substantial energy into her school work, bringing fellow students home for study sessions, organizing a car pool (for which she did most of the driving), and even helping some of her classmates find part-time jobs. "She was a wonderful person," Julia Deaton told author Jack Mendelsohn in 1966. "If it wasn't for Vi some of us wouldn't have gotten through school. Vi used to tape the lectures and play them back to help us prepare for exams."[7]

By the end of the term the study sessions at 18491 Marlowe had turned into debating sessions. The students, most younger than Vi, discussed their lives and current events and shared things that were important to them. Julia Deaton remembers that once the group stayed up all night discussing civil rights. One young woman said, "I'm as much for it as you Vi, but what about your daughter marrying a Negro?" Vi said that was a very old argument. She said she believed people had a right to make their own decisions about whom to marry and, no, that wouldn't bother her a bit.[8]

Shortly after graduating from Carnegie (tied with another student for top honors), on March 15, 1962, Vi got a job as a medical assistant at Parkview Medical Center. She enjoyed her work, but within a few months she began struggling with her supervisor over work rules. Because of Jim Liuzzo's position as a union organizer, Vi was familiar with labor contracts. Some of the regulations imposed on the secretaries at Parkview seemed unreasonable to her — especially the uneven distribution of overtime: men got it, women didn't. Then, when a secretary was laid off without severance pay, Vi turned over her own paycheck to the woman, hoping it would embarrass the administration into reconsidering a severance allowance. When it didn't, Vi decided to call wider attention to what she felt was an injustice. She stayed after her shift and phoned the Detroit police and told them she was thinking about stealing a microscope. She gave them a description of her car and left.

On her way home a patrol car stopped her. She demanded to be taken to the police station, knowing that local reporters would be interested because of Jim's connection with the Teamsters. Since she hadn't stolen anything, no charges were filed. But Vi used the attention she got as a platform to vocalize her opinions about the unfair labor practices at the nonunion Parkview Medical Center.

"She was a fighter," Jim said, "she never gave up when she thought she was right."

Right up through her school board challenge two years later, Vi's protests would be personal and dramatic. Her appeals for justice were re-actions to specific incidents—a secretary's dismissal, the denial of over-time to women, regret about her own decision to drop out of school as a teenager. But Vi's passion for fairness could blind her to the needs of peo-ple she most deeply loved. Her demonstrations sometimes cost her more than they accomplished.

Vi's activism cost her her job at Parkview hospital, but she found an-other, almost immediately, in the tissue lab at Sinai Hospital. There she was assigned to a visiting Nigerian medical researcher who praised her competence and encouraged her to continue her education. The doctor assured her she had the ability to handle college work, despite the fact that she had never finished high school.

On his advice, Vi took entrance exams for Wayne State University in October 1962. She passed them and was permitted to enroll as a condi-tional student in the spring of 1963. She did so well from the start that a year later she was fully matriculated.

Vi's determined pursuit of education was unusual for a white middle-aged woman in 1962. While her neighbors were taking cooking classes, raising funds for the March of Dimes, or doing volunteer work for the church, she was preparing herself for a career, crusading for workplace rights, and trying to get herself admitted to college at thirty-six.

The deafening silence my letters to the Liuzzo family produced was frus-trating. *Are any of them going to respond?* I wondered. Time passed. Three weeks. A month. Two months. I went to work, picked up Chinese take-out on the way home, watched the news, and waited impatiently while the rest of the world moved on. In April a U.S. district court awarded Rodney King damages for the beating he received at the hands of the Los Angeles police. In May, Jackie Kennedy died. Nelson Mandela be-came president of South Africa. In June, O. J. Simpson was charged with two counts of murder. Then one sticky night in August, while I was stretched out on my couch watching two experts debate the wisdom of ad-mitting female cadets to the Citadel, my phone rang. I considered letting the answering machine pick up but changed my mind on the third ring.

"Hello?"

"Hello. Is this Mary Stanton?"

"Yes."

"Hi. . . . This is Penny Liuzzo."

I nearly dropped the phone. "Oh, my God! Oh, *my God*! Penny! I'm so glad you called!"[9]

Penny

████████████   Mothers are . . . the first book read and the last put aside in every child's library.

—C. Lenox Remond

Penny Liuzzo Herrington is a warm, friendly Californian. Her voice is full of engaging humor as she asks—long distance—why in the world I want to write a book about her mother.

When I tell Penny how long I have been thinking about it she is amazed—and curious—but it strikes her as okay. Live and let live. A person could, after all, do worse than write a book.

We find we have a lot in common. Penny and I were born in 1946, we are both older sisters, both grew up in the city, both divorced. My father was also a Teamster. Penny asks about my mother, my family, my ex-husband, and about what it was like growing up in Queens. "Sounds like the old Marlowe Street," she laughs.

Penny has four sons. Between them the Liuzzo siblings have twelve children, none of whom their mother lived to see.

"What was she like?" I ask. I had prepared a list of "penetrating" questions, but Penny is so open and animated that I just put my list down and let the conversation take its course.

"Mom was for real," she says simply. "She believed in social justice and wanted to help black people get it. Am I proud of her? Sure, of course. But mostly I miss her. It would've been great to have her around to talk to when I was in my twenties or thirties, when I would have appreciated her more. You know what I mean? I'm angry sometimes because she's gone and I missed so much of her."

"Are you angry that she went on the march?"

"No. I don't think so. I get invited to speak to the social studies classes in the high schools out here. They ask me to talk about the march and the civil rights movement and who my mother was. I'm proud of what she did. My boys are too. She was a strong person."

I ask what Penny remembers most about life with her mother. "Well," she sighs, "the first thing that comes to mind is that she was always up to something. She had a lot of energy, you know? Once, on Halloween she snuck down to the basement and put on this fright wig. She covered her face in white pancake makeup and got into my brother Tommy's black cassock—he was an altar boy. Then she went outside and banged on the window. Well, she scared us so much we all started screaming.

"Mom thought it was great fun, but we fixed her wagon. We locked her out until we figured we'd evened the score. You can imagine what the neighbors thought with her in that get-up trying to break into her own front door!

"She really loved holidays—our house was always the one covered in Christmas lights. One year our neighbors, the Vogels, had a bad fire the night before Christmas. Mom called the owner of the local toy store and badgered him until he opened up for her—at ten at night—and she replaced all their gifts. She was always doing things like that.

"Then there was the time the pound got one of our dogs, Rex—he was this big German shepherd and we all loved him. I was sure the dog catcher took him because our neighbors were always complaining that he barked too much. Mom promised if he was in the pound she'd get him back. I called for two days before the dog catcher finally located him. By that time my mother was sick in bed with the flu. When my brother Nino (that's what we called Tony) ran upstairs to tell her that we found Rex she dragged herself out of bed, put a coat on over her nightgown, and told Tommy to go find the car keys. 'Are you going to the pound like *that?*' I asked her. 'Got a better idea?' she said. And we all piled into the car to get Rex. Life at our house was hectic, but we managed to get the important stuff done."

"She sounds incredible!" I laugh.

"Well, she had a million interests, that's for sure. She used to take me and my sisters to the symphony and to the art museum downtown, and she went rock collecting and camping with my brothers. I sat in on her college classes once in a while—she'd always be telling us about what she was studying, talking about what was going on in the world, and in the next second she'd be out there rescuing stray animals, feeding the bums and giving them spending money, or volunteering for fund-raising drives for the church or at our schools—she was always up to *something*. It drove my father crazy."

Penny thinks her mother's relationship with her and her brothers and sisters wouldn't seem unusual today, but for the 1960s it was revolutionary.

"Mom talked to us like we were her contemporaries," she said. "She believed it was more important to instill a sense of responsibility in us and build our self confidence than it was to control us. When I was eighteen she told me I had no more curfew, that I knew right from wrong and she expected that I'd behave accordingly. We had our battles, but I never had to fight for *my* freedom," Penny laughs. "*Mom* was the freedom fighter of the family. She was never on our backs, either. She believed she could trust our judgment.

"Why does my mother mean so much to you?" she asks, suddenly.

"I'm not sure. . . . I'm trying to figure it out."

"How can I help?"

"There are so many things I want to ask you," I tell her. "But my head's spinning. Can I call you?"

"Sure," she says warmly. "Call whenever you want. I like talking with you. I don't think you'll get much from the others though. It's been hard. I'll ask my sisters, but I know my brothers won't talk to anyone anymore."

"I think I understand," I say.

"I don't think so," she says gently. "Nobody could ever really understand. It was a nightmare. We lost our mother, then we had to listen to her name being dragged through the mud." Penny changes the subject abruptly, "But anyway, you might hear from Sarah."

"Sarah?"

"Sarah Evans. My mother's best friend."

After we hang up, I rummage through my stacks of copied microfilm until I find the picture of Penny Liuzzo in the *New York Times*. She is sitting in her living room with her two little brothers and her sister Sally. The boys are on opposite ends of a couch. Penny's arm is around her sister, reaching over to touch Tony's arm. Her other hand is holding Tommy's. All the other children are crying. Penny looks dazed as she comforts them. She is pretty, with delicate features like her mother's. Her dark hair is teased into the bouffant style of 1965, and she is wearing a sleeveless shift dress. In another picture she is in church, standing in the first pew with her family at her mother's requiem mass. Penny is a head shorter than Mary, who looks straight ahead. Mary's eyes are wide with disbelief. She grips the pew in front of her tightly, as if to steady herself. The others touch each other, but Mary is self-contained. Little Sally is gripping Penny's hand. As Penny glances sideways, the photographer catches the terror in her eyes, now frozen in time.

What does she look like now, I wonder? She is nearly ten years older than her mother was when she died. She is the mother of four children herself. Is she gray? Does she beat it back with Clairol like I do? Does she wonder, like me, how fifty came so quickly?

As I wait impatiently for Sarah Evans to call, I keep on digging. I could kick myself for not asking Penny more questions, like what she thought about the school board feud and how it affected her mother and her sister. And what about the incident at Parkview hospital? Did the rest of the family feel these issues were worth getting the police involved? And what about the cross-burning in their yard?

I call Penny a few days later. She says she is glad to hear from me. We chat for a long while. About my work, her boys, life in New York, about the man she lives with who is good to her sons and makes her happy. It's comfortable. We begin to feel like we've known each other a long time. I have trouble keeping the conversation on track, though, when we talk about her mother. I can hear tension build in her voice. I sense her reluctance to go into too much detail. What is it? Am I pushing too hard?

"Look," she says, finally. "Be careful what you write about that school board thing. That's what people used to drag out when they said my mother was crazy."

"I wouldn't—"

"She didn't just pull my brothers and Mary out of school because she woke up one morning and felt like it, you know." There is real heat in her voice. "She did it because the ordinance dropped the age when you could quit school without permission from eighteen to sixteen. She didn't think that was right. It was a reaction—a protest—against the new law."

"Did she do it for publicity?" I ask, carefully.

"Of course! How else do you call attention to something? How else do you get other people to care about it? They said she just did it for attention. Well, I guess that's partly right—but the press insinuated it was theatrics or hysterics or some damn thing. Look, you had to know her. She'd just gone back to school, and she loved college. She was sorry that she'd quit so young—she kept pushing me to apply to college." There is a long pause. I don't know what to say, so I just hold on.

"Anyway, I was supposed to start community college that September, but I never went. Things just got too complicated."

We talk a little more, about places we would like to go for vacation, old rock-and-roll songs, first loves. . . . Our conversations are like that. I like her. She wants to trust me, but so many others have taken this same information and twisted it. I feel her struggling. I feel her anger sometimes. Sometimes there is impatience in her voice. Sometimes there is ambivalence too.

During another conversation I ask how the family was able to cope with all the criticism about their mother leaving them to take part in the march. "People never gave that old rag up," she says. "But you know, I also think about whether I could have done what Mom did. I have four children, and when I ask myself if I could have left them the answer is always no." There is a long pause. "I don't have the confidence she had, I guess. She was always so sure about everything."

I'm increasingly grateful Penny has agreed to talk with me at all.

Motor City

Detroit stands for an America that is over.
—Jerry Herron

Downtown Detroit is a paradox—a city crumbling and expanding at the same time. Once the last stop on the Underground Railroad, Detroit experienced the worst racial rioting in American history on July 23, 1967. The night before, a group of blacks were arrested at an illegal after-hours club. The scuffle that began between the black patrons and the white police quickly escalated. Six days and nights of arson and vandalism followed. When the smoke cleared, four thousand fires had destroyed thirteen thousand buildings; five thousand blacks were left homeless and five thousand more jobless.

The Michigan National Guard was activated, and the frightened weekend soldiers began firing into buildings, unnerved by persistent rumors of snipers. A *Detroit Free Press* independent investigation concluded that guardsmen not only killed one of their own, two black citizens, and a four-year-old girl but were also responsible for the deaths of a fireman and a Connecticut woman visiting Detroit on business.[10] Forty-three people were killed, and more than a thousand were wounded. Ultimately President Johnson sent in tanks and paratroopers. The U.S. National Advisory Commission on Civil Disorders blamed the violence on the "explosive mixture of poverty, unemployment, slum and segregated housing."

A week after the riots, rumors circulated in the black community that three white Detroit police officers killed three young black men and beat two white girls because they caught them together in the Algiers Motel on Woodward Avenue. The police insisted that the black men were snipers. In *Detroit: City of Race and Class*, B. J. Widick recounts how suspicion began to grow when it was discovered that the motel owner, not the police, had reported the murders of the unarmed men. Eighteen months later, the three suspended white policemen and a black private guard were tried on charges of conspiring against the civil rights of the dead black men. Four years after the murder of Viola Liuzzo, an all-white jury declared them not guilty.

Professor Widick observed that "What the Negro community knew in August 1967 was confirmed by later events: No white policeman would ever be tried and found guilty of murdering a black man caught with a white woman."[11]

A labor relations conference brought me to Detroit in October 1995, and determination got me an interview with Sarah Evans. Mrs. Evans called, as Penny expected she would, and I spoke with her several times during the next few months, but I was anxious to meet her face to face.

"Nobody but her parents knew Mrs. Liuzzo longer than you," I said.

"That's true," she chuckled, "and nobody knew her better."

But now that I had actually come to Detroit, Mrs. Evans seemed less anxious to talk. I called her from my room at the Detroit Athletic Club on Thursday morning. She hesitated. Sunday was really the best time for her, but it would have to be after church. "Where?" she asked, with some trepidation.

"The St. Regis Hotel?" I wasn't going to ask her to meet me at the Athletic Club; if you looked out my window onto Madison Avenue and couldn't remember where you were, Dresden after World War II would be a reasonable guess. I picked the St. Regis out of the phone book. It sounded classy.

"Oh yes, the St. Regis." She sounded more relaxed. "I know where that is. How about two o'clock?"

"Two o'clock is fine."

"Good. I'll see you then."

My conference ended Friday at noon. First order of business would be to tell the clerk at the front desk that I needed my room until Sunday. I couldn't see how it would be a problem.

I'm sure the Detroit Athletic Club was very elegant thirty years ago. Built in 1915, President Theodore Roosevelt was one of its first guests. The walls are covered in rich, dark wood, and leather upholstered chairs still fill the lounges. But the rugs are thin, the halls are worn, and shabbiness is settling over everything. While the dining room still fills each night, I would guess few people linger very long over coffee in this part of town. Keeping my room over the weekend was either a bold act of courage or the height of recklessness.

I used the extra time to explore. By two o'clock Friday afternoon I was in a cab heading to the Wayne State University campus to see where Viola Liuzzo experienced the thrill of ideas and joined the excitement of a generation that knew it was going to change the world.

The Wayne campus is big and sprawling, three times larger than it was when Vi attended. Most of its buildings are new; some are still under construction. Wayne State is a commuter school, as it was in 1965 when it was still known as "the working man's college." Today's typical student is black, in his or her twenties, holds at least a part-time job, and has family responsibilities.

Wayne State was never Berkeley. Founded in 1868 with the motto "Industry, Intelligence, Integrity," by 1965 it had become a conservative institution that tolerated a core of committed activists who harangued the administration on issues of free speech, fair housing, and economic and social justice.

In 1965 the campus newspaper the *Daily Collegian* chronicled both civil rights demonstrations and accounts of Tau Kappa Epsilon's First Annual Cigar Bowl, where fraternity men competed to produce the best smoke ring while a band played "Smoke Gets in Your Eyes." Vista and the Peace Corps recruited on campus, Students for a Democratic Society protested the troop buildup in Vietnam, and Dr. Marion Edman, professor of education, was honored as one of the Ten Top Working Women of Detroit. Dr. Edman was praised by her colleague Professor Charles H. Sechrest as someone who never tried to boss a man. "If you don't like Marion," Professor Sechrest asserted, "there is something wrong with you."[12]

In this admixture of conservatism, apathy, and activism, the ideas that shaped Viola Liuzzo's destiny were forged. Here she made the personal decision that changed many lives.

From the campus I walk out to Woodward Avenue and over a few blocks to the Detroit Public Library. I spend the afternoon rolling microfilm, scanning old issues of the *Detroit News* and the *Detroit Free Press*. "Mrs. Liuzzo Dared Highway of Hate," "Priest Raps Martyr's Critics," "Governor Wallace Defends His State," "Martyr Comes Home in Peace, with Honor," "Romney Visits House of Sorrow," and "Burn Cross in Liuzzos' Backyard." The Detroit Public Library houses the Burton Collection, Detroit's archives. I thumb through the card catalog but find no entries under *Liuzzo,* so I check the computer bank. There is one there—a reference to Beatrice Siegel's *Murder on the Highway.*

I cross the street and enter the Detroit Historical Museum. On the third floor the Detroit Historical Society has its offices. They have no information on Viola Liuzzo at all.

Finally, I head back to the campus. Surely the university archives will have something! The archivist is friendly and warm and tries to be helpful. He gives me a folder less than half an inch thick. It contains a copy of the chapter on Viola in Sara Bullard's *Free at Last*, a few copies of the campus paper that covered Detroit's Selma sympathy marches, a picture of the Liuzzo memorial service at Wayne State, and a newspaper clipping about the twenty-fifth anniversary of the voting rights march, which devotes a single line to Viola Liuzzo.

"That's it?" I ask.

"Yes," he replies. "Were you looking for something special?"

When I return home I find a confirmation of my written request for information from the Burton Historical Collection. I can't accept that they have nothing in their files. Three months later I receive two copies of articles that appeared in the *South End* (successor to the *Daily Collegian*) in 1979. These articles are not even on file in the Wayne State Archives. The letter reads, "In reply to your recent research request enclosed are copies of materials concerning the Liuzzo family's lawsuit against the federal government. Sadly, I have no data on any memorials or services in Detroit."

Sunday morning I take another cab to the corner of Vassar and Marlowe Streets. I ask the driver to wait while I get out at 19375 Marlowe, a two-story brick house with a white birch tree on the front lawn—Viola Liuzzo's last home. Pots of geraniums sit on either side of the front entrance, and morning glory covers the north wall.

It is one of the few two-story homes on the block. Most of the others are brick ranches. Once solidly Jewish, later integrated middle-class, this is now a black middle-class neighborhood. This end of Marlowe Street reminds me of the Long Island neighborhoods of my childhood—Floral Park, Little Neck, Hempstead. It is pleasant, thriving, more comfortable than the blue-collar borough where I grew up.

The Liuzzos' former home is a corner house with a backyard that faces onto Vassar Street. As I walk around the outside I can easily imagine how someone could jump a short fence, set a burning cross on the back lawn, and have time to disappear down Marlowe to the busy Seven Mile Road and get away. A Florida room has been added, connecting the house with the garage, so you can no longer see into the yard. I suspect Jim Liuzzo had it built. The construction looks old enough.

I walk back around front and ring the bell. Nobody is home. Probably a good thing. What would I say? *Can I come in and look around? Can I walk into your yard? Do you know that Viola Liuzzo once lived here? Do you know who she was?*

On the way back, the cabby takes the Lodge Freeway—Route 10 to downtown—the route Vi Liuzzo would have taken to her classes at Wayne State. It is a twenty-minute drive. I bet she made it in ten.

Sarah

██████████ Best friend, my well-spring in the wilderness!
—George Eliot

Mrs. Evans is a tall black lady with salt-and-pepper hair, an arrow-straight back, and jeweled glasses. She walks directly over to me, sunken as I am in a massively overstuffed chair in the lobby of the St. Regis Hotel. "I knew you right away," she smiles.[13] I couldn't say the same. She has to be near eighty—Vi would have been seventy, and Penny told me there was about ten years between them. But there isn't a line on Mrs. Evans's face, not a wrinkle. Her eyes sparkle, she is wearing a brocade jacket and pearl earrings, and her hair is pulled back in a style that suits her distinguished features. "I'm having a little problem with my knee, which is why I'm on this cane," she explains. I'm probably gawking. I expected a fragile old lady.

A man is with her—in his forties maybe, dapper and smiling. "This is my grandson, Tyrone," she says. "He can tell you a lot about Vi, too. Tyrone grew up in the Liuzzo house."

He nods. "Penny and I went to school together. Sit down, Momma," he says, pulling a chair out for Mrs. Evans. A waitress comes and we order lunch. We've missed brunch, she tells us, and we're too early for dinner, so we order sandwiches.

"What do you want to know?" Mrs. Evans asks.

"I guess what she was like. What kind of a person was she, Mrs. Evans?"

"Oh, call me Sarah," she laughs. "Vi was an original, that's what. She knew what was right and couldn't hold back. She wanted to be part of what was happening in this country in the 1960s. That girl had some of that same stuff in her that Dr. King had in him."

Tyrone nods, "Vi was smart."

Sarah thinks for a moment. "You know, she said to me once, 'Sarah we're all created equal yet they'll give me more justice than they'll give you. That's not right. You keep a better house than me.' You see, I was fussier than she was—"

Tyrone laughs. "You can say that again, Momma. She was a terrible housekeeper! I didn't believe white people had messy homes until I saw Vi's!"

Sarah smiles. "People ask how I could be friends that long with a white woman, but we were like sisters."

"She wasn't like other white people," Tyrone offers. "She didn't think this country belonged to whites—and that, you know, we should either shut up and take it or swim back to Africa."

"If you don't have the right kind of heart you can't understand her," his grandmother says. "I won't ever believe that all white people are bad because I knew her. She asked me once if anything ever happened to her would I take care of her children. I said I would. And I kept that promise, too. I stayed on and lived in with the boys and Sally after Vi died. Sally's grown now. She named one of her twin babies after me, you know, and they all call me 'grandma.'" Mrs. Evans clears her throat. "But Vi had a real temper, too. Don't get me wrong—she was no angel. She could be real hardheaded."

"What do you mean?" I ask.

"Well, you know Jim, her husband, he liked to gamble. One day he lost a lot of money and Vi got furious. She told me she was going to teach him a lesson. She took the house money and asked me if I knew anybody 'safe' who could help her play the horses."

Tyrone laughs, and Sarah glares at him.

"Anyway, I told her my uncle knew a little about the horses, but I warned her not to do it. I told her using the house money was crazy, but she was determined. Finally I got her to promise to only play half of it.

She closed her eyes and pointed to a horse's name on the racing sheet and placed the bet with my uncle. She won, too! And *big*—it was a long shot. Vi wouldn't talk to me for almost a week because I stopped her from gambling the whole thing!"

"She was like that," Tyrone nods. "The light in the room. I mean it. I remember talking with her about Emmett Till when I was a kid. He was that black kid who got killed in Mississippi for whistling at a white woman. Remember?"

I nod.

"I was eleven when it happened. They beat him, shot him in the head, gouged his eye out, then they threw him in the river. I didn't believe anybody would do that to another person. How could people do that to each other? Vi said it was ignorance, but it seemed like pure evil to me."

Mrs. Evans shakes her head.

"I don't know," Tyrone sighs. "Vi always kept up hope that things could get better. I figured nothing could ever get better again for Emmett Till, but she believed marching for a voting bill could change things." He pauses for a moment and rubs his chin. "See, she didn't think like other people. Jim, he had a lot of money, but money never mattered much to Vi. Things didn't either. She gave a lot of stuff away. She was always giving me the keys to her car. And Penny and Mary would bug me to drive them over to Woodward to meet some boys Vi didn't want them hanging with. They put me in some binds, let me tell you! But Vi was just a good person. She even told me she'd send me to college if I wanted to go."

"She would have, too," his grandmother adds. "She was generous like that. See, she knew poverty when she was a little child. Vi had it made, but she didn't take advantage of it. She was no phony. Once I remember there was this little boy selling puppies outside the house. Vi went and chased him—told him to get home. Said he had no business being out so late at night. Then she bought all three of his puppies and brought them in. She was always bringing in stray dogs and cats. It used to make Jim crazy!"

"What was their marriage like?" I ask.

"Well, Jim went along with the things Vi did, but he didn't believe in them like her. He didn't always understand about what was important to her, but he did try. Jim was real proud of her when she graduated from medical technician school, and the Christmas after she started college he bought her a cabin in the woods up near Grayling. Vi loved the woods. She was always taking the kids camping and rock hunting. Now Jim, he preferred the city, but he wanted to give Vi a place to escape, to do her studying, you know? He was having plumbing and electricity put in while Vi was in Selma. It was going to be a surprise for her birthday."

"That was nice."

"Yes, he tried. But I think he really wanted a more traditional wife."

"In what way?"

"Well, Jim and Vi were intellectual equals, I'd say. They used to play Scrabble together at night a lot, but they were very different types, you know? He was a businessman and he liked to go out and party—drink a lot. But Vi, she wasn't a drinker, and she liked home. She loved to cook and make parties and sit out in the yard with the kids." Mrs. Evans smiles, remembering. "Vi walked around barefoot, and she kept a messy house full of cats and dogs and kids, and she was into something new every day. I used to tell her, 'Honey, you're so pretty, why don't you fix yourself up?' But she'd only laugh and tell me, 'Sarah, pretty is as pretty does.'"

"What about the children?"

"They argued a lot about the kids. Vi thought Jim was too strict—and he thought she was too soft. Sometimes Vi would get to feeling guilty and she'd write Jim long letters saying how she'd like to be more the way he wanted her to be and she would be that way if she could. But I think they really loved each other. Jim fell apart when she died. He never remarried. It seems to me he just went down like the *Titanic*. I don't know, maybe he felt that if he'd supported her more, that if he was with her more on her projects and things, that the end might have been different."

"That's sad," I say.

She nods. "Vi couldn't help how she was. She couldn't be different. She expected people to be like her and that got her into trouble. I told her once, 'Vi I know you're sincere, but face the truth, honey, most people don't see things the way you do.' And it's true, nobody was like her, not her parents or her sister or even the kids. None of them really understood her."

"Why do you say that?"

"Because, well, she was very spiritual, she saw things—*felt* things— deeper than anybody I ever knew. She used to have these premonitions."

I must have looked skeptical, because Mrs. Evans shakes her head. "All I can tell you is Tyrone and Sally and I went down to Montgomery when they opened that Civil Rights Memorial in 1989. There's a marker on the highway, at the place where Vi got shot. I wanted to see it, so Tyrone drove me out there after the ceremony. There it was, up on a hill over the road. I told Tyrone to look up. When we passed the spot the whole car shook and there was a popping sound—right there where they killed her."

I look over at Tyrone. "I heard it," he says.

I remembered the thoughts that had filled me as I stood at that same spot just a few months before. Surely they weren't telling me it was haunted?

"What do you think it was?" I ask.

Tyrone shrugs and Sarah looks away, uncomfortably.

"I went there, too," I tell them. "This summer. I stood by that marker and thought about what happened, I even imagined for a minute that I could see the car chase."

"Is that all?" Tyrone asks.

"Yes."

We sit in silence. Tyrone pokes at his club sandwich, I fumble with my notes, and Sarah stares straight ahead. My eyes drop down to a question I wrote the night before, and I ask it just to break the tension.

"Sarah, do you think Vi was happy? Did the movement give her what she was looking for?"

"When I think about it, no," she says slowly. "I don't believe she was happy. I don't think she found what she was looking for—she was still searching, still looking for something. She was so restless! Vi couldn't settle into her life. She hadn't reached her goal when they killed her."

A mind without peace, I think of Yeats's description of Maud Gonne. *A mind without peace.*

"And you think she's still looking?" I ask, carefully.

"Don't matter what I think, honey. Only matters what God thinks, and if He wants us to understand He'll see to it."

Tyrone sighs. "Look, if Vi had come back everything would be different. She went away for just a week, remember. A lot of people leave their kids to go on *vacation* for a week! And she left them with my grandmother who was like a sister to her. Twenty-five thousand people went down on that march and only Vi and Reverend Reeb didn't make it back. The odds were pretty good that she *would* come home, don't you think? She never intended to get herself killed down there."

On the flight back to New York I revisit the subject of my sanity. *What in hell are you doing?* I ask myself. *Who runs around the country like this— with no agent, no book contract . . . in debt big time from long-distance calls, plane tickets, hotel bills, and car rentals—and I still can't say for sure what Vi Liuzzo was all about! Who have I ever known who was possessed like this?* Possessed? *Oh, right.* Good. *Possessed!*

This is probably a creeping (but curable) middle-age craziness, I reason. They say women without children sometimes get "funny." They take up strange causes. Maybe I'm in an atypical depression brought on by my divorce or by my fast-approaching fiftieth birthday. Still, I don't *feel* crazy, but if I were watching someone else doing what I'm doing, I would probably think *she* was.

But I'm smiling. I can't help it. Hell, I am so far into the woods that the way back is longer than the way out now. Do the dead really haunt us? I wonder. . . . Do they drive us to tell their stories? Vi Liuzzo doesn't seem like a good candidate for resting in peace to me.

"What do you want?" I hear myself asking out loud. The man in the seat next to me looks uncomfortable. If it *is* possible for a pushy, bossy spirit to hound a human being, that is what is happening. Are you one of those southern haints, Vi? What do you want me to find?

Why did you get so careless in Montgomery? If you had left on Thursday afternoon like everybody else you probably would have gotten home. Was somebody watching you in your green Oldsmobile with your Michigan plates as early as Sunday or Monday? Did you suspect? Did you *know* something?

What was it they saw in you that needed killing? What was it about you that even after you died they couldn't let you be? Sarah says "they turned something good into something evil," but it's worse than that. They stole every chance you had to be remembered. What can *I* do? You must have been half nuts to get up into the faces of monsters like that. What did you think you were doing?

4 Outside Agitator

What was so striking about the civil rights fight, looking back, was how it galvanized ordinary people.
—Jonathan Kaufman

Despite J. Edgar Hoover's depiction of Vi Liuzzo as a bored northern housewife interfering in southern affairs, the fact is that Viola Fauver Gregg was raised a southerner. She was born on April 11, 1925, in California, Pennsylvania, a mining town on the Monongahela River less than fifty miles from the West Virginia border.[1]

Her father, Heber Ernest Gregg, a coal miner, had grown up in Tennessee. He had lost his left hand in a mining accident when Vi was twelve and was in and out of veterans' hospitals for the rest of his life. Heber Gregg was a self-educated man who had only completed elementary school but who read widely. Her mother, Eva Wilson Gregg, a teacher, had studied at the University of Pittsburgh. The Wilsons were of German-English descent; the Greggs, Scotch-Irish, with a smattering of Native American blood.

When Vi was six the Greggs moved to Georgia, and for the next ten years—the years of the Great Depression—they lived in a series of rented homes in rural Georgia and Tennessee. Life was hard because work was scarce. Factories, stores, and mines were closing all over the nation in the 1930s. People who had never been without a job suddenly found themselves living in grinding poverty. Although Mr. Gregg couldn't work, Mrs. Gregg was able to get temporary teaching positions.

The family did little better than eke out a living in Georgia. Often they lived in one-room shacks without running water, and they moved so much that Vi seldom started and finished a school term in the same place. Women like Mrs. Gregg who were lucky enough to find jobs had to face the hostility of men (and other women) who felt that working women took positions away from men.

Blacks who held jobs during the Depression were especially resented and often became the targets of southern racists. In 1932, Atlanta whites hung signs all over downtown declaring NO JOBS FOR NIGGERS UNTIL EVERY WHITE MAN HAS A JOB. Lynchings increased dramatically between 1932 and 1935. Those who insisted that Viola Liuzzo didn't know what she was getting into by going to Selma were wrong. She knew from personal experience what segregation, discrimination, and hatred were all about.

Vi was clearly aware of what she was doing thirty years later when she rode in Alabama at night with a black man in the front seat of her car. She had lived in Jim Crow Georgia with its "colored" rest rooms, department store dressing rooms, water fountains, hospitals, churches, and cemeteries, and she wanted to be part of a movement whose goal was to put an end to this humiliation and injustice. She understood that poor as the Gregg family was they could expect to enter the front door of a movie theater if they had the price of a ticket, while black people, no matter how much money they had, were forced to enter by a side door and sit in the balcony called "nigger heaven." Even as a six-year-old this outraged her sense of fairness. And when that sense was outraged Vi Gregg took action. Once, when her mother managed a small Georgia grocery, Vi was punished for taking money out of the cash register and giving it to a black child from a family poorer than her own. After her daughter's death, Eva Gregg recalled that Vi had been concerned with human rights all her life. "She was tender toward anybody in distress," she remembered. "She was so tender, even as a little child."

Vi couldn't sit still, Mrs. Gregg recalled. Once she surprised her parents by washing their wooden floors with kerosene because it made such a beautiful shine. "One spark and it would have been the end of all of us," Eva sighed.

Vi loved the movies and hunted up odd jobs all week to put enough pennies together for the Saturday matinee. She was a bright, lively little girl whose favorite food was Campbell's chicken noodle soup.

Ultimately the Gregg family settled in Chattanooga, Tennessee, where in 1936 a second daughter, Rose Mary (called Mary), was born. Then, while Mrs. Gregg was unable to work after Mary's birth, the family applied for "home relief" for the first and only time.

In Tennessee Vi attended school with children who told her that because blacks had started the Civil War over slavery they shouldn't be free like white men. Her parents told her to ignore them. Neither Heber nor Eva Gregg shared such racist beliefs.

Vi grew up in a society segregated by law and custom. Tennessee and Georgia were two of the twenty-nine states that then strictly forbade people of different races from dating, marrying, or having children. Interracial marriage was not recognized and was even voided by many states, and both partners in such unions could be charged with lewd and lascivious conduct and fined, imprisoned, or both. Children from interracial marriages were often declared illegitimate, and children from previous marriages could be taken away from an interracial couple by the state. In Georgia, when Vi was ten, the penalty for interracial marriage was two years in prison.[2]

During the Depression children were sometimes forced to assume responsibility at an early age, and Vi, like many teens of her generation, became self-reliant very early. Constant moving from place to place also left her with a lifelong sense of restlessness. In her mind there always seemed to be something just beyond her present circumstances, something waiting for her. Change didn't frighten her.

As a high-spirited, sassy, fun-loving teen, Vi sometimes found herself at odds with her more serious-minded father. She was an attractive young woman with a good singing voice who loved country music and dancing. Vi was sure of herself, determined to make her own decisions, and when she left school in the ninth grade her father was bitterly disappointed. He told her that lack of education had limited his opportunities all his life and she would regret her careless attitude.

Although the teenage Vi would be considered tame by today's standards, in her father's eyes she was wild—assertive, outspoken, sexual. It frustrated him that his eldest was the apple of her mother's eye. Vi would remain close to her mother, and the rocky relationship with her father would warm over the years as education became as important to her as it was to him. She saw how much Penny and Mary adored their grandparents, and Vi appreciated how patiently Heber Gregg helped the girls with their school work and encouraged them to achieve.

Mrs. Gregg would often shake her head and joke with Sarah Evans about Vi's willfulness. "Ever since Vi was a baby she was stubborn," she would say. "She wouldn't keep a diaper if she didn't want it on. She was always bound to have her own way."

When she was sixteen Vi ran away to Knoxville and eloped. She married William Phillips, who was thirty-four years old. The marriage was annulled the next day by mutual consent, and Vi returned home. All her life she would retain that impetuous nature—solving her problems and registering her protests by taking dramatic action.

When Vi's sons Tommy and Tony were eleven and nine she took them camping in Kentucky, Tennessee, and Georgia. She wanted to show the boys where she had grown up. They went barefoot for nearly the entire trip.

Tony remembers his mother telling him to "look at the stars and the woods. They're your heritage. Not what you see in the cities. This is what people were born for." She wanted them to know that crowded, bustling Detroit wasn't the whole world.

Sitting around the campfire she explained to her sons that their bodies were only shells and that what really mattered about them—and everybody else—was what was inside the shell: the spirit. The spirit, she said, is love, and without love the body is empty.

Sally remembers a similar conversation with her mother. When Sally was five, Vi took her to visit the grave of her brother Joseph, a child born between Tony and Sally who had lived only a few hours. "I was scared," Sally said, "and when Mom asked what I was afraid of I told her *dead people*." She laughed and told Sally that we have much more to fear from the living than the dead, that dead people are no longer tied to their bodies—which are only shells anyway—and that the spirits of the dead are free to watch over the people they love. She said that Joey's spirit is always with his family, even though his body is gone. "I believed her," Sally said, "and I was never afraid of cemeteries again."

During World War II, when Vi was seventeen, the Greggs moved to

Ypsilanti, Michigan, to look for defense work at Ford's new Willow Run Bomber Plant. Between 1941 and 1945 Ford hired forty-two thousand people at Willow Run to build B-24 Liberators. By the time the plant closed in June 1945, it had produced 8,685 planes.

The Greggs found an apartment in a barracks-like housing project, and Mrs. Gregg got a job right away. Their next door neighbor, Gordon Green, then an instructor at the University of Michigan, says the Greggs were open, warm-hearted people. "There wasn't a trace of selfishness in any of them." The Greens and the Greggs kept in touch for the next twenty years. Green particularly remembers Vi as strikingly beautiful. She was a petite, energetic redhead, just over five feet tall, with gray eyes and a mischievous smile.

In 1942 Vi moved to Detroit by herself. She was eighteen years old. Wartime Detroit was an exciting if sometimes dangerous place. The streets of the Arsenal of Democracy, as the city was known because of all its war plants, were lined with elm trees. It was a city of parks, theaters, music, and art deco ballrooms. Electric streetcars ran along Woodward Avenue through a shopping district that boasted the biggest store in the world—J. L. Hudson's.

Detroit was home to Polish, German, Greek, and Irish immigrants, poor whites from Appalachia, and poor blacks from all over the South. In 1912 Henry Ford's offer of a five-dollar-a-day wage at his Highland Park plant had attracted the first wave of unskilled immigrant workers. In the 1920s these immigrants were joined by the people who made up the black migration, and in the 1940s war production work attracted hundreds of thousands more immigrants. Like Birmingham, Alabama, Detroit's diverse workers lived together in uneasy proximity. The tense atmosphere was not helped by Father Charles Coughlin, whose radio program, *The Golden Hour of the Shrine of the Little Flower,* spewed anti-communist, anti-Semitic, and pro-fascist rhetoric throughout the 1930s. Fascist sympathies were also publicly expressed by Henry Ford, an unabashed anti-Semite, who strictly circumscribed what jobs were open to blacks in his plants.

When Vi arrived, Detroit was one of the most segregated northern cities in America. Hudson's department store refused to hire black sales help, and blacks could not drive Checker cabs. White Checker cab drivers would refuse black fares in front of Hudson's when they had the opportunity to pick up white passengers. All the "better" restaurants and bars downtown generally refused blacks service. Arthur Johnson, former executive director of Detroit's NAACP, remembers that "if [a black customer] ordered a drink, very fine places wouldn't hesitate to say, 'you've had too much to drink.' If you ordered food, they'd say, 'we're closing.' In many cases, particularly during the day, places would actually close rather than serve a black person."[3]

Detroit was home to nearly half a million white southerners who had simply transplanted their prejudices to a better economic environment. To them, any black man or woman was a "nigger." On February 27, 1942, as the first black families were preparing to move into a new federal housing project on Detroit's east side, a mob of more than a thousand whites picketed the complex and burned a cross.

The following year, the summer after Vi arrived, Detroit broke out in widespread racial rioting. After a fistfight on June 20, 1943, between a black and a white man over a dice game on Belle Isle—a popular amusement park on the Detroit River—fighting and violence quickly spread.

Before sunset, rumors ran all through Paradise Valley, the black section of the city, that a black mother and child had been thrown into the Detroit River by a group of white men. Mobs of blacks began to attack white men who entered Paradise Valley. Cars were overturned and stores were looted.

Whites retaliated by attacking blacks as they left the all-night movies in downtown Detroit. Black and white mobs roamed the city for thirty hours beating and murdering each other. When it was over, twenty-five blacks and nine whites were dead, six hundred people of both races were injured, and two million dollars in property had been either stolen or destroyed. Many of the war plants had to be temporarily closed because workers were afraid to leave their homes. Malcolm Bingay, one-time managing editor of the *Detroit Free Press*, compared what he saw to a near-riot he had once witnessed in Atlanta, Georgia. "On the streets of Detroit I saw again the same horrible exhibition of uninhibited hate as they fought and killed one another—white against black—in a frenzy of homicidal mania, without rhyme or reason. Their faces were all the same, their lips drawn back, their teeth bared like fangs, their eyes glazed—bestial faces bereft of all human expression."[4] It was the beginning of a pattern of racial fear and animosity that would haunt the Motor City for the next thirty years.

Despite the social unrest, war industry jobs were plentiful in Detroit in 1942, especially for white women. Posters depicting Rosie the Riveter hung all over the city, beckoning women to "do the job he left behind." Vi quickly found a job as a cashier in the employee cafeteria of the Champion Spark Plug Company. There she met and began dating George Argyris, the manager. She was eighteen and he was thirty-six.

Detroit, like many large cities, was filled with young soldiers and sailors on furlough anxious to meet girls. Vi wasn't interested in young men, however. Throughout her life she was drawn to men at least ten years her senior. Maybe she was looking for financial stability, or maybe she had grown up too quickly to have much in common with young men. In any case, Vi and George Argyris married on February 3, 1943, and rented an apartment at 2460 Blaine Street near Highland Park.

One Saturday morning as Vi was shopping she met Sarah Evans, a cashier in a grocery on Linwood. "It was during the War," Sarah remembers, "and this pretty little redhead came into my store looking for pepper. Pepper was still being rationed, and my boss used to save it for his special customers. I don't know, there was just something about this lady—she was so open and friendly, so lively. When my boss told her we didn't have any pepper I reminded him there was some under the counter. He could have killed me—probably should have fired me—I never did anything like that before. Anyway, he had to sell Vi the pepper.

"She realized right away what happened and whispered to me, in her southern drawl—she still had one in those days—'You're my kind of people.' She invited me to come over to her apartment for coffee sometime, and I went."

Vi and Sarah had a lot in common. Sarah had also been raised in the South—in rural Mississippi. "We talked about the South a lot," she said. "For all its foolishness, it was a place we both missed."

Vi became pregnant two years later. After Penny's birth, in 1946, Vi asked Sarah to baby-sit. With that request a twenty-year friendship and business arrangement began.

The Argyrises had a second daughter, Evangeline (called Mary), in 1947, and Sarah continued to baby-sit for the family. After Mary's birth Vi went back to work. Staying home with two babies under three years old felt confining, and she knew she could count on Sarah. Instead of returning to the cafeteria, however, Vi took a job as a waitress at the New Olympia Bar on Grand River Avenue, near Olympia Stadium—the famous Big Red Barn. The Barn, home of the Red Wings hockey team, also hosted boxing, wrestling, and rodeo events. It supplied the New Olympia Bar with a steady stream of customers. Vi made a good salary, and the tips were excellent. But her job became a point of contention between her and her husband. George Argyris felt his wife belonged home with their children, and he didn't like the idea of her working as a waitress. But Vi was restless. She was twenty-four years old and wanted to be back out in the world earning her own money.

In 1949 Vi brought suit for divorce against her husband, for reasons that were never specified. She later dropped it and then refiled in 1950. An uncontested divorce was granted to George Argyris who had countersued, and Vi was granted custody of the girls. She sent them temporarily to live with her parents back in Ypsilanti. George Argyris always remained close to his children, and the night before Vi went to Selma she went to see George, to apologize, Penny said, for her part in what had happened between them.

At the New Olympia, Vi met Anthony "Jim" Liuzzo, a handsome, outgoing union organizer who worked for the Teamsters. Vi was twenty-five and Jim thirty-seven. They both enjoyed music, dancing, and night life. Late in 1950 Jim asked Vi to marry him. When her divorce from George Argyris became final she did, and in 1951 Penny and Mary returned to Detroit to live with them. There would be three more children—Tommy was born in 1951, Anthony Jr. ("Nino") in 1955, and Sally in 1958. Jim adopted Penny and Mary in 1956, and Sarah Evans's role in the family gradually evolved from baby-sitter to full-time housekeeper.

Marriage to Jim Liuzzo seemed to suit Vi. By the time Sally was born, her high-spirited mother was focusing her substantial energy on family life. The twenty-four-year-old woman who had grown restless caring for two babies now seemed to delight in her five young children, sometimes to the consternation of her more social husband. She was thirty-three years old and a full-time mother.

The friendship between Sarah and Vi continued to deepen. Sarah got Vi involved in the Detroit chapter of the NAACP. In 1964 they drove to New York City to attend a civil rights seminar at the United Nations, sponsored by Detroit's First Unitarian-Universalist Church. Outside their hotel the women tried to find a cab to take them uptown. Sarah hailed cab after cab but none would stop. Finally one passed her and pulled over for Vi who was standing a few feet away. Vi refused to get in. "Boy, did she go after that cabby!" Sarah smiled, recalling the incident thirty years later. "She always spoke out for what she believed in. 'Sarah,' she'd say, 'you and I are going to change the world. One day they'll write about us. You'll see.'"

After the conference they took time out to see the Statue of Liberty and to visit Staten Island so Vi could do some rock hunting. "She loved to collect rocks," Sarah said, "and out in Staten Island she climbed down on this ledge and got stuck. I had to go find somebody to help me get her back up! That was the way she was. She always got totally involved in whatever she was doing."

Mary

■■■■■■ Childhood is the kingdom where nobody dies.
        —Edna St. Vincent Millay

One afternoon, a few weeks after I had spoken with Penny, I sat at my desk in the agency, where not much was getting done (at least not by me), folding and unfolding a small piece of paper. The telephone number on it belonged to Mary Liuzzo Ashley. Penny was right; neither of her sisters had called me. Well, I mused, I could call them. The worst that might happen is they would hang up on me, but I doubted they would. Penny hadn't.

It struck me as curious but not all that amazing that the staff of the four departments under my supervision at the agency were just as pro-

ductive, effective, and efficient then as they had been when I had taken an
active role in daily operations. A good lesson. It was two o'clock—eleven
in Oregon, where Mary was. I dialed her number.

"Hi, it's Mary. I'm not in right now, but if you leave me a message I'll
get back to you." The voice was warm, friendly. I hung up.

At midnight I was asking Mary Ashley if she would mind talking with
me about her mother. She didn't mind at all. An hour later we were still
on the line.

"We didn't know my mother as a civil rights activist," Mary said. "Her
response to the movement just flowed naturally from how she felt about
everything. She loved nature, animals, children, adventure, other people—it was all one piece to her. But don't get the idea that it made her
easy to live with! She questioned and challenged *everything!*"

I laugh. So does she. "As Penny and I got into our teens Mom's out-
spokenness sometimes embarrassed us, but when we were kids it was
great. I remember one summer when Penny was about ten—I was nine,
Tommy was probably five, and Nino maybe three—we all went to the
drive-in. It was a double feature—*Pinocchio* and some old war movie.
Hell and High Water, I think. *Pinocchio* was supposed to come on first,
but when it got dark and the movie started rolling *Hell and High Water*
came on. Well, you could hear moaning from all the other cars—a few of
them started honking their horns, too. Mom just bolted out the door and
headed for the projection tower. On her way she stopped at other cars
inviting the other mothers to come along with her to help change the pro-
jectionist's mind. About twenty of them did. Before they got back, we
were all wrapped up in *Pinocchio*, and my stepfather was laughing. God,
all my friends loved her! They thought she could do anything."

"So she was fun?"

"Oh yes, she was fun, and smart, but stubborn too. When she thought
she was right you couldn't get anywhere with her. And there were other
times, harder times, when she had a lot of self-doubt. See, she was very
conflicted about not fitting in—with my stepfather's family especially, and
with other women her age. She wasn't traditional, and she wasn't domestic. Everything I know about housework—cleaning, sewing, shopping, taking care of my clothes—I learned from Sarah. Sarah was the

stability in our house. Mom wanted so much out of life, but sometimes she felt like she was all alone. She had no one to share her search with. Other women didn't understand the things she did, and we were her kids, what did we know? We thought everybody's Mom was like ours.

"Now I know better. See, she never lied to us—never made things up to manipulate or frighten us. She always encouraged us to try things, to investigate, and draw our own conclusions. Mom believed if parents lied to their children, the kids would grow up doubting themselves, and she didn't want that for us. I think that was pretty advanced for 1963!

"I remember when I was about thirteen or fourteen she caught me drinking. She wasn't really angry, but she asked if I'd gotten sick. When I told her no, she said that was too bad, because I'd likely do it again. 'If you got sick,' she said, 'your drinking days might be over.'

"The first time I got an inkling that maybe we didn't live like everybody else was when I was in junior high school. We'd grown up with Tyrone, Sarah's grandson, being like one of our brothers. In the lower grades he and I and Penny played together, walked to school together, and we'd run up and kiss him when we saw him, just like we'd do with any member of the family. When I got to junior high, though, I began to feel the stares. I saw that a lot of people—even other kids—had problems with how we were around Tyrone. Even walking home with him was a problem, so I backed off. I began to avoid him because of the pressure I felt—society's pressure. That's how strong it was. It was certainly against everything I ever learned at home. I don't think my mother saw those barriers. It wasn't that she ever told us to ignore them or to fight against prejudice, I think she just didn't feel it and was surprised and hurt when she saw it in other people. Sarah was more realistic. She accepted that some people would just go out of their way to hurt you. I'm not sure that my mother ever did.

"She did get depressed sometimes, though. I believe it had a lot to do with all the babies she lost. There were five of us, but Mom had actually been pregnant nine times. She had two early miscarriages, a still birth, and a baby boy that only lived a few hours. She was devastated after each loss."

"Everybody seems to remember how much she loved children," I say.

"That's right. As much as she looked for challenges beyond mother-hood, Mom found it hard when Penny and I got to be teenagers and our friends were more important to us than family. I think she missed us, and I think it surprised her that she felt that way. Mom and I had some very difficult times when I was sixteen, seventeen. She wrote me a note while we were still battling, that was about six months before she died. She said she never wanted me to blame myself for our troubles. It was all a part of growing up. That one day it would pass and we'd be 'chums in joy, and comrades in distress,' again, just the way we used to be."

The Lane Report

██████████ Nobody's interested in sweetness and light.
—Hedda Hopper

On May 11, 1965, Walter Rugaber, a *Detroit Free Press* reporter, called Jim Liuzzo to alert him that a confidential report about his wife, written by Marvin G. Lane, police commissioner of Warren, Michigan, and for-mer chief of detectives of the Detroit Police Department, had been sent to Selma's sheriff Jim Clark in April. Early in May, Imperial Wizard Robert Shelton was seen passing copies of this report to newsmen covering the Wilkins trial. Rugaber told Jim Liuzzo that the *Free Press* would be breaking the story May 12.[5]

Jim was livid. He wanted to know why Commissioner Lane was in-vestigating his murdered wife. Jim was so upset he called the Detroit FBI office. Lane's jurisdiction was in suburban Warren, Jim told the agent on duty. The Liuzzos never lived in Warren. They had never received so much as a parking ticket out there, and no one from the Warren Police Department had ever questioned Jim about his personal affairs. The agent took the information and said he would look into it.

Who authorized Lane's report? Detroit Police Commissioner Ray Girardin vehemently denied that his department's criminal intelligence bureau had any part in compiling it. Commissioner Lane refused to name his sources, insisting that confidential reports were routine. Lane said he often supplied other police departments with confidential reports and re-ceived them in return. This, despite the fact that it was highly irregular to prepare a detailed personal history on a murder victim after the suspects had been apprehended.

Commissioner Lane's note to Sheriff Clark, however (written on City of Warren, Department of Police stationery), clearly stated that on March 26, one day after her murder, "the Criminal Intelligence Bureau began an investigation regarding the background of Viola Liuzzo." Lane went on to request Clark's assistance. "We would like," Lane wrote, "if it is at all possible to determine the method of transportation to Selma by Mrs. Liuzzo, and who may have accompanied her."

When the *Free Press* story broke, William Immergluck, president of the Warren-Center Line Human Relations Council, demanded an explanation of the Lane Report, saying "We [on the council] feel that the people of Warren are entitled to know about Commissioner Lane's involvement in a case that concerned neither the City of Warren nor the police agency in Alabama to which it was sent."

The South Macomb Council for Human Relations voiced "profound shock and opposition" to what it called Lane's "invasion of the privacy of the murdered Mrs. Liuzzo." In a written statement prepared for the *Free Press* the council asked, "Why did Commissioner Lane want Sheriff Clark to determine how Mrs. Liuzzo got to Alabama and who accompanied her there? What does Commissioner Lane plan to do with that information? And who are the *'we'* who Lane says want it?"

Warren County Councilman Howard Austin argued that the report was a routine police courtesy, but the editorial that appeared in the May 13, 1965, issue of the *Free Press* disagreed.

The *Free Press* posed three critical questions. What business of Lane's was it to compile a report on Mrs. Liuzzo, since she was not a Warren resident? By what distorted judgement did Lane decide such a report was any business of Sheriff Clark's, since the murder did not take place in Dallas County but in Lowndes? And on what authority did Lane ask Sheriff Clark to determine the method of transportation Mrs. Liuzzo took to Selma and who may have accompanied her?

Sheriff Clark finally admitted that he had asked Lane, who he knew through a "national police association," to provide him with background on the Liuzzos after he had been threatened by a man who identified himself as a Teamster. "You killed the wrong one this time," Clark said the anonymous caller told him. "Now we're going to kill you and your family."

On May 14, Walter Rugaber reported that virtually every detail of Lane's confidential report was smuggled out of a file in the Detroit Police Department. Rugaber identified the file specifically as #1782, which contained material gathered by both the Detroit police and the FBI. Chief of Detectives Vincent Piersante admitted it was "an obvious conclusion" that Lane's information had come from the Detroit Criminal Intelligence Bureau.

Police Commissioner Ray Girardin found himself in over his head. A former crime writer for the *Detroit Times*, Girardin had no experience in police work.[6] He had been appointed by Mayor Jerome Cavanaugh in 1965 on the basis of his knowledge of organized crime. Girardin stalled, publicly supporting Lane until he had no choice but to ask Piersante to investigate.

On May 17, Inspector Earl C. Miller, director of the Criminal Intelligence Bureau, admitted supplying his ex-boss, Marvin Lane, with File #1782. Former St. Clair County sheriff Ferris Lucas, who was serving as executive director of the National Sheriffs' Association in Washington, D.C., admitted that he had encouraged Clark to ask Lane for the information. (Lucas had introduced Clark to Lane several years earlier when Clark was in Detroit to extradite a prisoner. At that time Lane was Detroit's chief of detectives.) Commissioner Girardin relieved Inspector Miller of his duties with the CIB and transferred him to the detective bureau desk, commenting that Miller's "motives were right, but his judgment wasn't."

Chief Piersante explained, "The Liuzzo funeral was going to be here in Detroit, and we wanted to know what sort of security arrangements we would have to maintain. Demonstrations and counterdemonstrations were anticipated, and we were just trying to prepare ourselves."

Commissioner Girardin was called before Detroit's City Council to explain why Inspector Miller would assume that Lane, who no longer worked for the Detroit police, had a right to view confidential information. Girardin replied, "You must remember that Lane is a retired chief of detectives who spent thirty-three years in the department. If he asked to check a record, he would probably get cooperation."

Girardin assured the council that he would meet personally with Jim Liuzzo. He wanted, he said, to "spare the Liuzzo children from embarrassment," a quotation that was picked up by the *Detroit Free Press* and subsequently by the wire services. Jim went wild. When he couldn't reach Girardin by phone he dashed off a telegram demanding to know what the commissioner meant by his statement. Distortions, half-truths, and outright lies were being circulated about Vi. Aspersions were being cast on her sanity, her morality, and her sense of responsibility in going to Selma. Girardin's statement fed the aura of mystery surrounding the Lane Report. His posture with the council only encouraged further conjecture about Vi. Bits and pieces of Viola Liuzzo's history were taken out of context and distorted beyond recognition. The *Jackson Mississippi Daily News* was soon reporting that Mrs. Liuzzo had a police record four pages long!

The FBI's need to defame Vi in order to cover its own tracks is an understandable if not a forgivable motive, as is the press's desire for a good story. The connection between the Selma police, the Detroit police, and the Klan is, however, more ominous. Detroit was one of America's most racially troubled cities in 1965. Relations between the white police department and the black community were as angry and violent as any in Black Belt Alabama. In 1925 the Detroit Police Department had recruited officers from the Deep South, and many of them, their sons, nephews, brothers, and cousins, remained on the force forty years later. Members of the Detroit and Selma police forces reached out empathetically to one another. Many, on both sides, believed that a white woman who would leave her family to go off on a freedom march and live with blacks, ride in cars with black men, and advocate for their rights was if not crazy at least a traitor to her race and very likely immoral.

Detroit had always been a segregated city of homeowners. Block busting was a hot issue in the Motor City around this time, and extremists linked it with civil rights demonstrations. Restrictive covenants, forbidding the sale of homes in white neighborhoods to blacks or Jews, were written by realtors and signed by clients. As late as the mid-1950s a seller who violated such a covenant could be sued by his neighbors, and new owners could be prevented from occupying a house.

Certainly it occurred to more than a few Detroiters to wonder if Vi really wanted blacks moving into white neighborhoods, "destroying property values, intermarrying, and dragging white people down to their level" and to conclude that if she did, if that's what she was trying to prove by her "freedom march," then good riddance.

What exactly was in the Lane Report? In six pages Commissioner Lane documented Viola Liuzzo's marriages, arrest and probation records, civil rights activities, work and school history, a missing-persons report Jim had filed in 1964, Jim's income history, a record of the family's charge accounts at Hudson's and Winkleman's, and references to both Vi's and her father's medical histories.

Apparently nothing was too personal to be omitted. Information that Vi and Jim were having difficulty with their teenage daughters was noted. Lane reported that both girls ran away from home and that Vi sought family counseling at Wayne County General Hospital. What Lane *didn't* say was that Penny and Mary went to stay with their grandparents in Georgia temporarily when friction grew between them and their stepfather, who they considered too strict.

The fact that Vi had a nervous breakdown was documented, as was her outpatient psychiatric treatment at the Northland Center in Southfield. Lane did not acknowledge, however, that these incidents were connected, nor did he recognize in them the actions of a woman who had become overwhelmed and had the courage to seek professional help.

Vi's labor protest and subsequent dismissal from Parkview Medical Center was recorded. Lane incorrectly added that Vi had also been fired from Sinai. In truth, she resigned from Sinai to concentrate on her college work. Her personnel file contained a handwritten letter addressed to Bernard Fuss, then associate director of the hospital, explaining her reasons for resigning, including needing more time for her classes.

Furthermore, on April 1, 1965, FBI agents interviewing Vi's Sinai coworkers found one who didn't wish her well—a fellow medical technician whose name has been blacked out in the FBI report. She described Vi as being "of questionable character" and portrayed her as disruptive during a staff presentation. Vi kept interrupting the instructor, she said, and asking too many questions. It was this woman's opinion that Vi looked down on the other technicians and had ambitions of becoming a doctor. She incorrectly reported Vi had been dismissed and said she heard Vi was admitted to Sinai as a psych patient shortly after being fired. There is no record that Vi ever received psychiatric treatment at Sinai, yet this impression of her—as an angry, destructive individual too sick to work—found its way into the Lane Report.

The Lane Report focused on the problem areas of Vi Liuzzo's life, exaggerating them and ignoring her strengths and resourcefulness. Referring to the fact that she had returned to school at thirty-six and was successfully pursuing a college degree, despite finishing only one year of high school, Lane dismissed her as an "on and off" student. He never mentioned her charity work or the positive comments that were made about her by neighbors, friends, colleagues, fellow students, and the people she had met and worked with in Selma.

After citing the Detroit School Board hearing in 1964, in which her parole officer noted that Vi was "probably above average intellectually, but appeared to be confused and emotionally disturbed," Lane pronounced her "possibly mentally unbalanced."

Jim was not spared. His sixteen-year history as a business agent for the Teamsters was scrutinized. In 1953 Jim had been arrested on a charge of conspiracy to "request and accept money"—a charge subsequently dismissed. That same year he had been implicated in an unspecified Labor-Management Relations Act violation, but he was later dropped as a subject of the investigation. Neither incident had any effect on his employment, yet both were included in the Lane Report.

An editorial in the *Detroit Free Press* on May 13, 1965, observed, "The [Lane] report is inaccurate, derogatory and totally uncalled for. It makes insinuations which are not supported by facts, and dwells on irrelevant and unfavorable minutiae not only about Mrs. Liuzzo, but about her whole family. What Lane ignored was that Mrs. Liuzzo was not accused of any crime, and her murder was not the result of any provocation on her part. She was involved in no bar room brawl. She had broken no laws."

The effects of the Lane Report were insidious. Public sympathy was withdrawn from the Liuzzos. The image of Vi as a spoiled, neurotic housewife abandoning her family to run off on a freedom march began to stick. *Time* magazine referred to her as "the much-married Mrs. Liuzzo," while *Newsweek* described her as "a plumpish perky blonde, belatedly a sophomore at Wayne State University who liked a cause."[7]

In 1990, Scholarly Resources, an educational publishing service, released *The FBI File on the KKK Murder of Viola Liuzzo* on microfilm. When I read it I discovered that J. Edgar Hoover had preserved in his own Liuzzo file a letter from a concerned citizen from Corpus Christi who wrote, "I believe if this lady had been at home tending her duties as a wife and mother she would still be alive. You yourself know what an insult Mrs. Liuzzo made to the people of Alabama by cavorting around with a Negro Buck after dark in their state." Every negative observation, every slur, every comment that questioned Viola Liuzzo's motives or her sanity was carefully catalogued in Hoover's file.

Jim was smeared as well. In the minds of many Americans at that time, racial justice, socialized medicine, and militant unionism were all manifestations of one great evil—communism. In the minds of others the word *Teamster* was synonymous with *gangster*.

Jim held a responsible management position with the Teamsters, and he knew the president, Jimmy Hoffa, well. In 1964, when Hoffa was convicted of conspiracy and mail fraud, Vi wrote a letter to the *Detroit Free Press*, criticizing the government's treatment of the union leader. This letter was included in her FBI file and also documented in the Lane Report.

Hoffa made the Teamsters' plane available to return Vi's body to Detroit after her murder. His assistants, Charles O'Brian and George Kirchner, identified themselves as friends of the Liuzzo family when they met the plane and helped with funeral arrangements. Union officials also announced they would be setting up a fund to provide for the education and support of the Liuzzo children. Suddenly, Jim found himself identified in the press as a "strong-arm union extortionist" with ties to organized crime—echoing allegations Hoover had made to President Johnson the day after Vi's murder.

Jim's requests to reclaim Vi's personal belongings were ignored by the Justice Department. When Jim persisted, Hoover took the opportunity to remark publicly that Mr. Liuzzo seemed more interested in getting his wife's possessions back than in the fact that she had been killed. In desperation Jim finally wrote to the Johnson White House asking for Vi's wedding ring. His letter found its way into Hoover's files, where it remained unanswered for more than ten years. Vi's ring was finally returned to Jim in 1976, two years before his death.

This wasn't the first incidence of sullying the reputation of a victim of a civil rights murder or her family. Journalist William Bradford Huie, writing about the Schwerner, Goodman, and Chaney killings in Mississippi just a year before, noted that "After the murder, in their treatment of Rita Schwerner [wife of Michael Schwerner] the people of Mississippi had to try to degrade her. To risk showing her any sympathy would be to risk showing respect for her murdered husband."[8]

Viola Liuzzo's funeral was scheduled for March 30 at the Immaculate Heart of Mary Church in Detroit, with burial following at Holy Sepulchre Cemetery in Southfield. When a solemn requiem mass was announced, angry Catholics called the chancery demanding to know how a divorced woman could be granted Christian burial. In the next edition of the diocesan weekly newspaper *Michigan Catholic* the editor charged that these callers were not making innocent inquiries. "There was belligerence and hatred in their voices. . . . They deeply resented the prayers on her behalf and the consolation that was offered to her family."

Pat Fry, a fellow parishioner remembered, "The reaction to her death from the parishioners was 'how dare she leave her children and go down south with *them* people.' I was horrified . . . even though I wasn't very aware of the civil rights movement . . . I *did* have a strong reaction to discrimination; it really repelled me."[9]

A letter written by Elaine Landry to the As Our Readers See It page of the *Detroit Free Press* almost two months later touched the very heart of the Liuzzo family tragedy. "It's sad enough to lose a wife and mother," Mrs. Landry wrote, "but to have the family's personal life bared to the public after death is reaching a new low. Whether she was a saint or not, whether she belonged in Selma or not—she was still murdered—and she does have a family who must go on living."

Crazy Lady

Every why hath a wherefore.
—William Shakespeare

Two months after Viola Liuzzo's murder and shortly after the discovery of the Lane Report, journalist Anthony Ripley wrote a feature for the *Detroit News* entitled "The Enigma of Mrs. Liuzzo." In it Ripley described Vi as "a woman bright, determined, perhaps erratic and sometimes troubled."

In the 1960s, civil rights activists—especially *white* activists—were often considered troubled. Some whites, angered or frightened by the movement, believed that white activists were not seriously interested in the rights of blacks but were instead immature rebels or neurotics who got involved in "the black movement" to work out their own problems.[10] Furthermore, a majority of white Americans believed that public protest against segregation and discrimination (rather than those evils themselves) showed the United States in an unfavorable light to the rest of the world.

Blacks were sometimes ambivalent about white activists. While they were glad to have the visibility and financial support liberal whites brought to the movement, they were not sure just how much whites could really empathize with them, and they sometimes accused them of trying to take over.

While Viola Liuzzo was involved in neighborhood activism most of her adult life, it wasn't until she entered college in 1962 that she began to get seriously involved in the organized civil rights movement.

The early 1960s were turbulent years for the Liuzzos. The 1963 move to 19375 Marlowe Street had not brought the happiness that Jim expected it would. Tensions were building between Jim and his adopted daughters, who were now in their teens. The girls saw their own father regularly, and they resented their stepfather's strictness. Vi was also becoming increasingly concerned about Jim's gambling habits. She didn't like the people who were involved in that aspect of Jim's life, and the couple argued about it.

In July 1964, less than two months after her battle with the school board, just weeks after her arrest and Mary's move to Georgia, an emotionally overwrought Vi got into her car and left home without telling anyone where she was going. When Jim didn't hear from her for two days he called the Detroit police and reported her missing.

Vi drove for five days through New York State and Canada. She often released tension by fast long-distance driving, and this time the tension had built to an unbearable level. Ultimately she stopped in Montreal to visit Gordon Green and his wife, former neighbors from Ypsilanti. She called Jim from Montreal to assure him that she was all right.

In 1964 Gordon Green was teaching at Chateauguay High School and was an editor at the *Montreal Star*. He told Ripley that Vi came up to Canada "for a rest and to take time to let things cool down. I think we would have to admit that she was disturbed when she reached us," he said, "a bit erratic, but she was better when she left. I don't possibly see how this could be used against her." Green stressed that Vi called Jim frequently—two or three times a day. "She was a little excitable. I can't doubt that she was capable of a nervous breakdown. But she was a clear thinker about most things."

Ripley asked Green to comment on the rumors, traceable to the Lane Report, that Vi had pulled her children out of school, abandoned them, fled to Canada, and wrote bizarre and despondent letters home from Canadian cemeteries. Exasperated, Green explained that Vi was a rock collector. She had often taken field trips with her sons on which they sometimes visited cemeteries and quarries in search of rock samples. She did this alone during her stay with the Greens in Canada. Jim had bought her a rock polishing machine for her birthday the year before.

Jim flew up to Montreal, and the Greens drove back to Detroit with the Liuzzos. On the way, Gordon Green recalled, Vi convinced Green's wife that she should also go back to school. One can only imagine her conversation with Jim, however. Vi was temperamentally high-strung and terribly stubborn. Jim admitted that their life together could be difficult. Both had tempers. At times Vi would rail at Jim for being an "autocrat," he said, telling him he needed to "snap into focus." Tony remembers that once during an argument his mother rammed his father's car. "She would bring down-and-out people home," Tony recalled, "feed them and get them help. Then they'd rip us off and my dad would go crazy. 'Why do you do this?' he'd ask her."

"Vi and I had our troubles and our bad days," Jim said. "She used to storm at me for sitting around talking instead of doing something about things—the things she was interested in. . . . We had our blow ups, lots of them, but she was a great person. There was never a dull moment with her."[11]

The stress didn't ease, however, after Vi returned home. In September she angered Jim by pleading guilty rather than allowing the school board to drop charges against her. Her relationship with her mother also deteriorated. Eva Gregg was upset with Vi for using the children in her protest. The last straw came when Judge Gillis called Vi a "do-gooder," reducing the protest that had caused so much family disruption to a joke. On September 28, 1964, Vi suffered a nervous breakdown and was admitted to Detroit Memorial Hospital.

Shortly before her hospitalization Vi went to the Detroit office of the NAACP, where she and Sarah were members, to report that during her court hearing she had seen a young black girl who looked as if she were suffering from malnutrition. She said she had wanted to give that girl some money but didn't want to offend her. The young woman had been convicted of some minor offense. Vi asked an NAACP staff member to try to find the girl's name and address through the court system, and she left a check to help her out.

As a result of her guilty plea, Vi had to report to a parole officer once she was released from the hospital. The officer reported that Mrs. Liuzzo described her marriage as "good, except that her husband did not understand the children, and that she had no formal religion, but believed in basic good conduct which is the basis of all religions."

At the time of her mother's arrest, eighteen-year-old Penny was working in Ann Arbor, but she returned home periodically to help out. In early November 1964, Penny accompanied Vi to her first parole appointment. By this time, Mary was married to a young man in Georgia who Vi had never met. Mary's rebellion brought back memories of Vi's own, and it upset her to realize that the freedom she had granted her daughters because she had hated the restrictions that her father had placed on her had not resulted in a better outcome. Ironically, both girls fled to the same Gregg household Vi had run from as a teen more than twenty years before.

Vi's weight had fluctuated over the years because of her many pregnancies, but she had always managed to bring it under control. Only five foot three, she added twenty pounds to her usual trim 125. She was so distracted she couldn't attend the fall 1964 semester at Wayne State, although she returned in January 1965 for the spring term.

Vi's nervous breakdown, eight months before Selma, her subsequent psychiatric treatment, rumors that she had "disappeared" for a week, and the discovery that Vi had called Jim from the campus of Wayne State on March 16, surprising him with the news that she was not coming home but heading straight to Selma, gave credence to Anthony Ripley's portrait of Vi as a troubled white activist.

The picture of Vi Liuzzo filling my imagination is one of a stylish, stubborn woman who drove too fast and smoked too much. Bossy and overbearing one minute, loving and generous the next, she had a tendency to offer her opinion before it was asked for. Impulsive, headstrong, passionate, ambitious, and smart. A full-blown extrovert with a big heart, she took on more than she could handle through the spring and summer of 1964, made a series of poor judgments, and became temporarily overwhelmed by family stresses and personal depression. Ripley, however, suggested something very different. He profiled Vi as the classic troubled white activist. Ripley's article was only the beginning of a general disqualification of Vi Liuzzo as a civil rights martyr or a feminist pioneer. His exposé led to speculation that she was a manic depressive who had gone to Selma in a frenzy and brought about her own death. If that was true, and her contemporaries felt there was reason to believe it, then there was no story. Vi Liuzzo's death might therefore be seen as tragic but it could never be considered heroic.

Ripley's article was written for the *Detroit News*, the major daily newspaper of a city that defined itself as white. White Detroiters, especially working-class whites, were frightened by the steady increase in the black population in their city and the steadily rising crime rate. They could remember a time when they walked the streets safely after midnight and never locked their doors. They might wonder about the sanity of a white lady from a comfortable neighborhood who would associate herself with the cause of those who they felt were destroying the Motor City.

Was Vi manic depressive? She had abundant, often unfocused energy. She was restless, impulsive, headstrong, and sometimes aggressive. She had a voracious appetite for education and could read as many as ten books a week. Sometimes she sat up half the night writing in her diary, reading, or listening to classical music. Sarah claims Vi had a photographic memory.

Vi occasionally suffered from periodic mood swings and migraine headaches. Penny remembers that sometimes her mother's energy would get so drained that she would have to stay in bed for a day or two.

In 1957 Vi was diagnosed with an overactive metabolism. The condition was discovered during routine tests ordered by her physician to determine the cause of two miscarriages she suffered after Tony's birth. She was put on medication, and Sally, her last child, was born the following year.

But the medication interfered with Sally's prenatal development. She was born fragile and malnourished, and she was not expected to live. Sally was given the last rites of the Catholic church, but Vi refused to accept her poor prognosis and focused her attention on keeping the baby stimulated. By 1959 the doctors conceded Sally would probably live but predicted that she would never be able to lift her head or walk. Again, Vi ignored every hint of negativity and continued to work with her daughter. The older children assisted with Sally's exercises and lavished attention on her. By the time she was three, Sally Liuzzo was walking, talking, and laughing. It might be conceded that Vi Liuzzo was *obsessive*.

Obsessive, restless, searching . . . Vi was looking for something she couldn't fully articulate—something she felt was missing from what looked like a full life. She enthusiastically shared that search with her family—reading the essays of Thoreau and the dialogues of Plato to her children, discussing her ideas and new discoveries and listening to music with them, taking them on field trips, and celebrating every holiday and every birthday with a party.

Vi was always an enthusiast, never a leader. She consistently chose the role of worker. After her death the Reverend Malcolm Boyd commented, "She epitomized the very strong person in the freedom movement who doesn't ask to be a leader. People like her make up the moral backbone of movements."[12]

Sarah's grandson Tyrone told me that money never meant a lot to Vi. She didn't spend wildly, but she did give a lot of things away. She often brought down-and-out people and stray animals home to Marlowe Street, offering them shelter, food, and assistance. In the 1960s Detroit was filled with refugees from the South, like Vi had been twenty years before. Black and white, they came north looking for work and found instead grinding poverty and despair. Well into the 1960s transplanted Appalachian whites were referring to Detroit as "the capital city of Hell." Vi remembered how it felt to be hungry.

"Sometimes she drove me crazy," Jim said. "She always had to be doing things for other people whether they deserved it or not."[13] Hers might have been irritating, or even eccentric behavior, but it was hardly pathological.

Still, it is difficult to draw conclusions about a person's behavior outside his or her own times. In the 1960s some women were called eccentric simply because they were aggressive or strong-willed. According to Sigmund Freud, the ability to stand up for one's convictions and to act on one's whims is more likely to be present in those who retain a childlike openness to experience. Freud did not consider such openness to be a symptom of neurosis.

In the 1960s women who complained to their doctors of being restless, exhausted, frustrated—describing a whole panorama of psychosomatic disorders—were usually diagnosed as anxious or depressed. Middle-class white women with such complaints were often over-medicated with tranquilizers. By 1960 tranquilizer consumption (most of it by women) had soared to over a million pounds a year. Doctors believed strong tranquilizing medications were appropriate for homemakers because the drugs appeared to relieve their discomfort.

In 1971 Dr. Robert Seidenberg wrote, "The drug industry openly acknowledges the enslavement of women, as shown in an ad with a woman behind bars made up of brooms and mops. The caption reads: *'You can't set her free but you can make her feel less anxious.'* Another one pictures a woman who, we are told, has an M.A. degree, but who now must be content with the PTA and housework. This, we are advised, contributes to her gynecological complaints, which should be treated with drugs."[14]

An abnormal-psychology college textbook, published in 1960, listed among psychosomatic disorders "various disturbances in the menstrual cycle (irregularity, unusual pain or tension associated with the menses, disturbances in parturition and lactation, and extreme reactions to the climacteric)." The authors explain that "The essential psychodynamic focus is the patient's insecurity and her immature approach to fulfilling the role of wife and mother."[15]

Dr. Joseph Rheingold, a psychiatrist at Harvard Medical School wrote in 1964 that "Anatomy decrees the life of a woman. . . . When women grow up without dread of their biological functions and without subversion by feminist doctrine, and therefore enter upon motherhood with a sense of fulfillment and altruistic sentiment, we shall attain the goal of a good life and a secure world in which to live."[16]

In 1971 therapist Naomi Weisstein noted while exploring how women are characterized in our culture and in psychology that they are considered "inconsistent, emotionally unstable, lacking in a strong conscience or superego, weaker, 'nurturant' rather than productive, 'intuitive' rather than intelligent, and if they are at all 'normal,' suited to the home and the family. In short, the list adds up to a typical minority group stereotype of inferiority: if they know their place, which is in the home, they are really quite lovable, happy, childlike, loving creatures."[17]

In 1963 Vi summed up her frustrations in a college notebook. Under the heading Personal Convictions and Objectives, she wrote, "I protest the attitude of the great majority of men who hold to the conviction that any married woman who is unable to find contentment and self-satisfaction when confined to homemaking displays a lack of emotional health."[18] This was the same year that *Mademoiselle* and *Ladies Home Journal* began running excerpts from Betty Friedan's soon-to-be-published *The Feminine Mystique*. Friedan's experience resonated with American women—mostly white, educated, middle-class women—who felt a gnawing void in their lives.

Friedan called the emptiness "the problem that has no name." The problem she said had lain buried and unspoken of for many years. "It was a strange stirring, a sense of dissatisfaction, a yearning that women suffered in the middle of the twentieth century in the United States. Each suburban wife struggled with it alone. As she made the beds, shopped for the groceries, matched slipcover material, ate peanut butter sandwiches with her children, chauffeured Cub Scouts and Brownies, lay beside her husband at night—she was afraid to ask even of herself the silent question—*Is this all?*"

"American women," Betty Friedan said in 1963, "no longer know who they are." What *was* the problem that has no name? Certainly not manic-depressive illness! Friedan wrote that "Sometimes a woman would say, 'I feel empty somehow . . . incomplete. . . . I feel as if I don't exist.' Sometimes she blotted out the feeling with a tranquilizer. Sometimes she thought the problem was with her husband, or her children, or that what she really needed was to redecorate her house, or move to a better neighborhood, or have an affair, or another baby. . . . Sometimes the feeling gets so strong she runs out of the house and walks through the streets. Or she stays inside and cries."[19]

Why was it important for some journalists and commentators to insinuate that rather than being genuinely motivated by a desire to help the civil rights movement or even frustrated by the lack of opportunities for personal growth that were available to women of her generation Vi Liuzzo may have been mentally ill? Ripley specifically called attention to Vi's driving ambition, energy, and impulsiveness, her nervous breakdown, and information garnered from the Lane Report that Vi's father, Heber Gregg, had been hospitalized on several occasions for "a nervous disorder." (Manic-depressive illness was by then known to run in families.) The true nature of Mr. Gregg's illness, however, was unknown.

The Lane Report, bolstered by J. Edgar Hoover's self-serving portrayal of Mrs. Liuzzo as a drug-taking middle-aged adulteress with a black teenage lover, set her reputation in stone. Reporters looking for a story about her always leaned toward the sordid. They began, perhaps unconsciously, with the presumption that this woman was *different*—that there was something basically "not right" about her. If she wasn't outright immoral, then perhaps she was sick.

A common symptom of full-blown manic depression (in the manic stage) is sexual promiscuity and abuse of alcohol or drugs. Fitting Vi with such a diagnosis would give weight to Hoover's assertions. However, Vi was not sexually promiscuous, and she drank very little. A neighbor, outraged about the gossip after her murder, told a *Detroit News* reporter that "She was never a run around. She wasn't a drinker, either, but she did smoke a lot. [A carton a week.] Her biggest pleasure was having her children in her backyard. I just can't believe that this could happen to her. She meant no harm to anyone."[20]

To propose that Vi Liuzzo was manic depressive was, in a strange way, an attempt to be helpful—to explain what in 1965 seemed inexplicable. A manic-depressive diagnosis would clearly explain what a thirty-nine-year-old white woman with a family was doing driving a car alongside a nineteen-year-old black man at 8 P.M. on an Alabama highway. Portraying Vi as a woman functioning in a high manic cycle, impulsively drinking or taking drugs and using the march as a cover for sleeping with a young black man—at *least* one—resolved a number of conflicts. Manic-depressive illness became a facile rationalization of what drove Vi. What might have passed for eccentricity in a more affluent, better-connected, or better-educated woman was theorized as pathology in her case. She was, therefore, *not* the lady next door. Not the sister, daughter, wife, or mother in *your* house. Her cause, her motives, her actions could all be suspect. She was a crazy lady.

5 Never!

History will have to record that the greatest tragedy of this period of social transition was not the strident clamor of the bad people, but the appalling silence of the good people.
—Dr. Martin Luther King Jr.

On May 3, 1965, jury selection began at the Lowndes County Courthouse for the trial of Collie Leroy Wilkins Jr., youngest of the three Klansmen indicted for the murder of Viola Liuzzo. The panel from which the jurors were selected, taken from local voting rolls, consisted of one hundred white males and one black man—farm foreman Arthur Means, who asked to be excused for health reasons.[1]

The courthouse in Hayneville, a one-hundred-year-old white wooden edifice with a domed steeple, built by slaves, faces the town square park and the Confederate War Dead memorial. Outside, in the blazing sun, journalists, law enforcement officials, lawyers, Klansmen, civil rights advocates, and locals milled around watching each other and waiting for the trial to begin. One hundred and fifty blacks came to register to vote that morning and were sent to the old Hayneville jail where voting registrars had set up two tables in a room where an antique gallows was prominently displayed.

Inside the courthouse the defense team and the team for the prosecution huddled in separate corners as people entered and left continuously, making use of the three rest rooms marked White Women, White Men, and Colored.

Few locals doubted that Wilkins would be acquitted. A court clerk told Paul Montgomery of the *New York Times* that he believed the real defendant was Tommy Rowe. People were disgusted with Mrs. Liuzzo, he said, but they *hated* Rowe. Defense counsel Matt Murphy was determined to use their anger to full advantage by portraying Rowe as a race traitor and Viola Liuzzo as an outside agitator.

Imperial Wizard Robert Shelton told reporters that the Klan could prove that the deaths of Mrs. Liuzzo and Rev. James Reeb had been planned by the communists to blacken the name of the Klan. He said the Klan Bureau of Investigation was looking into the background of the lady from Detroit for possible communist connections. "I understand that she hasn't been home for the last few months," he said. "She's been around the country on these demonstrations."[2]

Unfortunately, the blackening of Vi's character went virtually unchallenged. Viola Liuzzo had no organized constituency to defend her. She had gone to Selma as a private citizen. Not a teacher, a lawyer, or a member of the clergy, and not representing any professional, ethnic, or other interest group, she had simply volunteered, like thousands of others, to help when Martin Luther King Jr. made his national appeal after Bloody Sunday.

The State of Alabama's case against Collie Leroy Wilkins Jr. was presented by Circuit Solicitor Arthur Gamble Jr., Lowndes County Prosecutor Carlton Perdue, and Assistant State Attorney General Joseph Breckenridge "Joe Breck" Gantt.

Gamble, like the presiding judge, Thomas Werth Thagard, was a native of Greenville, Alabama. Gamble, a veteran World War II navy pilot, had entered the state Senate for a short time before becoming solicitor for the Second Judicial Circuit. Joe Breck Gantt, the son of a Covington County sheriff, was a graduate of the University of Alabama who had served in the army's judge advocate general's corps. Fifty-nine-year-old Carlton Perdue, the oldest member of the team, was a lifelong resident of Lowndes.[3]

Gantt began by telling the jury, "I don't want to talk about the Communist Party, or the Teamsters' Union, or the NAACP, or segregation, or integration, or whites, or niggers, or marchers, or demonstrators. I want to talk about a murder case that happened in Lowndes County."

He argued that no man had the right to kill just because the sight of a white woman and a Negro man sitting together enraged him. "I'm a segregationist too," he assured the jury, "but we're talking about murder today."[4]

Arthur Gamble continued in the same vein. "I don't agree with the purpose of this woman either," he said, "but gentlemen, she was here and she had a right to be here without being killed. This was a cold-blooded middle-of-the-night killing that you cannot overlook."

Gantt, Gamble, and Perdue seemed either unwilling or unable to create sympathy for Viola Liuzzo as the victim of a brutal murder. All openly agreed with defense counsel Matt Murphy that Mrs. Liuzzo's actions were wrong. They also failed to produce a single character witness whose testimony might carry weight with the jury. Willie Lee Jackson, who Vi roomed with in Selma, and Amelia Boynton, president of the Dallas County Voters' League and a colleague of Vi's, were certainly not candidates since both were black. Nor were any of the hated northern clergy or members of the SCLC appropriate choices. The doctors, nurses, and social workers Vi had assisted at a first-aid station in Montgomery during the march had all gone home. Therefore, the prosecution simply appealed to the jury's sense of fairness in their efforts to hold Viola Liuzzo's assassins accountable for inflicting a punishment far greater than her "crime" warranted.

The defendant's crime—first-degree murder—was prosecuted with little reference to its victim. Even Viola Liuzzo's possessions, introduced into evidence, were tossed about the courtroom carelessly. They were stuffed into four cardboard cartons—clothes, shoes, a sociology textbook, and a tan pocketbook with bloodstains still on it. Neither Perdue nor his fellow prosecutors ever spoke of Viola Liuzzo as someone deserving respect or consideration.

Carlton Perdue, the county prosecutor, was an avid segregationist. Although he tried not to let his personal beliefs interfere with his responsibilities, he was not always successful. Two weeks before the Liuzzo trial, a part-time Lowndes deputy sheriff had been indicted for the cold-blooded shooting of two civil rights workers in Hayneville, and Perdue commented to a *Selma Times Journal* reporter that if they "had been tending to their own business like I tend to mine, they'd be living and enjoying themselves today."[5] On May 5, two days into the trial, Perdue informed reporters, "We got ways to keep nigras in their place if we have to use them. We have the banks, the credit—they can't live without credit. We could force them to their knees if we would so choose."

The state's case rested on the eyewitness testimonies of Tommy Rowe and Leroy Moton, the testimony of Alabama state trooper James Haygood, who had given Thomas a speeding warning notice on Highway 80 approximately two hours before the murder, and the fact that the bullet that killed Mrs. Liuzzo was traced to a .38-caliber pistol registered to Gene Thomas and found in Thomas's home. Rowe testified that since Thomas was driving he had passed his gun to Wilkins, who fired it twice. Eaton, he said, fired a .22-caliber gun at Mrs. Liuzzo. The autopsy report showed it was the .38 slug that had killed her.

"How much stronger could the evidence be?" Perdue asked the jurors.

Back in Detroit, Penny asked Sarah, who was now living-in and caring for the younger children, if she thought the murderers would be convicted. "No honey," Sarah told her. "That jury's just going through the motions. They're glad it happened."

Wilkins's defense attorney, Matthew Hobson Murphy Jr., fifty-one, was chief legal counsel ("klonsel") for the United Klans of America Knights of the Ku Klux Klan. Jimmy Breslin, reporting for the *New York Herald Tribune* in 1965, described Murphy as "six foot three and weighing 235 pounds with two fingers missing from his right hand from an industrial accident during his career as an engineer. In 1946 Murphy came out of the army and became a lawyer without ever passing a bar exam. He claims the Jews own the Federal Reserve Bank and that Alger Hiss runs the country through Felix Frankfurter, his godfather."

Murphy's father ran for lieutenant governor on a Klan-supported ticket in 1925 with Hugo Black. Black won a U.S. Senate seat and ultimately became a Supreme Court justice. (Black was the brother-in-law of Virginia Durr.)

Trafficking with the Klan was not unusual for politicians in the late 1920s. At that juncture, the Klan nearly succeeded in re-inventing itself as a patriotic fraternal organization as benevolent as the Lions or the Elks. In 1924, thirty thousand fully robed Klansmen marched down Pennsylvania Avenue in Washington, D.C., as part of an organizing drive.

The "New Klan" appealed to urban middle-class businessmen because of its anti-union and anti-pacifist positions. Recruitment flyers read, "Every criminal, every gambler, every thug, every libertine, every girl ruiner, every home wrecker, every wife beater, every dope peddler, every moonshiner, every crooked politician, every pagan Papist priest, every shyster lawyer, every Knight of Columbus, every white slaver, every brothel madam, every Rome-controlled newspaper, every black spider—is fighting the Klan. Think it over. Which side are you on?"

Klan members held offices in the Democratic Party in the South and in the Republican Party in the North and West. The KKK campaigned for (and elected) mayors, congressmen, and even senators. Hugo Black and Harry Truman were only two of the best-known politicians who had accepted Klan support early in their careers. Black joined the Klan in 1923. In 1925, after his election to Congress, Senator Black attended a victory celebration given for him and for governor-elect Bibb Graves by the Birmingham Klan. There he accepted a gold-engraved Grand Passport to the Invisible Empire from the imperial wizard himself. This was the same Hugo Black who was a sitting justice when the Supreme Court *unanimously* struck down racially segregated education with the *Brown vs. Board of Education* decision in 1954.

In 1922 Harry Truman, running for judge for the eastern district of Jackson County, Independence, Missouri, paid a ten dollar membership fee and joined the Klan at the urging of his supporters. Truman, whose executive order as president of the United States desegregated the armed forces, insisted that he never completed the initiation ceremony, though rumors persisted well into the 1950s that he had taken part in the Klan ritual in a pasture south of Independence.[6]

At the time of Wilkins's arrest, Klonsel Murphy was not aware that Tommy Rowe was an FBI informant. During a news conference on the day after the murder Murphy announced that the FBI offered Rowe a bribe of 580 acres of land in Minnesota if he would give them information on the murder case but, Murphy said, Rowe refused. "These four boys will be exonerated," he had gloated. When he discovered Rowe's undercover role two weeks later, Murphy went wild. He told reporters he intended to prove that Rowe "was a traitor and a pimp and an agent of Castro and I don't know what all."[7]

Rowe completely overshadowed the victim at the trial, just as the imperial wizard stole the spotlight from the morose defendant.

Wilkins was a twenty-one-year-old high school dropout who lived with his parents, sixteen-year-old sister, and two little brothers, twelve and four, in Fairfield. He worked as a self-employed auto mechanic. At five feet nine inches tall and 195 pounds, Wilkins appeared pudgy, but his dark brown hair and blue eyes highlighted his handsome features. Wilkins had recently served time for petty larceny and malicious destruction of private property.

The imperial wizard moved easily through the restricted areas of the courtroom, coaching Wilkins, conducting impromptu news conferences, and sitting at the defense table during the opening arguments. Finally, Judge Thagard told Shelton to find another seat, so he took the chair next to Grand Dragon Robert Creel.

When Normond Poirier, a correspondent for the *New York Post*, asked Arthur Gamble if he didn't think the presence of the imperial wizard was intimidating to the jurors and witnesses, Gamble had no comment. When Poirier asked Perdue the same question, the county prosecutor replied, "Well . . . I don't know . . . uh . . . actually the trial hasn't really started yet. All we've done is pick a jury."

Another reporter asked Shelton if he thought Rowe was in danger. "Well, I'd hate to have to think I'd have to look over my shoulder everywhere I went," Shelton replied. He also told the reporter that the Klan knew where the FBI was hiding Rowe. "I don't think he can go anywhere we won't know where he is." When asked for his thoughts about Viola Liuzzo, Shelton replied, "They portrayed her as being the mother of five lovely children and a community worker. . . . The fact is she was a fat slob with crud that looked like rust all over her body. She was braless."[8]

Wilkins sat at the defense table biting his fingernails. He had been charged with drunk driving two weeks before the Liuzzo murder, in Hueytown, Alabama. When the Hueytown police searched his car they found a sawed-off shotgun, a small baseball bat, a slingshot, a Kloran (book of Klan rituals), and a Klan robe. He was on probation for possession of the shotgun.

Throughout his opening statement, defense Klonsel Murphy hammered at the two themes he would repeat endlessly during the trial—that Rowe had broken his Klan oath of loyalty in testifying against his fellow Klansmen and therefore could not be trusted and that because Mrs. Liuzzo was a white woman alone in a car with a black man at night whatever happened to her was her own fault.

Today it seems incredible that an attorney would employ such blatant racism in his appeal to a jury, but thirty years ago diehard segregationists believed that a woman who would socialize with a black man to the extent of riding in a car with him was inviting the possibility of sleeping with him and producing a mulatto. Some white men would argue that such actions incited to murder.

"I'm proud to be a white man," Murphy told the Wilkins jury, "and I'm proud that I stand up on my feet for white supremacy, not the mixing and mongrelization of the races . . . and not with the Zionists that run that bunch of niggers." (Kivie Kaplan, a Jewish businessman, was president of the NAACP; Jack Greenberg was head of the NAACP's Legal Defense Fund; and Martin Luther King's chief white adviser, Stanley Levison, was a Jewish lawyer.)

Murphy called Vi "a white nigger who turned her car over to a black nigger for the purpose of hauling niggers and communists back and forth."[9]

"And here is another strange thing," he ranted. "This white woman . . . *white woman?*—where is that NAACP card?" He held up Vi's membership card, "Mrs. Liuzzo was up there singing 'we will overcome, we will overcome, we will overcome.' What in God's name were they trying to overcome? God himself? . . . Integration breaks every moral law God wrote. Noah's son was Ham and he committed adultery and was banished and his sons were the Hamites and God banished them and they went to Africa and the only thing they ever built was grass huts. No white woman can ever marry a descendant of Ham. That's God's law. . . . I don't care what Lyndon Johnson or anybody else says!"[10]

His opening statement completed, Klonsel Murphy proceeded to direct his fury at Tommy Rowe, who had been brought into the courtroom under heavy guard. Rowe was a five foot eight stocky redhead with a ruddy complexion. The divorced father of four, he had been born in Savannah, Georgia, but then lived in Birmingham. He was a restless, anxious man who had worked sporadically as a bartender and an ambulance driver, and as a laborer in a dairy, a novelty store, and a meat-packing plant. At the time of the trial he was unemployed and behind in his child support payments. Rowe testified that he had pretended to fire shots at Mrs. Liuzzo so he wouldn't "blow his cover" but that he had not hit her and he had been powerless to prevent her murder.[11]

Murphy called Rowe a liar. He asked if Rowe had taken an oath when he joined the Klan. Rowe said that he had. Then Murphy turned to the jury and read them the Klan vow of secrecy. "I swear that I will never yield to bribery, flattery, threats, punishment, passion, persuasion or any other enticement. . . . I will die rather than divulge."[12] Spinning back on his heels, Murphy asked Rowe if he had sworn that same oath on the Bible. When Rowe admitted he had, Murphy asked the jury, "Could you believe him on oath when you know he's a liar and a perjurer, holding himself out to be a white man and worse than a white nigger?"

Murphy asked Rowe, "On the way to Selma, didn't you say continually that you hadn't come all that way for nothing, that you were going to cause some niggers some trouble?"

"No sir," Rowe said. "Very definitely not. It was Wilkins who said that."

Finally Murphy asked Rowe, "Did the FBI promise you five hundred acres in Minnesota and enough money to live on the rest of your natural life if you'd help break the back of the United Klans of America?"

"No," Rowe replied. "*You* instructed me to put that information out, and that's how it got out, Mr. Murphy."

Murphy slammed his fist on the table. "Are you telling me I *told* you to say that?" he shouted, throwing his hat on the floor. Judge Thagard pounded his gavel and called for a recess. The following day the imperial wizard himself testified that *he* was present when Rowe told Murphy that he had been offered a farm in Minnesota by FBI agents.

The next day Murphy asked the jury what they thought Leroy Moton was doing "all that time, in that car, *alone* with that woman." He asked Moton point blank if he had "had relations" with Mrs. Liuzzo. Although Moton emphatically denied it, Murphy repeatedly implied that there was a sexual relationship between them. "Why," he asked, "would a white woman from Detroit desert her husband and children to ride around in a car with a black man?"

Instead of defending Wilkins, Murphy prosecuted Viola Liuzzo as Judge Thagard watched in silence. Murphy deliberately and repeatedly mispronounced Mrs. Liuzzo's name, stressing its unfamiliar and "foreign" Italian sound. Referring to her as *Mrs. LOO-zee-o*, he insisted that she and Leroy Moton were lovers, despite the fact that Dr. Paul Shoffeit, the Alabama state toxicologist who performed her autopsy, said he found no indication of recent sexual activity. The only admission Murphy got from the toxicologist was that Mrs. Liuzzo's feet had been dirty when she died. He speculated that she had recently been walking barefoot.

Leroy Moton was a tall, thin young man. He wore dark-framed glasses that kept slipping down the bridge of his nose, and his six-foot-three-inch frame was stooped. He was visibly nervous on the witness stand, having to repeat several of his answers because his voice dropped so low. Murphy asked Moton if he had been drinking. Moton said no. He asked if he had touched Vi's body. Moton answered no again. Then he asked if Moton hadn't fired the shots himself. Moton looked horrified and said he had not.

Murphy tried unsuccessfully to get Moton to say that he was carrying a gun that night and had shot holes in the windshield of the Oldsmobile in order to cover up a theft. "I suggest to you," Murphy thundered, "that you fired those two shots and rifled her pocketbook and took her money."

Despite all his thunder, Murphy never produced a single witness to discredit the eyewitness testimonies of either Rowe or Moton. During his twenty-three-minute defense presentation he called Lorene Frederick, whose Bessemer Cafe the Klansmen had visited after the murder in order to provide themselves with an alibi. Mrs. Frederick testified that she had seen all three men in her cafe between 9:30 and 10 P.M. on the night of

March 25. On cross examination Arthur Gamble reminded her that Tommy Rowe testified that the men arrived at Lorene's cafe at 10:20 P.M. "Could they have been there after ten?" the chief prosecutor asked. "They could have been," the elderly and very arthritic Mrs. Frederick agreed. "I didn't time 'em in, and I didn't time 'em out."

Murphy made a number of attempts to introduce material from the Lane Report, but Judge Thagard repeatedly overruled him. Then he tried to manipulate the FBI weapons expert, Marian Williams, into agreeing that he had been pressured "from Washington" to produce evidence that would result in a conviction. Williams wouldn't yield.

In his summation, Murphy took a parting shot at Moton. "You remember what the nigger Moton said on the stand?" he asked the jury. "'No. Yeah. No. Yeah.' Like a ten-year-old boy. He should have been saying 'Yes, Sir,' and 'No, Sir' before this honorable white judge. But the buck hasn't got the sense, the morals, or the decency. . . . You notice his eyes?" he continued. "You see him sitting up there. You look at his eyes? Oh, I did. Eyes dilated. You see them? You see them staring? Pupils dilated? You see him talking under the hypnotic spell of narcotics? You didn't? Well, I did. And I tell you as one white man to another that Jim Clark says *Never* and I say *Never* myself![13] You know that [Viola] was in the car with three black niggers? One white woman and three black niggers. Black nigger communists who want to take us over!"[14]

In his twenty-five-minute charge to the jury, Judge Thagard instructed that if they determined Tommy Rowe was an accomplice (as Klonsel Murphy tried to establish) then they could not convict Wilkins on the strength of Rowe's testimony alone. That left Leroy Moton's eyewitness account.

On May 6, 1965, the jury began its deliberation. After an hour they asked if they could select a charge less serious than first-degree murder. Judge Thagard told them that both second-degree murder and first-degree manslaughter convictions could be returned. After another three and a half hours they said they were not near a decision and Judge Thagard ordered them sequestered in a Montgomery hotel for the night.

The following afternoon the jury reported that they were hopelessly deadlocked—two against and ten *in favor* of conviction. Foreman Clifford McMurphy said, "I wouldn't say we've made any progress. We've been hung from almost the outset. It's been right constant." The 10-2 ballot was for conviction of manslaughter, which carried a ten-year sentence. The jury had very early ruled out first-degree murder. They appeared to be more influenced by the fact that Tommy Rowe had broken the Klan oath of silence (which made him a confirmed liar in their eyes, since he had made the oath to God on the Bible) than they were that Wilkins and his accomplices had viciously murdered an innocent woman.

When a hung jury was declared, Wilkins's mother ran up to him, kissed his cheek, and said, "There now, I told you, didn't I?"

It wasn't the outcome the klonsel had hoped for, and he had to cancel his "acquittal party," but when journalist William Bradford Huie asked Murphy what he thought his chances were of getting an acquittal at a retrial he replied, "Acquittal is certain. All I need to use is the fact that Mrs. Liuzzo was in the car with a nigger man and she wore no underpants."[15]

Juror Edmund Sallee commented on Murphy's summation to a reporter from the *Alabama Journal*. "I think a great many of us were insulted to a great extent and he must have thought we were very very ignorant to be taken in by that act."[16]

Two local woman spoke with reporters outside the courthouse. One said the fact that a majority of the jurors voted to convict should show the country that Alabama was trying to do the right thing. The other disagreed. "I don't know why they kept calling Mrs. Liuzzo a mother of five children," she said. "A mother wouldn't have gone off and left her children and come here."[17]

Some in the Motor City felt differently. "This is the home town of Mrs. Viola Liuzzo," an editorial in the May 11, 1965, *Detroit Free Press*, began. "Wilkins is charged with killing one of us. Some of us may feel differently about what Mrs. Liuzzo was doing. About her right to live, there can be no disagreement. The defense that mixed white supremacy, anti-communism and motherhood into one confused tirade wasn't effective. . . . The nation's spotlight was on Hayneville. It saw a lawyer's transparent appeal to racism. It saw racism so ingrained it couldn't be moved by evidence. . . . Still, in the heart of the Black Belt ten out of twelve men said a man should go to prison for killing a civil rights worker. They were willing to face the hostility of many neighbors and the possible vengeance of the Klan. . . . The trial may not have brought justice for Mrs. Liuzzo, but it sped the day of justice for her cause."

Wilkins was freed pending appeal, and he, Murphy, Thomas, and Eaton began a tour of Georgia, Alabama, and the Carolinas to assist with local Klan membership drives and raise funds for their own defense expenses. Crowds cheered them during a parade through Atlanta. The four Klansmen were treated like the heroes of a resistance movement. At each rally Klonsel Murphy, dressed in a red sheet with a purple lining, introduced Collie Leroy Wilkins as "the trigger man" and "the hope of America." Wilkins was given a rock-and-roll star's reception. At the Atlanta parade a young girl told a reporter she thought Wilkins was "dreamy." The paunchy cigar-smoking auto mechanic became a celebrity, continually swamped by autograph seekers.[18]

Klan rallies generally consisted of prayer, a cross burning, and speeches warning the crowd against mongrelization. "White man, is this your country?" the imperial wizard repeatedly asked the crowd. Each time the crowd would respond with a thunderous "Yes!" He was followed by the Klan chaplain or "klud," who assured them, "Your horse won't mix with your cow, and your cow won't mix with your pigs. The nigger-man is an inferior race. Nobody can force the white man to mix with him. But we got a dictator in the White House who thinks he can. God help you to wake up and do what God wants you to do!"

On May 6, 1965, Butler Alabama's *Choctaw Advance* reported that Klonsel Matt Murphy introduced his clients, Collie Leroy Wilkins, Gene Thomas, and Orville Eaton, at a Klan rally in Bladon Springs by asking, "Do these men look like murderers to you?" Grand Dragon Robert Creel, dressed in an emerald-green robe, spoke about the Klan's opposition to integration, testifying that he would never send his three children to school with "runny nosed niggers." Commenting on the recent incidents in Selma, the grand dragon informed the crowd of more than two hundred that Rev. Reeb's body had been cremated because it was "rotten with cancer and syphilis."

The rally ended with the Klan benediction, led by the klud. "Our Heavenly Father, we invoke Thy Divine Benediction upon us. Keep us unfettered from the world that we might fight the good fight and run a true course and be worthy to claim the prize. May we as brethren and Klansmen be steadfast and unremovable, always abounding in the work of Our Lord, knowing that our labor is not in vain. Through Jesus Christ we pray. Amen."[19]

Only twenty weeks separated the first Wilkins trial in May 1965 from the retrial in October, but they were turbulent, fearful weeks. On July 10 a Klan rally was held in Hayneville where more than two hundred whites protested the invasion of Lowndes by the civil rights movement and the federal government. All summer the White Citizens' Council held its meetings at the Lowndes County Courthouse. July was tense, but August would be hot.

On August 20, 1965, Klonsel Matt Murphy was killed when he fell asleep at the wheel of his Chrysler convertible on a trip from Birmingham to the United Klan headquarters in Tuscaloosa. At four in the morning he swerved and hit the side of a gasoline tank truck. When Jim Liuzzo heard of the death he told author Jack Mendelsohn "I don't wish anybody dead, not even Matt Murphy, but I can't help feeling there's a kind of poetic justice here. I wonder if that truck driver was a Teamster."[20]

Then Stokely Carmichael began to organize. Twenty-four hours after the news of Vi's murder broke, Carmichael had left the Mississippi Delta SNCC project where he had been serving as field director and headed to Lowndes. Carmichael understood that the Liuzzo murder had been a message to outsiders to stay away and a warning to local blacks that life was not going to change because of a march.

On March 27, 1965, *New York Journal American* reporter Victor Riesel observed, "Terror is marching into racially troubled Alabama as federal troops move out and the national guard returns to the control of Governor Wallace. Some 10,000 Klansmen are ready to occupy the Cotton State when the guard is defederalized. In Montgomery, Birmingham and Bessemer negroes and whites who took part in the March expect retaliation by the Klan. For negroes it will mean not being able to leave their ghetto area without fear of attack. The murder of Mrs. Liuzzo was only the beginning. It was only a warning."

In the Mississippi Delta, Stokely Carmichael had learned how far the segregationists were willing to go to keep blacks away from the polls. Arriving in Selma with only a sleeping bag, he began working with a coalition of SNCC workers (who had maintained a field office across the street from the Dallas County Courthouse in Selma since 1963) and local militant blacks who had vowed to keep voter registration moving in Lowndes. The murder of Mrs. Liuzzo had only served to make them more determined.[21]

Carmichael's arrival would change the direction of the Lowndes movement from a struggle for equality with whites to a drive for black self-determination.

On August 6, 1965, President Johnson signed the Voting Rights Act, and on August 10 federal registrars arrived in Lowndes. Blacks were suddenly guaranteed the opportunity to register without having to submit to a literacy test. Increased black voter registration, however, brought increased resistance by whites. When white land owners evicted black sharecroppers and tenant farmers for registering to vote, Carmichael and his colleagues erected a tent city. Journalist Walling Keith observed in the *Birmingham News* on August 25, 1965, that "The white people in Lowndes County have been living with and under a set of guidelines handed down from grandfathers and great-grandfathers. It has been an accepted way of life. And when things have 'always' been one way it does not come easy to have a stranger come in to disrupt things."

August 1965 was also the month when an integrated group of young civil rights activists (two white males and two black females) were arrested in Ft. Deposit for picketing white stores that refused to hire blacks. They were told they were being placed in the Hayneville jail for their own protection, then were abruptly released a week later. Less than an hour after their release on August 20 the two white males were shot by Tom Coleman, a white part-time deputy sheriff. Jonathan Daniels, an Episcopal seminarian from Keene, New Hampshire, who had returned to Selma after the voting rights march and ultimately became involved in the

Lowndes voter registration movement, was killed and Rev. Richard Morrisroe, a Catholic priest, was seriously wounded. Jon Daniels was the seminarian Joanne had told me about when I was in Selma. He was the student who had roomed with Alice's family—Alice, who I had tried so awkwardly and so unsuccessfully to speak with.

The second cold-blooded murder of a civil rights agitator near Big Swamp made local black activists even more determined to organize their neighbors to vote. Stokely Carmichael fired up an audience at one evening rally with "We're going to tear this county up. Then we're going to build it back, brick by brick, until it's a fit place for human beings."[22]

Black voter registration efforts were bitterly resisted by Lowndes whites who did not want black candidates running in their Democratic primary. The state party, led by George Wallace, had "White Supremacy" as its rallying cry, so blacks were not enthusiastic about joining it either.

Carmichael proposed forming an independent black political organization. Through his efforts the Lowndes County Freedom Organization was created, with Lowndes resident John Hulett serving as chairman. LCFO produced an independent slate of candidates and held its own primary. Since many blacks were still illiterate, LCFO needed a party symbol to make it recognizable to voters. Alabama state Republicans were using a red elephant and the Democrats a white rooster. After some discussion, LCFO chose a black panther. "We were illiterate," one local said, "but we could tell a black cat from a white rooster and a red elephant."[23]

The symbol was appropriate, John Hulett explained. "The black panther is an animal that when it is pressured moves back until it is cornered, then it comes out fighting for life or death."[24]

The white population of Lowndes was therefore already dangerously agitated when, in mid-August, in the Watts area of Los Angeles, five thousand blacks rioted. The national wire services reported that Watts was a war zone with blacks roaming the streets chanting "Burn baby, burn." L.A. Police Chief William Parker angrily told reporters that violence was only to be expected "when you keep telling people they are unfairly treated and teach them disrespect for the law."[25]

The brief window of hope for convicting Wilkins—based on the close vote at the May trial—slammed shut. A car full of Klansmen rode through the streets of Hayneville with a loudspeaker blaring "What happened in Los Angeles will happen here if we don't take care of these niggers now!"

As the second trial of Collie Leroy Wilkins Jr. for the murder of Viola Liuzzo approached, Lowndes County was in emotional turmoil. Someone painted a swastika on the Hayneville water tower, and the impression of a cross was burned into the courthouse lawn.

On October 18, 1965, the retrial of Collie Leroy Wilkins Jr. opened at the Hayneville courthouse. Arthur Hanes Sr., who had been a pallbearer at Klonsel Murphy's funeral, replaced Murphy as Wilkins's defense attorney. A former FBI agent, Hanes was serving as legal counsel for Hayes Aviation in Birmingham, a firm that repaired and modified planes for the air force. Hayes had provided pilots to train Cubans for the Bay of Pigs invasion. Two Hayes employees—a flight engineer and a technical inspector—were killed during the failed plot to overthrow Castro in 1961.[26]

Arthur Hanes Sr. had also served as the mayor of Birmingham when white rioters attacked Freedom Riders as they entered Birmingham's bus station on Mother's Day in 1961. On January 15, 1962, when a federal court issued an order desegregating the city's public places—parks, playgrounds, swimming pools, and golf courses—Mayor Hanes padlocked the parks, removed the swings and slides from the playgrounds, closed the swimming pools, and cemented up the holes on the golf courses rather than permit them to be integrated. Hanes was still Birmingham's mayor when Martin Luther King Jr. carried his civil rights campaign to the city and Police Commissioner Bull Connor turned fire hoses and police dogs on the black marchers. Mayor Hanes had bitterly denounced King at that time. Two years later, when King was assassinated and James Earl Ray was charged with murder, Ray would request that Art Hanes Sr. defend him, and Hanes would accept.

Alabama State Attorney General Richmond Flowers personally directed the prosecution at Wilkins's second trial. He asked for a continuance "in view of the local racial situation" and was granted time for the state Supreme Court to review his petition. During jury selection Flowers, a tall red-haired man who towered above the jury box, asked each can-

Viola Gregg (third row, second from right) as an eleven-year-old sixth grader in Atlanta, Georgia. *Courtesy of Penny Liuzzo Herrington.*

Viola Gregg and George Argyris on a hiking trip with friends in 1942. They married on February 3, 1943. *Courtesy of Penny Liuzzo Herrington.*

Viola Argyris with eight-week-old daughter Penny in August 1946. *Courtesy of Penny Liuzzo Herrington.*

Viola Argyris at twenty-four. This is the picture the news media distributed widely after her murder. *Courtesy of Penny Liuzzo Herrington.*

The Liuzzo children at Viola's parents' home in Ypsilanti, Michigan, Thanksgiving Day 1954. Left to right: Mary, age six; baby Tony; Tommy, age three; and Penny, age eight. *Courtesy of Penny Liuzzo Herrington.*

Penny, nine years old, and seven-year-old Mary with Vi at Penny's First Communion in 1955. *Courtesy of Penny Liuzzo Herrington.*

Viola Liuzzo at thirty-four. *Courtesy of Penny Liuzzo Herrington.*

Jim and Viola Liuzzo with three-year-old Sally at 18491 Marlowe Street, in 1962. *UPI/Corbis-Bettmann.*

Viola Liuzzo mopping up while on vacation at a summer rental cottage in Newton Lake, Pennsylvania, in 1957. *Courtesy of Penny Liuzzo Herrington.*

19375 Marlowe Street, Viola Liuzzo's last home. *Courtesy of Kathleen McSherry.*

Nuns resting along the Jefferson Davis Highway during the Selma to Montgomery
voting rights march in 1965. *AP/Wide World Photos.*

Viola Liuzzo's bullet-riddled 1963 Oldsmobile. *AP/Wide World Photos.*

Jim Liuzzo, Penny, and Tommy at 19375 Marlowe Street on March 26, 1965. *UPI/Corbis-Bettmann*

Liuzzo family during solemn requiem mass for Viola Liuzzo at the Immaculate Heart of Mary Church in Detroit on March 30, 1965. Right to left: Jim, Tommy, Barry Johnson (husband of Mary), Mary, Penny, Sally, and Tony. *AP/Wide World Photos.*

Sarah Evans and the Liuzzo children read some of the more than sixteen thousand pieces of condolence and hate mail that began to arrive hours after Vi's death. Left to right: Tony, Mary, Sarah, Tommy, and Penny. *Edward E. Roberson, Jet Magazine.*

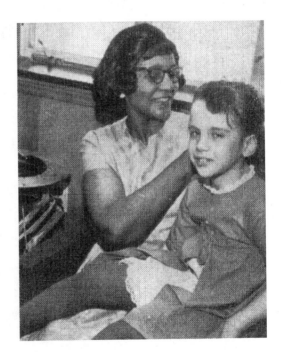

Sarah and Sally, May 1965. *Edward E. Roberson, Jet Magazine*

Collie Leroy Wilkins Jr., twenty-one, taken into custody in Birmingham, Alabama on March 26, 1965. *UPI/Corbis-Bettmann.*

Gary Thomas Rowe, thirty-one, arrested on March 26, 1965 in Birmingham. *UPI/Corbis-Bettmann.*

Robert M. Shelton, imperial wizard of the United Klans of
America, and Klonsel Matthew Hobson Murphy Jr., defense
attorney for Wilkins, Rowe, Eaton, and Thomas. *AP/Wide World
Photos.*

Leroy Moton, nineteen, who was riding in her car the night Viola Liuzzo was murdered, stopped by newsmen as he walks to the Hayneville courthouse as the first trial begins on May 4, 1965. *AP/Wide World Photos.*

Tony Liuzzo in 1982. *William Archie/
Detroit Free Press.*

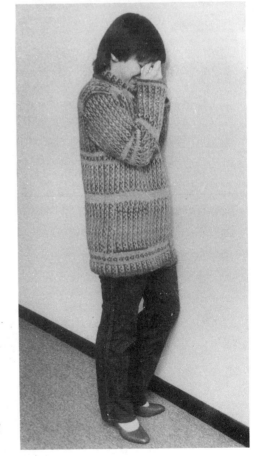

Sally Liuzzo weeps after federal district
judge Charles W. Joiner ruled that the U.S.
government was not responsible in the
1965 death of her mother. *AP/Wide World
Photos.*

Alabama activists pray at the defaced monument to Viola Liuzzo on February 5, 1997. The memorial has been vandalized three times since 1991. The SCLC Women plan to leave the Confederate flag painted on its face to serve as a reminder that racism still exists. *AP/Wide World Photos.*

didate about his or her racial views. This was revolutionary in the Deep
South in 1965.

"Do you believe a white person is superior to a nigra?" Flowers asked.
Most did. "How about a white who like Mrs. Liuzzo associates with nigras . . . people who come down here and try to help nigras integrate our
churches and schools?" Most stated that they thought a person like that
was also inferior.

Flowers lost his appeal to the Alabama Supreme Court to dismiss
eleven of the jurors on the grounds of racial bias. Despite the fact that the
Civil Rights Act of 1964 had been the law of the land for a year, jurors in
Alabama could not be disqualified for holding racist views.

"It's the strongest case I've ever had," Flowers said, "complete with the
eyewitness testimony of an FBI agent." Still he did not feel confident of
achieving a conviction. The all-male jury panel included six self-identified
white supremacists and eight current or former members of the White
Citizens' Council. He knew what was important to them—and to their
elected officials. Flowers was aware that when Mrs. Liuzzo's shattered
body was taken to the state laboratory in Montgomery the first thing the
lab had been asked to do was to test to determine if she had recently had
intercourse. The white population of Hayneville firmly believed its Way
of Life was under siege by the federal government, and they were terrified
by what they saw as their worst fears being confirmed by the Watts
rioting.

Only a month earlier, Flowers's office had prosecuted the Jonathan
Daniels case under the leadership of Joe Breck Gantt. When the jury acquitted Tom Coleman, Flowers called the verdict appalling. He said the
democratic process was going "down the drain of irrationality, bigotry
and improper law enforcement . . . now those who feel they have a license
to kill, destroy and cripple have been issued that license."[27]

At the retrial of Collie Leroy Wilkins, Flowers told the jury, "the blood
of this man's sin, if you do not find him guilty, will stain the very soul of
our country for an eternity."

Defense counsel Hanes characterized the trial as "the parable of the
two goats." He referred to Rowe as the Judas Goat and to Wilkins as the
Scape Goat. Hanes produced two witnesses who swore that they had seen

Wilkins drinking beer at a VFW hall near Birmingham (125 miles from the murder scene) less than one hour after Viola Liuzzo was shot. He asked the jury to consider that "Maybe the murderer is from the Watts area of Los Angeles."[28]

Then Hanes introduced the fact that the first police broadcast had described the murderers' car as a red Sprite, not the red-and-white Impala driven by Gene Thomas that night. This, he said, was grounds for reasonable doubt.

During his summation, Flowers, who had received death threats throughout the trial, reminded the jurors that Rowe's testimony was well corroborated by both the circumstantial evidence and the other witnesses. Angrily, he ripped a fistful of papers out of a lawbook. "If you don't render the true verdict of guilty," he told them, "you might as well tear the meaning of true verdict out of the book!"

As the jury deliberated, Jim Liuzzo was alerted by the Detroit police that an anonymous caller had contacted the Chicago FBI office. "Wilkins is innocent," the caller said. "If Wilkins gets convicted I'm going to get a bus tomorrow for Detroit and kill Liuzzo's husband."[29]

Despite the eyewitness accounts of Rowe and Moton, on October 22, 1965, a second all-white, all-male jury took one hour and forty-five minutes to find Wilkins not guilty of either murder or conspiracy. The jurors refused to convict a white man for stopping one of the outside agitators from destroying their Way of Life. When the foreman announced the verdict, the courtroom burst into applause. Dr. Martin Luther King said the shameful acquittal only underscored the need for new legislation to make civil rights murder a federal crime.

Throughout Lowndes County, bumper stickers declaring OPEN SEASON began appearing on cars, trucks, and farm machinery.

On November 5, 1965, Eugene Thomas, Orville Eaton, and Collie Leroy Wilkins were indicted on federal charges of conspiracy to violate the civil rights of Viola Liuzzo. These charges were based on the Federal Conspiracy Act of 1870 (title 18, section 241 of the U.S. Code) passed during Reconstruction, whose provisions had been extended by the

Supreme Court to protect interstate travelers. The statute declared it a federal crime "for two or more persons to conspire to injure, oppress, threaten or intimidate any citizen in the free exercise of any right or privilege secured him by the Constitution of the United States." The indictment charged that "It was part of the plan and part of the conspiracy that the defendants would harass threaten and pursue and assault citizens . . . in the area of Selma and Montgomery who were participating or had participated in, or who were lending or had lent their support to, the demonstration march." The murderers of Col. Lemuel Penn and the three Mississippi civil rights workers, Goodman, Chaney, and Schwerner, would also be indicted under this statute.

This time the trial was conducted at the federal courthouse in Montgomery. The U.S. assistant attorney general for civil rights, John Doar, served as chief prosecutor. Federal judge Frank Johnson presided. Johnson was the judge who had declared Montgomery's city bus segregation ordinance unconstitutional in 1954 and who had enjoined Governor Wallace to prevent any interference with the Selma marchers. Despite the fact that he had attended law school with George Wallace, Judge Frank Johnson was known as one of the great judicial enablers of the civil rights movement. In 1989, when he was seventy-one years old and still serving on the federal bench, Johnson told journalist Fred Powledge that "The biggest problem was white folks not doing anything. The large majority of white people were not active in opposing the rights of blacks. Their inactivity allowed those that were willing to be active in opposing to be more effective."[30]

Judge Johnson allowed the government to exclude former White Citizens' Council members from the jury this time and also allowed the defense to strike NAACP members. Initially the federal jury also deadlocked, but Judge Johnson refused to accept their stalemate. He told them that there had been about fifty witnesses and as many exhibits, that the trial had been thorough and expensive, and that they had not "commenced to deliberate the case long enough to reach the conclusion that they were hopelessly deadlocked." He assured them that there was "no reason to suppose that the case would ever be submitted to twelve more intelligent, more impartial, or more competent people to decide it, or that more or clearer evidence would be produced on one side or the other."[31] Then he sent them back to try again.

In an unanticipated landmark victory, the all-white, all-male southern jury returned a verdict of guilty. On December 3, 1965, Wilkins, Eaton, and Thomas were given the maximum sentence under the federal statute—ten years. President Johnson noted that "The whole nation can take heart from the fact that there are those in the South who believe in justice in racial matters and who were determined not to stand for acts of violence and terror."[32]

Wilkins began serving his sentence on January 4, 1966. Civil rights murder would not, however, become a federal crime until after the death of Dr. Martin Luther King Jr. in 1968.

The state murder trials for Orville Eaton and Gene Thomas were scheduled for spring 1966. But balding, pasty-faced Orville Eaton, who had walked through his indictment, federal trial, and the Klan parades looking dazed, died of an apparent heart attack on March 9, 1966, before he could stand trial. Eaton's only previous brush with the law had been a violation of prohibition laws—he had been caught distilling alcohol, which got him a two-year suspended sentence. A port helper at U.S Steel, he was retired and living in Bessemer on a disability pension for a heart condition. He was married and had four sons between the ages of seven and fourteen and a four-year-old daughter at the time of his arrest.

Eugene Thomas, the gaunt, thin-faced man who drove the Impala on the night of the murder, was given a trial date in May, but it had to be postponed because of the unavailability of Tommy Rowe, now protected by the Federal Witness Protection Program. Thomas, who was born in Bessemer and lived there all his life, had been employed by U.S. Steel for twenty-four years as a machinist. He was married with three sons, one serving in the air force. Like Wilkins, Thomas had been arrested for a series of petty crimes, including carrying a concealed weapon, assault and battery, and reckless driving. Despite his record he had been issued a card and a badge by the Fairfield Police Department designating him a special constable for the purpose of law enforcement for the City of Bessemer. He was carrying both the card and his badge on the night of the Liuzzo murder. Like Wilkins, Thomas was an active Klan member. In 1961 he had been elected assistant klokan chief of the Eastview Klavern 13, and in 1964 while serving as exalted cyclops, he was questioned by the FBI in the course of their investigation of the bombing of the Sixteenth Street Baptist Church in Birmingham.[33] After a Klan rally in September 1964, Thomas had taken part in a plot to bomb the Flame Club in Fairfield, where blacks and whites had attended a function together. The plot was aborted, however, when police arrived unexpectedly.

Thomas's trial finally opened on September 26, 1966, with a jury composed of eight blacks and four whites. It was the only biracial jury of the four trials associated with the Liuzzo murder. By this time Attorney General Richmond Flowers had decided not to call Tommy Rowe as a witness, based on the extensive publicity the Wilkins trials had focused on him and on the general opinion in Lowndes that he was a liar and a race traitor. Flowers also decided against calling Leroy Moton, who he felt had been an ineffective witness at the first trial. Like Wilkins, Thomas never took the stand in his own defense. On the day after the trial opened, the jury brought in a verdict of not guilty.

Tommy Rowe, using his new Federal Witness Protection Program identity, headed out to California. Leroy Moton left Selma to take a job as a cook in an SCLC Freedom House in Atlanta.

Back in Selma, as federal voting examiners arrived, the number of blacks registered rose from less than 10 percent to more than 60 percent in just two months. As the election for sheriff drew closer, Jim Clark threw away his NEVER! button and hosted a barbecue for Dallas County's black voters. It was too little too late. He was soundly defeated.

"Martin Luther King ruined Selma's way of life," Clark complained bitterly. "We had a way of life we liked." Ultimately the sheriff left Selma, and in 1967 he wrote The Jim Clark Story: I Saw Selma Raped. Ten years later he would be convicted of smuggling marijuana and sentenced to two years in federal prison.

In the fall of 1967, back in Detroit, Jim Liuzzo was coping with a gunshot blast fired through his living room window and paint splattered inside his car eighteen months after his wife's murder.[34]

The Decision to March

■■■■■■■■ The point is, simply, of course, that one's motives are usually mixed, and
one had better know it.
—Jonathan Daniels

Jim Liuzzo was convinced that his wife had made up her mind to go to
Selma on March 7, 1965, during the eleven o'clock news, as she watched
the Alabama state troopers beat voting rights demonstrators on the
Edmund Pettus Bridge. Sarah Evans was certain her friend went south because she believed she could change the world. Thirteen-year-old Tommy
thought his mother went to help people. "If there was a mountain to
climb, she could always make it," he said, "Some of the rest might fall
down, but she'd make it."[35] Like much in Viola Liuzzo's passionate, restless life, her decision was complicated.

When Vi started classes at Wayne State University in the spring of 1963
she became enthralled with college life and resigned her job at Sinai
Hospital to concentrate on her studies. Jim was earning almost twenty
thousand dollars a year—good money in 1965—and she didn't have to
work. In 1963 a dozen large eggs cost twenty-seven cents, a good suit
$60, and a sports jacket $35. You could buy a brand new two-door Ford
Falcon for $1,789, a T-Bird for $3,995, and four tires for $39.95. A
Kelvinator three-speed clothes washer was listed at $187, a family-size
refrigerator $117, and a Magic Chef Early American range "with fluo-
rescent back panel" retailed at $157, but you could do better than that at
a sale.

Vi's supervisor at Sinai asked her to reconsider and possibly work
fewer hours, but she refused, determined to focus her energy on the new
life she had discovered at Wayne. The people she met on campus and the
courses she took stimulated her imagination. Sarah said Vi became fascinated with Plato, whose works she read over and over. The dialogues particularly appealed to her because of her love of discussion and debate.
What is beauty? What is courage? What is virtue?

Vi absorbed Plato's ideas about the importance of knowing oneself. He
defined courage as knowledge that involves a willingness to act for the
good, and this appealed to her. The idea that made the strongest impres-

sion, however, the one she repeatedly quoted to Jim, Sarah, and the rest of the family, was one she had found in the *Protagoras.* There Socrates insists that no one chooses evil except through ignorance. "No one who either knows or believes that there is another possible course of action, better than the one he is following, will ever continue on his present course when he might choose the better. To 'act beneath yourself' is the result of pure ignorance, to 'be your own master' is wisdom."

In the writings of the American philosopher Henry David Thoreau, Vi found a kindred spirit. Thoreau loved nature and took unconventional stands on public issues. He was described by his neighbors as a very stubborn, opinionated young man. He too expressed his deepest convictions through dramatic action.

In 1845 Thoreau refused to pay taxes to the federal government to protest the Mexican War and its enforcement of slavery. He went to jail for his refusal. When his friend Ralph Waldo Emerson asked him, "What are you doing in there, Henry?" Thoreau looked through his bars and replied "Waldo, what are you doing out there?"

In class Vi discussed the principles of self-reliance and civil disobedience. Thoreau's belief that a creative minority, even a minority of "one honest man," could start a moral revolution captured her imagination. "Things do not change," Thoreau wrote, "we change." In his essay "Civil Disobedience," Vi read, "There are thousands who are in opinion opposed to slavery and to the war, who yet in effect do nothing to put an end to them; who, esteeming themselves children of Washington and Franklin, sit down with their hands in their pockets, and say that they know not what to do, and do nothing."

Vi read to her children from *Walden,* Thoreau's journal. She helped them with their school work and shared hers with them. Mary remembers that when one of her mother's professors mentioned the theory of relativity in class and Vi didn't know what it was Vi and Mary sat with their set of encyclopedias looking up Einstein, relativity, and astrophysics until they pieced together the mystery and formulated a working definition of relativity together.

Mary also recalls her mother talking about Ralph Waldo Emerson's *Essays.* Vi was particularly drawn to the way Emerson linked God and nature in the belief that God's truth could be revealed by attention to nature. Emerson was a universalist. He believed when one finds what is true for himself (or herself) he has also found what is true for all. In his essay "Self Reliance," Vi read, "To believe your own thought, to believe that what is true for you in your private heart is true for all men—that is genius. It is a kind of genius that is possible for anyone who is willing to acquire it."

As Vi studied philosophy, sociology, and political thought she became increasingly engaged in the subject of racial justice. Professor Johan Bellefleur, her academic adviser, called Vi "very much an individual" who "tended to see things in terms of values."

Studying alongside young men and women in 1963 made Vi painfully aware of what she had missed by rushing headlong into adulthood. She had left school at fourteen, been married and divorced at sixteen, lived and worked alone in Detroit at eighteen, and remarried at nineteen! Although her parents, especially her father, had fought with her about quitting school, Vi hadn't understood the value of what she gave up. Now she was angry that the law had allowed restless kids like herself with poor judgment to make such life-altering decisions. This was why the challenge to the school board meant so much to her.

A hard-working B-minus student, Vi became a singular figure on campus—an outgoing, enthusiastic lady, always in a dress, carrying a pocketbook, and usually in a hurry. Sometimes she appeared frazzled, but she was always eager.

Vi internalized everything she read for her philosophy, psychology, sociology, and literature courses. She tried to make sense of the feelings that drove her in ways she couldn't always understand. Vi was a terrible poet, but lack of talent didn't stop her from putting some of her painful feelings into verse. She wrote a poem entitled "Eternity" in 1964.

Beneath a dark and dreary night
There stands a man within God's sight.
He, alone, can tear away
The power of night that forms a day.
So relentlessly this man treads on
To search for that something he fears long gone.

Hence from rising sun to an endless day
He is never still for he cannot stay.
So above or below the mud or the rain
He thrashes on through an unknown terrain
So often he's tired, so often he's pained
Yet he still struggles on to the peak he must gain.
This peak will he reach? Can this man refrain
From surrender to the pain, the cost of life's gain?
Oh! the peak he has reached, he did not refrain
Thus everything ventured was everything gained.
Tranquil peace is the peak and now also his right
So he now lies forever, joined with God in sight.[36]

All the doubts, regrets, fears, and religious longings that washed over Vi at midlife are evident in this poem. Here she expressed her fears that she had lost something irretrievable, that she would never find peace, that life is "unknown terrain" on which an individual must struggle, that everything is achieved at great cost with only the hope that God cares.

This struggle to understand herself drew Vi to religion. Her mother was a lapsed Catholic, and Vi had attended Catholic school for a short period (St. Mary's Junior High School in Chattanooga), but she had been raised essentially without religion. She formally converted to Catholicism when she married Jim, who was a practicing Catholic. Initially the mysticism of the Catholic Church appealed to her, as did the social gospel of Evangelical Protestantism that rang out in the speeches and sermons of Martin Luther King Jr., a Baptist preacher. But Vi's daughter Mary told me that when one of Vi's children was stillborn and she was told that because the baby was not able to be baptized its soul would remain in Limbo, Vi turned away from the church. She asked Jim, "Why would a loving God do that? *I* wouldn't do that! I can't believe it's true."

Vi believed, like the mountain people of her Appalachian roots, that God was partial to the poor and the suffering. Like Martin Luther King she believed that Jesus of Nazareth had come "to preach the good news to the poor, to proclaim release to the captive, and to set at liberty those who are oppressed."

Vi found little comfort in organized religion. She synthesized a personal religion from many traditions, believing deeply in the oneness of creation that Dr. King referred to when he said, "Injustice anywhere is a threat to justice everywhere. We are caught in an inescapable network of mutuality tied in a single garment of destiny. Whatever affects one directly, affects all indirectly."[37] Vi believed a loving God intervened in human history, and she became increasingly impatient to discover her own purpose in His plan.

Early in 1965 Vi began attending services at the First Unitarian Universalist Church on Cass Avenue, just two blocks from the Wayne State campus. The bulletin board outside the church still reads RELIGION FOR THE MODERN THINKER.

Unitarian Universalists are liberal Christians who follow the dictates of reason, conscience, and experience and are open to the insights of all world religions. They believe in a Unitarian (as opposed to a Trinitarian) God and salvation by personal accountability rather than through atonement, baptism, or predestination. Rev. Jack Mendelsohn wrote in 1964, "The atmosphere of a Unitarian Universalist Church encourages each person to make his best contribution to the group's enrichment. The emphasis is on sharing the results of personal thought and evaluation. Truth, we recognize, is vast and many-sided. . . . The UUC welcomes all who catch the vision of placing principles of freedom, responsibility and tolerance above uniform theological doctrines . . . we continue to evolve in the light of our growing knowledge of ourselves and our world."[38]

Detroit's First Unitarian Universalist Church congregation was committed to social justice, and many of its members were former Freedom Riders. Vi felt comfortable among them and convinced Penny to attend the church's college-age discussion group several times.

When Rev. James Reeb was killed in Selma, just days after Bloody Sunday, Vi attended a memorial service for him at the First Unitarian Universalist Church. Reeb, originally ordained a Presbyterian minister, had been re-ordained a Unitarian in 1958. In his application for re-ordination he had written, "I want to be a Unitarian minister because the Church does not prescribe for people what the ultimate outcome of their religious quest must be; rather it attempts to create a fellowship that will strengthen and encourage each member in his desire and determination to live the truth as he sees it."[39]

Jim recalled that Vi also spoke about Rev. Malcolm Boyd, the Episcopal chaplain at Wayne State whom she admired very much. Boyd defined himself as a Christian Existentialist who believed that social protest and religion met in what he called the "ethics of action." He told his students, "We are what we *do*, not what we think or say."

Vi agreed wholeheartedly. This was exactly what she needed to hear: meaning could be found in action. She became a regular at Rev. Boyd's weekly open house sessions where students gathered to discuss political, social, and religious issues.

Malcolm Boyd was a controversial figure on the Wayne State campus. When he was hired in June 1961 a *Detroit Free Press* headline announced "Colorado's Beatnik Priest Will Become Wayne's First Full Time Chaplain." Boyd had been criticized by Colorado Bishop Joseph Minnis for his "beatnik activities," including "sponsoring espresso nights for students, and occasionally holding religious discussions in taverns."[40]

Malcolm Boyd, dubbed "the espresso priest" before he ever arrived in Detroit, commented, "The church cannot wait for people to come to it, the church's whole reason for being is to go out to the people, where they are, and to learn to speak their language."

Like the Unitarian Universalists, Boyd believed in individual accountability. He told his students, "There are no born heroes or cowards, no predisposing conditions, no persons or situations in our lives which we can blame for what and who we are—salvation lies in action."[41]

Chaplain Boyd had also been a Freedom Rider. In 1961 Louisiana State University barred him from speaking on campus as he traveled with twenty-eight other Episcopal priests on a prayer pilgrimage from New Orleans to Dearborn, Michigan (one of his first activities upon assuming the Wayne chaplaincy). By 1963 he was in hot water with the Wayne State administration for meeting with Wilfred X, brother of Malcolm X, in the chaplain's apartment at 4863 Second Street, right in the heart of the campus.

In August 1964 Boyd accepted a national chaplaincy assignment for the Episcopal Society for Racial and Cultural Unity and officially left Wayne. The following year he received the Catholic Press Association's journalism prize for his articles on civil rights. Until he left Detroit in the late 1960s, however, Boyd continued to hold open houses for students. Many who attended his Espresso Nights were veterans of the 1964 Freedom Summer project in Mississippi.

Wayne State University seemed to come alive with protest activity during the 1965 spring semester. On March 11, a group of about one hundred students, demonstrating against police brutality on the Pettus Bridge in Selma, left the campus carrying posters that read STOP JIM CLARK and STOP JIM CROW. They marched down Woodward Avenue to the Detroit federal building. Senior Carol MacDonald told a reporter from the *Daily Collegian,* "This demonstration is the least we can do to show the people in Selma that we support them." A graduate student noted that the march was bringing the events in Selma to the attention of Detroiters and that "The university is finally taking a stand." Jim Krumm, a senior, said, "The turnout of one hundred students was very good considering that the demonstration was spontaneous," while a freshman commented, "It needs to be brought out that the university students aren't apathetic and that we care what's happening in Selma."[42] The following day fifty Wayne students and faculty members left for Washington, D.C., to take part in a march to the Capitol to demand federal intervention in Selma.

On March 16 Vi participated in a second Selma sympathy march to the federal building along with another 250 Wayne students. Mayor Jerome Cavanaugh and Governor George Romney led the march, which ultimately swelled to ten thousand people. Penny, who was eighteen, marched with her mother. They listened as students who had been to Selma told their stories. Ronald Helveston, a member of the University Law Students Civil Rights Research Council said he had seen vigilantes leering, laughing, and mumbling at the marchers before Bloody Sunday. They were menacingly twisting ax handles and drumming them in their palms. "I never saw such looks in my life," he said. Another commented, "I thought I could tell the new deputies. They had on uniform police tops and old corduroy pants. They were looking and laughing, rattling those handles. Men like these killed Rev. Reeb, only these were deputized."[43]

Vi told Penny, "See, it's everybody's fight."

It was during a discussion about Bloody Sunday, in Rev. Boyd's living room, among students who were planning to leave for Selma on March 16, that Vi decided she was going to march. She had been thinking about it since she had watched newscasts of the brutal acts of the state troopers. After her death, a handwritten letter was found in Vi's car. It appears to have been written to one of her professors shortly before she left. "Prior to today I felt that any personal contribution I might offer to those individuals in distress in Selma, Alabama was of little or no significance," Vi wrote. "I also had concluded that even if such efforts should prove at all helpful, they would have to wait until the quarter's end. Nevertheless, upon reading the content of our president's speech today, I am no longer able to sit by while my people are suffering. . . . I examined carefully my own possible reaction if I were one of the Selma victims, not just a spectator."[44]

With the school board struggle and her Canada odyssey less than a year behind her, however, it wasn't hard for Vi to anticipate Jim's response if she told him she was thinking about going to Selma. Racked with guilt yet determined to go, she decided to plan the trip without consulting him.

She finally confided in Sarah, who told her she was crazy, that she would wind up getting herself killed. But Vi was stubborn, Sarah remembers. "A few people started this mess and a few people can end it," Vi said. Then she told Sarah how much it meant for her to do something concrete with her life and that she thought the civil rights movement would give her that opportunity. "It's important," she said, "and I want to be part of it."

Years later Sarah would tell me "Vi was a loving mother. She took good care of her kids. She set it up for me to stay with them when she went to Selma. And remember, Penny was already eighteen—she helped, too." Sarah promised Vi she would take care of the children, explain to them where their mother had gone, and assure them their mother would call every night. Vi wrote out their schedules and left detailed instructions. She also made arrangements at Wayne. She was completing political science, English, and sociology courses that semester and had to apply for permission to postpone her final exams. Permission was granted, but she was told it would mean accepting two incompletes for the term. "I'll take the incompletes," she said. "I'm going to Selma. It's something I have to do."

"Before she left, Mom went to see my father, George Argyris," Penny remembers. "I didn't understand why at the time, but she said she wanted to tell him how sorry she was about the way things had ended with them. Then she told me that I ought to get married and have children. I thought that was strange, since she'd been encouraging me to go to college all along, but looking back I think she sensed that something was going to happen to her. She used to have premonitions."

It makes sense that Vi would tell Penny to get married. Vi must have noticed Penny's ambivalence about college, and she had learned from her sad experience with Mary that forcing her children to accept her values didn't work. Vi's own ambivalence was clawing at her too. Activism was demanding, and she had learned that even unflinching endurance couldn't ensure that injustices would be corrected or that others wouldn't get hurt. Years earlier, when she had worked so hard to make Sally well, Vi began to believe she could change anything she didn't like through sheer willpower. The experiences with Parkview hospital and the school board, however, caused her to question that assumption. At Parkview she had lost her job, and in her struggle with the board her relationships with Mary, Jim, and her mother had been badly strained. Increasingly, there were moments when Vi weighed how much her convictions had cost her. Might not Penny, after all, be better off following a more traditional, more acceptable path? Might not happiness for her daughter lie in becoming the type of wife and mother most men wanted, someone even Jim Liuzzo might have preferred?

Jim's sister, Josephine Florini, who still lived in the old neighborhood at 6366 Abington Avenue, was a woman like that. A successful homemaker, wife, and mother, Jo seemed to do everything effortlessly. Penny told me that Vi had once dyed her blonde hair black, just like Aunt Jo's. "It looked *awful!*" Penny laughed. "It just didn't fit." Vi could never make herself into Jo Florini. That was something even her strong will and determination couldn't accomplish.

Vi seemed unaware that other white, middle-aged, middle-class women were feeling some of the same restlessness and anger that she was experiencing. She knew few others besides her sister-in-law, neighbors, and the parents of her children's friends. Her closest friends were a black woman ten years her senior and college classmates twenty years younger. She assumed that she was just out of sync and struggled with her love for her family and her need to fulfill herself as if they were separate issues.

By 1965 her ex-husband George Argyris had also remarried, and he had another daughter. Vi's growing insight allowed her to own up to her part in his pain fifteen years earlier. Argyris had remained close to Penny and Mary despite the fact that Vi had struggled with him until he agreed to allow Jim to adopt them. She realized her Selma decision would likely bring more pain, this time to Jim and the kids. I believe it was this pain she anticipated in her premonition, not her own death. She knew her family would suffer as she attracted more criticism to herself, but she was driven.

"Things do not change," Thoreau said, "we change." Vi had changed, and she wanted another chance. She needed to feel alive again after her crippling bout with depression, and she wanted an opportunity to do something meaningful.

At Rev. Boyd's home on the evening of March 15, 1965, students who had participated in the 1964 Mississippi Freedom Summer recalled their experiences and discussed what was then happening in Selma. Rev. Boyd remembered that the conversation became very impassioned, and he recalled Viola Liuzzo participating in it. He said that like most of the students she was a sincere idealist, but he felt she had an added dimension of deep spirituality. She was "a truly religious person, not explicitly religious, but religious in a profound sense."[45]

Vi left Marlowe Street the following morning with a shopping bag full of clothes. Her tan pocketbook was slung over one arm, and at the last minute she tossed her sociology textbook into the bag. Sociology was her last class on Tuesday evenings. In the afternoon she and Penny marched to the federal building. After the demonstration, Penny went back to Marlowe Street and Vi finished her classes. Then Vi phoned Jim. She told him she was leaving for Selma with some students and that she would be back in a week. Shocked, he demanded that she at least come home and talk about it. "There are too many people who just stand around talking about it," she replied. When he got angry, she asked him to try to understand. She said she wanted to visit Mary on the way back. Mary had moved to Ringgold, Georgia, with her husband, Barry Johnson. There was nothing to worry about, Vi insisted. In the middle of their argument Penny picked up the extension phone. She also tried to reason with her mother. "Finally I told her if it was that important to let me go with her, but she said no. She was determined—stubborn. I had a very bad feeling during that conversation."

"Just be careful," Jim said finally. And Vi was gone.

Thousands of people all over the country were making the same decision. Journalist George Leonard writing for *The Nation,* described his reactions to the televised events of Bloody Sunday. "We were in our living room in San Francisco watching the 6 P.M. news. I was not aware that at the same moment people all up and down the West Coast were feeling what my wife and I felt, that at various times all over the country that day and up past 11 P.M. Pacific Time that night hundreds of these people would drop whatever they were doing, that some of them would leave home without changing clothes, borrow money, overdraw their checking accounts; board planes, buses, trains, cars; travel thousands of miles with no luggage; get speeding tickets, hitch hike, hire horse drawn wagons; that these people mostly unknown to one another, would move for a single purpose: to place themselves alongside the Negroes they had watched on television."[46]

Human Flotsam, Beatniks, and Prostitutes

We had every screwball in the United States down here.
—Roswell Falkenberry

Just a few decades ago, in the early 1960s, white women were both excluded from the powerful white-male world and dependent on it. Young white women (both northern and southern) were taught early that life was dangerous. Grown women were discouraged from going to a restaurant or a movie by themselves. Parents, teachers, and clergymen warned them that there were places women should never go unless accompanied by a man. If they were attacked because they ignored those warnings, they would be blamed for inviting trouble.

Vi Liuzzo ignored such warnings all her life. Being protected felt too much like being confined. She was a strong-minded, strong-willed woman who chose to balance family responsibility, work, and school. She was temperamental, high spirited, and determined, yet she could not bring herself to tell her husband face-to-face that she was going to Selma. Later feminists would theorize about the personal being political, but nothing crystallizes the experience of a white American woman in 1965 like Vi's ambivalence.

Viola Liuzzo loved her family. She encouraged Penny to settle down and have children because she believed children were critical to a happy life, yet she also felt compelled to join the wider world. The Selma voting rights march was a good cause with powerful backing, and it had a chance to succeed. It called out to individuals like her to become part of a collective act of social justice. Still, she felt she had to slip away to Selma. If she paused to explain or stopped to ask permission she might not get there.

"Vi thought people's rights were being violated in Selma and she had to do something about it in her own way," Jim said. "That was her downfall. So many times I told her 'one of these days the humanitarian things you do are going to backfire.'"[47]

The voting rights march was—to borrow Jim Liuzzo's expression—the backfire that jolted America. White marchers, white women in particular, would be accused of a variety of perversions—mostly sexual. On March 22—before the first demonstrator stepped out of Selma—Alabama's state legislature released Act 159, a resolution denouncing the anticipated march. It read, "Many innocent people of Alabama are being led by supposedly religious leaders from other parts of these United States who call themselves preachers, some of whom have been seen drinking strong drink and heard using the most vulgar and profane language on the streets of Montgomery. There is evidence [the legislators did not specify *what* evidence] of much fornication and young women are returning to their respective states apparently as unwed expectant mothers." Act 159 was printed in a half-page advertisement in the *Montgomery Advertiser*.[48]

On the second day of the march, Alabama's freshman congressman, William Dickinson, who represented the congressional district that included Montgomery, spoke on the floor of the United States House of Representatives declaring that "drunkenness and sex orgies were the order of the day." He read from a pamphlet that he said was passed out to the marchers inviting them to a burlesque show. He alleged the show was staged nightly during the march in one of the tents.

Dickinson testified that the whole demonstration was a communist plot, that orgies were being conducted in a hotel in Montgomery, and that there were many incidents of sexual intercourse in public between blacks and whites. "Negro and white freedom marchers invaded a Negro church in Montgomery and engaged in an all night session of debauchery within the church itself," he said. He described the marchers as "human flotsam, adventurers, beatniks, prostitutes, and similar rabble hired to march at $10 a day, free room and board, and all the sex they wanted. Free love among this group is not only condoned, it is encouraged," Dickinson said. "It is in fact their way of life. Only by the ultimate sex act with one of another color can they demonstrate that they have no prejudice."[49]

Responding to the congressman's accusations, a black marcher observed, "These white folks must think we're supermen to be able to march all day in the rain, eat a little pork and beans, make whoopee all night and then get up the next morning and march all day again!" Several nuns (in full habit) good-humoredly lamented their lost reputations to reporters, and Julian Bond, then a member of the Student Non-Violent Coordinating Committee, said, "I hope he realizes that he is accusing nuns, priests, rabbis, and other responsible citizens of misconduct."[50]

But anti–race mixing sentiment was blazing all over Lowndes and Dallas counties. It was fueled by the release of Albert Persons's *The True Selma Story: Sex and Civil Rights.* This magazine, issued by Esco Publishers of Birmingham in April 1965, was distributed through local truck stops and newsstands all over the South.

In the summer of 1997 I held a copy of *The True Selma Story* in my hand in the rare-book room of the Library of Congress. I had expected to find an ignorant, amateur, comic book–like production, since on August 22, 1965, the *New York Herald Tribune* reported that "The best selling book in Alabama today is *Sex and Civil Rights*. It reveals . . . that half the women in the Selma March wore no underpants." Such a "revelation" appears nowhere in the book, which turns out to be a thirty-two-page magazine produced on glossy paper, looking surprisingly like *Time* or *Newsweek*. It sold for one dollar in the days when *Life* magazine cost thirty-five cents.

"The True Selma Story" is one of four articles in the magazine authored by Persons. The others include "Bayard and Ralph: Just a Couple of Boys," which exposed Bayard Rustin's homosexuality and accused Ralph Abernathy of adultery with a teenage girl (both Rustin and Abernathy were close associates of Martin Luther King); "How the Birmingham Image Was Created," in which Persons attests that trick photography, expert photo cropping, and just plain lying by the national press had created America's poor image of Birmingham in 1963; and "Black Knight of the Civil Rights Movement," where Persons assembles evidence to support his theory that Martin Luther King was a puppet of the Communist Party. In summarizing his research, Albert Persons observed that "The greatest obstacle in the Negroes' search for freedom is the Negro himself and the leadership he has chosen to follow." The magazine's red-and-black cover carries the same silhouetted photo of voting rights marchers walking up a hill that the producers of the PBS series *Eyes on the Prize* would use as their logo in 1991.

Fully expecting to find something that would appeal to Klan scholars with third-grade educations, I was horrified to discover that Albert "Buck" Persons was a professional journalist—a stringer for *Life* magazine, who lived in Birmingham and covered the demonstrations there in 1963. A nephew of a former Alabama governor, Buck joined the Royal Canadian Air Force in 1939 and became a skilled b-26 bomber pilot and later flew dc-3 planes commercially. Like Mayor Hanes of Birmingham, Persons had ties to the Bay of Pigs invasion of Cuba. In 1961 he had been recruited by Major General Reid Doster to "train some Cubans down South."[51] Persons produced *The True Selma Story* while on research assignment for Congressman William Dickinson. It was from Persons's research that the congressman had assembled his "facts."

The Montgomery hotel Dickinson referred to was the Ben Moore, lo-

cated next door to the Montgomery headquarters of SNCC. Persons reported that "On one occasion, James Foreman, Executive Director of
SNCC [a black man] was observed in a sex act with a red haired white
girl." The church where public sex supposedly took place was identified
as the Jackson Street Baptist Church. A thirty-two-year-old unidentified
black Montgomery resident supposedly told Persons, "I saw numerous
instances of boys and girls of both races hugging and kissing and fondling
one another openly in church. . . . On one occasion I saw a Negro boy
and a white girl engaged in sexual intercourse on the floor of the church
while other boys and girls stood around watching and laughing."

The True Selma Story included a series of sworn, notarized statements
from supposed eyewitnesses. Those quoted included an employee of the
Montgomery City Police Department, a captain in the Montgomery sheriff's office, an unidentified Negro woman, a lieutenant in the Alabama
National Guard, and a deputy sheriff of Dallas County.

Persons carefully tailored his quotations, photos, and captions to suggest the kind of behavior that would most incense the white segregationists of the Black Belt. He made sure his "facts" were attributed to those
whom his audience would find most credible—white men in uniforms.

James Duke, captain in the Montgomery sheriff's office, reported that
near the state capitol on the day the marchers arrived, "At approximately
8 A.M. one of the leaders, a colored man whose name I cannot recall, but
whom I believe I could identify from existing photos if necessary, stood
and announced in a loud voice to the crowd, 'Everyone stand and relieve
yourselves.' Practically the entire crowd in every mixture of age, sex and
color rose and a large number exposed themselves and urinated in the
streets."

Lionel Freeman, a captain in the Alabama state troopers, attested, "In
Selma near Brown Chapel I observed smooching and lovemaking between
Negroes and whites. I saw a mixed couple in the act of having sexual relations. . . . I along with thirty of my men saw two men dressed as priests
and four young Negro girls cross US 80. The priests were holding hands
with two Negro girls each. The Rev. Reeb was beaten about two or three
hours later."

James Crowder of the Selma police department reported, "I saw a short Negro in a green sweater on three different occasions rub up against white girls feeling their breasts and other parts of their bodies and then take them off to the rear of the crowd and on to different apartments."

V. B. Bates, deputy sheriff of Dallas County, told Persons, "I saw white females from other counties, other states I believe, building up their sexual desires with Negro males. After a few minutes of necking and kissing the Negro male would lead them off into the Negro housing project. I watched this procedure many, many times."

And finally, Nettie Adams, an employee of the Montgomery police department testified, "This one particular couple on the lawn of St. Margaret's Hospital [in Montgomery] was engaged in sexual relations. It was a skinny blonde white woman and a Negro man. . . . In front of Chris's Hot Dog Stand this other red-haired woman and Negro man started making love and embracing one another as if they wanted someone to try and stop them. . . . My husband said 'let's get out of here. This is no place for a man to have his wife.'"

Buck Persons masterfully caricatured all the enemies of the South: outside agitators, horny white women, priest impersonators, and rapacious black men. "Here," he wrote, "for those who are willing to accept the kind of evidence which is accepted in our courts are some of the affidavits of people who were on the spot and have taken an oath that what they say is true."

United Press International photographer Phil Sandler commented, "I spent five days and nights on the March. None of those things ever happened."

The national press, however, couldn't resist a good story. A rumor ran through Selma that a white girl had died of exhaustion after making thousands of dollars "providing comfort to the visiting clergy," and all the wire services picked it up. During the first week of May 1965, *Newsweek, Time,* and *U.S. News* carried features entitled "Kiss and Tell," "Charges of Interracial Sex," and "Orgies on the Rights March."

Virginia Durr observed that "After everybody cleared out and things began to settle down, the story got around all over Montgomery of the rapes that had taken place in Selma. . . . The crazies put out pamphlets saying that nuns weren't nuns and priests weren't priests; they were just pimps and prostitutes who'd come down here. They said there'd been a wholesale rape at the black hotel in Montgomery. One girl had been raped forty-seven times. Mrs. Rutledge, who was living in Lillian, came up to Montgomery to a church meeting and all she heard about was these women and girls who had been raped—one of them forty-seven times. That's when she made the remark, 'Well, I think the poor dear would have done better if she'd screamed rather than counted.' What was so interesting to me—so terrifying—is that it always got down to sexual relations between a black man and a white woman. The fact was that the marchers slept on the ground, and the cold mud of Lowndes County is not very conducive to loving warmth, I wouldn't think. But people pictured the whole thing as a terrible sexual orgy."

John Lewis, chairman of SNCC (and a future U.S. representative from Georgia) agreed. "All these segregationists can think of is fornication," he said disgustedly, "and that's why there are so many shades of Negroes."[52]

Journalist Howell Raines recalls speaking with a white woman from Selma who told him, "You should have seen the filth that came down here. If you had seen the men and women lyin' out on the ground all together, it's something that anyone would have been upset about. You would see men and women of both races going in and out of the Headquarters right here in Selma."[53]

On March 28, 1965, in an attempt to stem the hysteria, the *Selma Times Journal* reprinted "Don't Let Rumors Get You," from the *Tuscaloosa News*. (Ironically, Tuscaloosa was the home of the national headquarters of the United Klans of America.) "Many people are asking in Tuscaloosa and elsewhere why the newspapers have not carried certain stories about horrible happenings that were supposed to have occurred in Selma," the article recounted. "The answer is that the events did not occur. . . . The *Tuscaloosa News* asked the Associated Press to check on reports of various crimes being committed by the hordes of visitors who have plagued Selma. The police department there says there has been no difference of importance between the rate of crime there during the last nine weeks and previously. . . . The difficult element of rumor is that a good juicy one can't be proved to be wrong."

The *Alabama Journal* agreed. "Most of us would like to believe that the demonstrators were, without exception, dissolute and base," their editorial the following day declared. "This is the comfortable belief and many people will go on believing it. This despite the fact that there were obviously, to any eye not blinded by rage, thousands of sincere morally impeccable people in the March."

But many sincerely believed the rumors. They despised the outside agitators and anyone who sympathized with them. Virginia Durr told me that one white Montgomery husband went so far as to place an advertisement in the paper to publicly refute his wife's activism. His notice attested that he, for one, believed deeply in the "Southern Way of Life."

The Southern Way of Life

> I only know one thing, that there are few troubles in this world that a woman, directly or indirectly, is not connected with.
> —Margaret Mitchell

I used to think I knew what people were talking about when they referred to the Southern Way of Life. I was sure they meant courtesy colonels, cotillions, mint juleps, and Scarlett O'Hara types who went with the wind. Wasn't it already gone? I had endured hours of American history classes in high school and college and not one person—*no one*—mentioned anything more about the Southern Way of Life than that it centered on nostalgia for a lost past—a largely imagined golden age.

The more I spoke with people like Virginia Durr, however, and the more I researched and read, the more I began to understand that the Southern Way of Life was code for a system built on sexual taboo to maintain white privilege.

The Southern Way of Life was based on the religious, political, and economic belief that racial segregation was essential to the stability of southern society. The organizing principle of the Way was that blacks were genetically inferior to whites and incapable of either bettering themselves or controlling their sexual urges. Therefore it was concluded that racial separation was a basic requirement of a civilized society.

White segregationists believed that if their schools were integrated, race mixing would become acceptable and intermarriage would ultimately result. It was "pollution" of white blood with black blood that they feared. In 1954, Mississippi circuit judge Tom Brady asserted that "one drop of Negro blood thickens the lips, flattens the nose, and puts out the lights of intellect."

White segregationists argued that racial separation was sanctioned by the Bible. This was based on a proslavery interpretation of Genesis 9:18–29 that describes the migration of Noah's three sons after the flood. Africans were supposedly the descendants of Ham, whose son, Canaan, Noah cursed in a drunken fit. Noah's curse on his grandson supposedly doomed all Canaan's descendants to slavery.

Leviticus 19:19 was widely quoted to justify the taboo on intermarriage: "Thou shalt not let thy cattle gender with a diverse kind; thou shalt not sow thy field with mingled seed; neither shall a garment mingled of linen and woolen come upon thee." Racial purity, segregationists insisted, was a requirement of God, and they pointed to the disasters David, Solomon, and Samson brought on themselves by their love of foreign women as proof.[54]

Author Eddy Harris, whose southern odyssey took him to Greenwood, Mississippi, in the early 1990s, described a conversation he had with a white woman whose mother belonged to a segregated church in the 1960s. When the older woman was asked, "Wouldn't Jesus have let those black people into his church?" she answered, "Of course he would have, but Jesus would have been wrong."[55]

A textbook used in elementary schools in several counties of Mississippi throughout the 1950s counseled white third and fourth graders that "God wanted the white people to live alone. And He wanted colored people to live alone. The white men built America for you. White men built America so they could make the rules. . . . The white man has always been kind to the Negro. We do not believe that God wants us to live together. Negro people like to live by themselves. Negroes use their own bathrooms. They do not use white people's bathrooms. The Negro has his own part of town to live in. This is called our Southern Way of Life. Do you know that some people want the Negroes to live with white people? These people want us to be unhappy. They say we must go to school together. They say we must swim together and use the bathroom together. God has made us different. And God knows best. Did you know that our country will grow weak if we mix the races?"[56]

During the afternoon I spent on Virginia Durr's porch in Montgomery she gave me an illustration of how this early indoctrination manifested itself in her life. When she was a teen, Virginia made a trip to Connecticut with her church's "young people's group" to attend a youth conference. It was a particularly hot summer, so the Connecticut pastor took all the teens to a public pool to cool off. Young Virginia and her friends were having a wonderful time until a black boy, about their own age, jumped off the diving board. At that point, each and every one of the southern girls scrambled out of the pool as if they were experiencing a tidal wave. "Everybody looked at us like we were crazy," she remembered. "They couldn't imagine what in the world we were doing. We looked to the pastor, and to the other young people attending the conference, but they were clearly just as puzzled. In the end we felt pretty foolish. We'd been trained very early, and very well. We just didn't know any better."

After the 1954 Supreme Court decision requiring that the public schools be integrated "with all deliberate speed," white southerners bitterly resented the interference of white northern agitators. They considered northern volunteers invaders who were undermining and destroying the Southern Way of Life.

In May 1961, *CBS Reports* dedicated a special one-hour television presentation to the question "Who Speaks for Birmingham?" Birmingham attorney Colonel William S. Prichard told a national audience that "All the nigras in Alabama have the same background. They were savages in Africa whose parents sold them into slavery. They were brought here without the concept of working to earn a living. The nigra knows the best friend he has in the world is the southern white man. These northern agitators spur them on to believe they are equal to the white man in every aspect, which they are *not*. This hurts the nigra, and estranges him from the white man."

Retired judge Hugh A. Lock agreed. "Racial unrest in Birmingham exists essentially in the minds of people outside Birmingham," he observed.

"Detroit, Chicago, Buffalo, and Washington, D.C., have more troubles than we do."

Rev. J. Carpenter, Episcopal bishop of Alabama, considered a moderate on racial issues, noted, "The negro is not able to talk in any terms less than complete integration and the white man will never speak of total integration. The gradual approach has been shelved. Everything came too quickly with the Supreme Court's decision. We were making progress, but we've been set back."

White segregationists passionately hated "mixers"—white people who were willing to mix with blacks. (It was assumed all blacks wanted to mix with whites.) Mixers were believed to advocate a kind of social sharing comparable to the communist theory of economic sharing and so were considered communists. Since communists were atheists and mixers were communists, it was only logical to assume that mixers were atheists too.

Writing in 1965, Calvin Hernton observed that "Sexual paranoia is an inextricable ingredient in that psychiatric terror known as racism. . . . Like any paranoiac the racist experiences himself as an authentic individual only when he projects his fears onto others and imagines they are attacking him. . . . In the mind of the Southerner, the word rape not only applied to sexual assaults on white women by black men, but to any attempt at changing 'our way of life.'"[57]

A liaison between a white woman and a black man was considered an affront to white male authority. White southern men assumed responsibility for protecting white southern women from black men, who were all potential rapists—savages who, given the chance, would revert to type.

Racial (and ultimately sexual) equality between white women and black men would break down the white social order—would destroy the Southern Way of Life. In Davis, Gardner, and Gardner's 1941 book *Deep South*, the authors observed that sexual taboo affected not only the Negro man but also was oppressive to the white woman. "Any white woman who has sexual relations with Negro men or even encourages advances is open to punishment and expulsion. Even white prostitutes are not allowed to accept Negro business; and should they be discovered the Negro is likely to be whipped, and the prostitute run out of town. There is, however, no taboo preventing sexual intercourse between white men and Negro women despite the inflexible taboo on marriage or offspring."[58]

Segregationists believed that black men desired intermarriage and that white women would be "open to proposals from Negro men" if they were not guarded from even meeting them.[59]

Vi Liuzzo, with her Michigan plates and a black man in the front seat of her car, symbolized everything the segregationists most feared and despised. Here was a white woman who had clearly stepped across the line. Her behavior removed her from the category of sacred white womanhood and motherhood (which in the chivalric code of the Southern Way of Life required male protection) and into the despised category of race traitor. Understanding that, I could see why Gene Thomas and Collie Leroy Wilkins had focused on another interracial couple in Selma as their original victims. What the Klan missionaries were planning that afternoon was a warning—a clear message to blacks that things were not going to change and to whites that a trip south to support change could prove fatal.

White Citizens' Councils, the self-appointed defenders of the Southern Way of Life, who organized after the *Brown vs. Board of Education* decision in 1954, distributed a recruiting pamphlet still in circulation in 1965 stating that "The Citizens' Council is the South's answer to mongrelization. We will not be integrated. We are proud of our white blood and our white heritage of sixty centuries. . . . The fate of our great nation may well rest in the hands of the Southern white people today. If we submit to this unconstitutional, judge-made integration law, the malignant powers of atheism, communism and mongrelizaton will surely follow, not only in our Southland, but throughout our nation. To falter would be tragic; to fail would be fatal. The white people of the South will again stand fast and preserve an unsullied race as our forefathers did eighty years ago. We will not be integrated, either suddenly or gradually."[60]

Reporter Don Beck wrote in the March 28, 1965, issue of the *Detroit News* that "In death Viola Liuzzo became a symbol of the lengths to which some in the South will go to maintain their control."

6 The Great March

It is hard for many to remember that there was a period when the civil rights movement harnessed the dreams and energies of the best among us, when it served as the catalyst for idealism and justice for many millions of white and black Americans.
—Vernon Jordan

The trip from Detroit to Selma took Vi Liuzzo three days. She drove more than a thousand miles through five states all alone. One by one the Wayne students who had planned to make the trip had backed out.

No evidence has ever been found of where Vi stopped—if she stopped —or of what route she took. The FBI, the Selma police, and Detroit's Criminal Intelligence Bureau were tenacious in their efforts to uncover anyone—motel owner, gas station attendant, restaurant worker, hitchhiker—who remembered seeing Viola Liuzzo or her green Oldsmobile between March 16 and March 19. If anyone had, they never came forward.

Vi arrived in Selma on Friday afternoon and drove to the Roy Brown African Methodist Episcopal Chapel to volunteer with the Southern Christian Leadership Conference—to become one of Dr. King's "shock troops." She had hoped to be assigned to a medical unit but was instead dispatched to the hospitality desk to welcome and register volunteers. She was offered, and she accepted, a bed at Mrs. Willie Lee Jackson's home in the George Washington Carver Homes. Mrs. Jackson managed Smith's Cafe on Griffin Street and was an active volunteer with the food service during the march. Vi was one of six women—four white and two black— who were rooming with the Jackson family. Mrs. Jackson remembers Kits from California, Pat from Boston, and Joan from Wisconsin—white women who arrived on Saturday and left with the marchers for Montgomery on Sunday. Two young black female students from Boston, Shirley and Dean, arrived Friday and flew home late Sunday night. Another white woman, whose name Mrs. Jackson couldn't recall, left abruptly on Saturday and never returned to collect her luggage.[1]

Vi stayed with the Jacksons from Friday night until the following Wednesday morning. Mrs. Jackson remembers her as friendly—"not a bit shy"—and very helpful with the children. "Seems to me she really loved children," Mrs. Jackson recalled. Vi told Mrs. Jackson that her husband had not wanted her to come to Selma but that he understood how much it meant to her.

During the four days Vi spent in the Jackson home she and Mrs. Jackson became friends. Vi invited Mrs. Jackson's teenage daughter Frances to come to Detroit and stay with the Liuzzos while she finished high school. Frances was an unmarried teen with a five-week-old baby. Vi thought she could use a new start. "We had made big plans for it," Mrs. Jackson recalled, "seemed like things were going to turn out so good and right." After Vi's death, when the rumor mill began to hum around Selma and Montgomery, Mrs. Jackson felt compelled to defend her guest. "I know the rumors going around," she said, "but she never went out anywhere. She stayed here with me and was home in bed every night. She came to Selma because she thought she could help. She just loved to be with people and to talk."[2] Mrs. Jackson said Vi went to a neighbor's home to call her husband and children every night because the Jacksons didn't have a phone.

On Saturday morning Vi reported to her station at the hospitality desk in the Brown Chapel parsonage, where she met Leroy Jerome Moton, nineteen, a voting drive organizer who also lived in the Carver Homes. Leroy was the same age as Sarah's grandson Tyrone. He and Vi talked about the civil rights movement, about life in Selma, and about his dreams of becoming a barber. Moton's father had been killed in an accident four years before, and the young man had become the primary source of support for his mother and the rest of his family. The young black man had lost his job as a short-order cook when his boss found out about his voter registration activities. He was convinced that voting was the only way to make changes in the South, and so he had risked his livelihood to help in the registration effort.

Leroy had proved such a successful organizer that when he became available full time he was asked to coordinate the volunteer transportation service. Vi offered him use of her car, and he accepted.

Saturday night Vi attended her first mass meeting in Brown Chapel and took an active role greeting people. Mrs. Amelia Boynton of the Dallas County Voter's League, the lady who had persuaded Dr. King to come to Selma, recalls Vi as "an attractive young woman, outgoing with a personality anyone could approach."[3] Mrs. Boynton had been beaten and arrested during a voter registration attempt at the Dallas County Court House only a few weeks before the Selma gathering.

Everything in Selma was turned inside out. There were more white faces in Brown Chapel that night than black ones. The "Negro section" had become "home" to thousands of whites. When whites walked the streets of black Selma at night they felt safe—that they were among friends. If they wandered into white Selma, however, they were quickly reminded that they were in enemy territory.

On Sunday morning Vi worked for a few hours fielding phone calls and registering volunteers at the hospitality desk, where she met the Reverend Carl Sayers, rector of St. Stephens Church in Birmingham, Michigan. Sayers recalled that he arrived in Selma with the Reverend James McAlpine, another Episcopal priest, "tired and scared after our drive in from Dannelly Field [Montgomery airport]. We were ushered into the parsonage and Mrs. Liuzzo saw how tired and concerned we were and went out of her way to be nice to us." They joked about coming all the way from Detroit to meet in Selma. Father Sayers lived less than fifteen miles north of the Liuzzos. They discovered they shared other connections. Carl Sayers was chair of the Bishop's Committee of Wayne State University's Episcopal Mission and was a friend of Malcolm Boyd, the campus chaplain who had so strongly influenced Vi's decision to go to Selma.

"I never will forget the attention we received and the kindness," Rev. Sayers said. "I was amazed to see her doing so many things, always to help people. She was a doer."[4]

At noon Vi joined with almost three thousand people for a pre-march rally outside Brown Chapel. Martin Luther King gave a rousing speech. "You will be the people that will light a new chapter in the history of our nation," he said. "Those of us who are Negroes don't have much. We have known the long night of poverty. Because of the system we don't have much education, and some of us don't know how to make our nouns and verbs agree. But thank God we have our bodies, our feet and our souls. Walk together, children, and don't you get weary, and it will lead us to the promised land. And Alabama will be a new Alabama and America will be a new America."[5]

A deafening cheer rose from the crowd, and the long-awaited march began. The demonstrators walked five abreast down Sylvan Street (now King Street), an unpaved red-sand road, to Water Avenue where they turned onto Broad. They were of all ages, all classes—blacks and whites. The least-represented group, however, was working-class whites—the class both Vi and Jim Liuzzo had been born into. As Vi made her way with the crowd toward the Pettus Bridge, an older black woman called out, "I can't walk, but I sure will pray for you." A white female reporter from Belgium, overcome with emotion, tore off her press badge and joined the marchers.[6]

Sheriff Jim Clark, standing on the sidelines wearing a tan Eisenhower jacket with gold braid, a military helmet, and a button that read NEVER!, watched the marchers leave his town with a military escort. He told a reporter for the *Selma Times Journal* that he considered the march a Roman holiday. "The United States has hit a new low today," he said.[7]

Members of Clark's posse placed themselves along the parade route. Some looked angry, others stunned. Historian Stephen Longenecker described them: "Clark supplemented his paid deputies with a volunteer posse composed mainly of uneducated poor whites. . . . Posse members wore khaki GI shirts and pants or work clothes. Some armed themselves with large pistols, which hung from leather holsters, and most carried unpainted, hand-turned billy clubs and cattle prods of varying length. Before the civil rights era Clark's posse performed flood-relief services in Dallas County, but later they traveled, with Clark, around the state to 'help' when civil rights demonstrators threatened the status quo."[8]

As the parade crossed the Edmund Pettus Bridge and entered Highway 80, a group of Birmingham Klansmen marched on the opposite side of the road with Confederate flags and banners that read BE A MAN, JOIN THE KLAN; YANKEE TRASH GO HOME; FAKE CLERGY & BEATNIKS GO HOME!; and RENT A PRIEST—$5 PER DAY. A young woman screamed at the marchers, "You all got your birth control pills? You all got your birth control pills?" Soldiers marched at the front and the rear of the parade. Low-flying helicopters searched for snipers, and demolition experts looked for dynamite.[9]

Gerald Frazer, a black reporter covering the march for the *New York Daily News*, reported, "This part of the White South has turned its wrath on Northern whites. 'You niggers beat the crap out of them whites there with you and I'll let you vote,' one cracker yelled to the marchers."

At the same time an eighty-three-car motorcade, led by Imperial Wizard Robert Shelton, was moving through downtown Montgomery. FBI records indicate that three men from the Eastview Klavern 13 (riding in a 1962 red-and-white Impala) were observed participating, as was J. B. Stoner, organizer of the anti-Semitic, anti-black National States Rights Party of Savannah, Georgia. Stoner also belonged to Eastview Klavern 13. In 1980 he would be tried and convicted for the 1958 bombing of the Bethel Baptist Church in Birmingham.[10] Rev. Fred Shuttlesworth, an associate of Dr. Martin Luther King and founder of the Alabama Christian Movement for Human Rights, was pastor of Bethel in 1958. When his church and parsonage were bombed, Rev. Shuttlesworth told CBS reporter Howard K. Smith, "We mean to kill segregation, or be killed by it."[11]

In the March 19, 1965, issue of *Life* magazine journalist Richard Stolley describing the voting rights marchers noted that "They came from everywhere—clergymen, nuns, students, doctors, plain Americans—Negro and white—to place themselves beside Martin Luther King in the streets, to stand against the police of Alabama in the name of human dignity. In all the turbulent history of civil rights, never had there been such a widespread reaction to the doctrine of white supremacy."

Shana Alexander, also in Selma on assignment for *Life*, was covering the march for her column "The Feminine Eye." She was issued a press pass and warned by one of Sheriff Clark's deputies to "watch out for them white niggers."

Three thousand marchers completed seven miles on Sunday. The weather was hot but the skies were clear. Amelia Boynton recalls watching a young black man carrying an American flag up near the front of the parade. "He was beaming with pride and every now and then he would burst into song, and we would join him, often singing "The Star Spangled Banner." It was that young man who drove for the SCLC transportation service," Mrs. Boynton remembers. "Leroy Moton."[12]

New York City Council president Paul Screvane, representing Mayor Robert Wagner and the City of New York, marched for six miles on the first day. "It's like living in another world," he said. "The attitude of the white people toward the negroes, and toward us who participated in the march is something difficult to describe. They called us dirty, foul names, and the slogans were just as bad. It doesn't make you feel like you're in America."[13]

That night, three hundred invited marchers made camp on land owned by black farmer David Hall near the Victory Baptist Church. They pitched four large circus tents. The others, including Vi Liuzzo and Leroy Moton, returned by specially arranged trains and buses to spend the night back in Selma. Only three hundred people would be permitted to complete the next leg of the march, which ran through Big Swamp, a lonely stretch of dense forest and snake-infested marshes in Lowndes County. No limits were placed on the number of marchers where Highway 80 was four lanes wide, but as the highway approached the swamp it narrowed to two lanes and was surrounded by water. Federal District Judge Frank Johnson, who had overridden Alabama state officials in permitting the march, stipulated that only three hundred people would be allowed to walk the twenty-two miles of narrow swamp road.

Sunday night the temperature dropped to thirty-one degrees and the marchers ran short of blankets. Some huddled around makeshift fires terrifying each other with stories of what might be waiting for them in Bloody Lowndes. Rumors of snipers, bombs, poisoned water, and snakes sent chills up their spines. By daybreak the pasture was covered with frost. After a breakfast of oatmeal and coffee they began a second day of walking, hoping to complete fourteen miles. Amelia Boynton remembers, "From Selma well into the rural sections there were groups of white rabble rousers carrying the Confederate flag, waving and cursing and many saying 'go back to Africa where you belong, you black jigaboos.' One youngster retaliated, 'I can't go back to Africa, you white folks took it away from us just like you took America from the Indians.' He was told not to say anymore, and he was obedient."[14]

Along the way an old black man with a cane joined them. "I just wanted to walk a mile with y'all," he said. "I been called a boy long enough, don't you think?"

A *Newsweek* reporter asked a seven-year-old black girl from Selma why she was marching. "For freedom and justice and so the troopers can't hit us no more," she said. Sister Mary Leoline, a white nun from Christ the King parish in Kansas City, Kansas, told him, "This is a great time to be alive."

Just before noon on Monday the marchers crossed into Lowndes County. There, a correspondent from the *New Yorker* overheard a middle-aged white woman speaking animatedly to a state trooper. "Look at them so-called white men," she said angrily, "them with their church collars that they bought for fifty cents! And them de-virginated nuns! I'm a Catholic myself, but it turns my stomach to see them!"[15]

Then, suddenly, the marchers were showered with flyers released from a plane with Confederate Air Force painted on it. UNEMPLOYED AGITATORS CEASE TO AGITATE, the flyer taunted. It was printed by White Citizens Action, Inc., of Tuscaloosa, Alabama.

Twenty-one miles into the march the activists approached Big Swamp. It was early afternoon. Sheriff Frank Ryals of Lowndes County, watching them enter the swamp, said that he had little respect for the white demonstrators who came in from other states. "I'm sure some of them are good people," he said, "but most of the ones I've seen are beatniks and screwballs and people like that. I don't think these professional agitators would be satisfied with anything you gave them."

While Sheriff Ryals ignored the thousands of clergy of all denominations who marched, Archbishop Thomas Toolen of the Mobile-Birmingham Diocese was irritated by them. "Certainly the sisters are out of place in these demonstrations," the archbishop told a reporter for the *Montgomery Advertiser*. "Their place is at home doing God's work. I would say the same thing is true of the priests. . . . What do they know about conditions in the South? I am afraid they are only eager beavers who feel this is a Holy cause. . . . Sane and sensible Negroes realize we are trying to bring them up to the standards they should have, but do we need crusaders coming in from other states to tell us how to run the state of Alabama?"[16]

Monday evening the large tents were raised once again in a pasture of Rosa Steele's farm, and Dr. King presided over a mass meeting. Heavily armed National Guardsmen and army regulars surrounded the camp for the night while helicopters periodically circled overhead.

Tuesday morning, as the three hundred marchers crossed Big Swamp, it began to rain. The marchers trekked through six hours of pelting downpour. The *Washington Post* reported that "A passing car with a white man and woman stopped at one point and through the window the man laughed and jeered at the marchers. The woman tugged at his sleeve. 'They're tired and they're weary,' she said softly. 'I don't think it's funny.' He rolled up the window and they drove on."

On Tuesday night they camped in ankle-deep mud on a farm belonging to A. G. Gaston. (Gaston was president of the Federal Savings and Loan Association of Birmingham. He was the black businessman who had bailed Dr. King and Rev. Abernathy out of jail during the Birmingham demonstrations in 1963.) The same *Post* reporter recalled that a white man told him that night, "Half these niggers will never make it. They've got no integrity. They never finish anything they start. If they do it's because somebody's paying them $14 a day. At least that's what I hear."

Another white man, a Presbyterian clergyman, leaned against the tailgate of a farm truck and ate a cold pork chop. "This is our finest hour," he told a reporter from the *Nation*.

Mrs. Ann Cheatham of Ealing, England, joined the marchers on Tuesday night. She told correspondent Renata Adler of the *New Yorker*, "It seemed to me an outrage. I saw it on the telly—people being battered on the head. I came to show that the English are in sympathy. I can see there are a lot of odd bods on this march, but there were a lot on the marches on Aldermaston [an anti-nuclear demonstration] and Wash-

.ington. This appalling business of barring white facilities to Negro children! People say it's not my business, but I would deny that. It's everybody's business."[17]

It's too bad Vi didn't camp with the marchers that night. She and Mrs. Cheatham might have enjoyed each other's company. But Vi spent most of the early part of the week registering volunteers at Brown Chapel. Only occasionally did she make transportation runs, ferrying marchers from the airport to the campsite and back to Selma. Soon she began to grow restless. She hadn't traveled hundreds of miles to answer phones and staff a welcome wagon while others used her car for the real work. Finally, she volunteered to help at the first-aid station at the last campsite. She was accepted because of her medical technician training.

On Wednesday morning at 7 A.M. Vi took a bus from Brown Chapel to the City of St. Jude, a forty-acre integrated Catholic church, hospital, and school complex on Fairview Avenue, one mile inside the Montgomery city limits. Three of Dr. King's four children had been born at St. Jude's. The marchers planned to camp on the grounds Wednesday night. Vi went to help set up the first-aid facilities. She planned to stay at St. Jude's Wednesday night and join the marchers for Thursday's walk into Montgomery.

Jim remembered that the last time he spoke with her Vi seemed very happy. She told him not to worry, that she would be coming home right after the Montgomery rally. He warned her to be careful, that the most dangerous time would probably be after the demonstration when the troops wouldn't be around to protect the marchers anymore. "I'm assigned to the first-aid station," she assured him. "I'm not on the front lines. Don't worry." Then he wired her fifty dollars for the trip home.

Wednesday morning the marchers woke on soggy, muddy ground. The hay they had spread to dry the soaked earth hadn't done much good. They were sore and uncomfortable, but everyone ate well. From the very first day the community's Loaves and Fishes Committee, funded by local donations and a grant from the National Council of Churches, had fed the marchers. Rev. Ralph Abernathy of the SCLC remembers that "Most of the black kitchens in Selma and Montgomery were pressed into service—kitchens in homes, restaurants, schools. People sent whatever they could, from loaves of bread to more substantial dishes like fried chicken, fish, ham, collard and turnip greens, peas, sweet potatoes and macaroni and cheese. And there was lots of soup—cooked in pots and brought in the back seats of cars—still hot when it was put on the folding tables."[18]

The marchers started the last leg of their journey at 7 A.M. National guardsmen checked out a concrete bridge just beyond the campsite before they allowed the marchers to cross. They had found dynamite in the woods of Lowndes county a few days before, and six homemade bombs were discovered in the black section of Birmingham on Sunday. The bombs had been set to go off at noon—the hour the march was scheduled to begin. As the three hundred marchers completed their trek through Big Swamp, Highway 80 expanded again into four lanes and they were joined by more demonstrators.

Approaching Montgomery, the number of marchers continually swelled. Andrew Young, at that time an aide to Dr. King, announced that chartered trains and planes were bringing people from New York, Washington, Los Angeles, Pittsburgh, Chicago, and Detroit. By Thursday morning there were almost twenty-five thousand demonstrators.

Dr. King was asked if he thought Governor Wallace would agree to see them. "Governor Wallace may not be at the Capitol that day," King said, "but he will see the marchers. There is no way that he can fail to see thousands and thousands of unarmed, courageous Negroes and whites who are marching to dramatize a tragic evil—a tragic expression of man's inhumanity to man."[19]

Wednesday evening the marchers joyously celebrated the end of their long trek, unaware that the Klan had threatened to "blow St. Jude's sky high." A stage was set up in the baseball field and musicians, actors, and politicians gathered for all-night entertainment. Harry Belafonte; Ella Fitzgerald; Joan Baez; Odetta; Peter, Paul and Mary; Mahalia Jackson; Pete Seeger; the Chad Mitchell Trio; and Sammy Davis Jr. were among the performers. Reporter Andrew Kopkind of the *New Republic* called it "a kind of Civil Rights Copacabana." At one point rain toppled the big tent, but the weather cleared once the show got under way. Andrew Young remembers, "That night at St. Jude's the magical musical celebration that went on in spite of all the problems and frustrations was a celebration of our determination to accomplish the dreams of our entire Selma campaign: to change Selma and towns like it forever. We were drenched with joy; in that sense, the relentless rain was in harmony with our spirits."[20]

Vi spent the evening assisting the medical staff and providing first aid for blisters, heat exhaustion, and pulled muscles. Many had walked the last twenty miles barefoot. Alfred Loeb, an engineer from Philadelphia commented, "My feet are awfully sore, but if someone had done something like this march in Munich before World War II maybe six million Jews wouldn't have died."[21]

The grounds of the City of St. Jude overflowed. Crowded conditions, confusion, a blaring public address system, and jammed parking areas increased tensions. People overcome by heat and excitement were constantly being rushed to the first-aid station. Vi was offered a bed in the basement of the church at the end of her shift, but she slept in her car to leave the bed open for a marcher. Father Timothy Deasy, who had been assigned to St. Jude's from his native Ireland (and had met a black person for the first time in 1958) later commented, "I felt very strongly about this woman and her goodness. She inspired us all. Her energy, enthusiasm, and compassion were contagious, and put many of us to shame."

Thursday morning as people began to move out toward the capitol, Vi asked Father Deasy if she could go up to the church tower to get a better look. He went up with her. They watched as thousands of people walked the four miles east to Montgomery. From the west, demonstrators were still arriving from the airport. When Vi came down from the tower, she became overwhelmed by an anxiety attack. She flushed pale, shook, and had some trouble breathing. She told the priest, "Father I have a feeling of apprehension. Something is going to happen today. Someone is going to be killed."[22]

Deasy tried to calm her, but she was very excited. She repeated her premonition to Father Edward Cassidy, a missionary priest from Chicago, and to some nuns who were with him. Vi said she thought someone was going to try to kill Governor Wallace and blame the marchers. When she calmed down she said she wanted to go into the church to pray. When she came out, she looked and felt much better. She assured Father Deasy she was all right and told him that she was going into Montgomery. When she got to Fairview Avenue, Vi took off her shoes and walked the four miles to the capitol barefoot, as many marchers were doing. She was wearing a blue suit with a white blouse, carrying her tan pocketbook in one hand and her shoes in the other.

In 1997, Father Deasy, then a retired monsignor, told me that he saw nothing strange or far-fetched about Vi's fears. St. Jude's had received bomb threats since the announcement was made that its grounds would be made available to the marchers as a campsite. One month after the march the complex remained under twenty-four-hour police protection. Besides, Vi wasn't the only one who had had a disturbing premonition. Malcolm X was assassinated in Harlem on February 21, 1965, one month before the march began. Twenty-four hours later, Martin Luther King began receiving death threats. His life had been continually threatened since the days of the Montgomery bus boycott, but this time he was certain he would be killed somewhere between Selma and Montgomery. His premonition was so strong that anticipation made him physically ill one evening.[23]

After King's assassination in Memphis in 1968, Attorney General Ramsay Clark commented that he had also been sure King would be killed in Selma. Clark had a very strong premonition that King would be assassinated on the way to the capitol. Clark was so uneasy that he personally walked up and down Dexter Avenue checking for snipers.

In spite of the fears for his life, Dr. King refused to leave the march. On Wednesday the SCLC senior staff was officially alerted of rumors of a plot to kill Dr. King in Montgomery. Andrew Young, knowing King would not be dissuaded from leading the last mile of the journey, provided a distraction. "Martin always wore the good-preacher blue suit," Young said, "and I figured since we couldn't stop him from marching, we just had to kind of believe that it was true when white folks said we all look alike. So everybody that was about Martin's size and had a blue suit, I put in front of the line with him. . . . There were some very important people who felt as though they were being pushed back, but all of the preachers loved the chance to get up in the front of the line with Martin Luther King. I don't think to this day most of them know why they were up there."[24]

The parade route took the marchers through the poorest section of Montgomery, down Holt Street to Mobile on their way to the capitol. Crowds, overwhelmingly black, lined the streets cheering and singing. The demonstrators carried signs that read WALLACE, IT'S ALL OVER; BALLOTS HAVE NO COLOR; THE PEACE CORPS KNOWS INTEGRATION WORKS; 50 MILES CAN'T TURN US AROUND; and OUT OF VIET NAM INTO SELMA. Hundreds of American flags waved, both in the parade and along the route. Many who came to watch ended up joining the marchers.

When the marchers turned onto Montgomery Street, the business district, the mood changed abruptly. Jeers and curses met them in downtown Montgomery. At one point they passed a dead skunk in the middle of the road. One marcher remembers, "First we advanced past cheering Negro homes, then through the business section of town with stony-faced whites peering hostilely from windows and balconies. We marched six abreast while helicopters buzzed over us. There was an amazing amount of restraint on both sides."

Black maids at the Jefferson Davis Hotel watched the marchers from top-floor windows. Outside the office of the Montgomery White Citizens' Council a man waving a Confederate flag was asked his name by a reporter. "None of your goddamned business!" he replied.

Amelia Boynton recalls that when they reached downtown "A young white woman, very pretty and intelligent looking, stood in the doorway of an office building. Seeing the integrated group passing seemed to enrage her and she screamed vile things. To be sure we saw her contempt, she held her nose, turned her back to the street and hoisted her dress."[25]

White female state employees were given the day off with pay. State Personnel Director John Frazer said, "We thought it was a good move on the state's part to let the women stay home. Traffic will be very heavy on Thursday." Men were not given the day off because it was felt they could cope with the traffic. Frazer's subtlety was not lost on either blacks or whites.

The marchers approached the capitol along Dexter Avenue, by the same route that Jefferson Davis's inaugural parade had followed. By this time they were the only ones carrying American flags. Over the capitol building only the Alabama state flag and the Stars and Bars of the Confederacy flew.

When the demonstrators reached the capitol building Governor Wallace refused to see them. From his executive office the governor watched the events through binoculars, unaware that he could be seen from the street through the parted blinds. The *Chicago Tribune* reported that Representative J. J. Pierce of Montgomery, who was standing on the portico of the capitol with a group of Alabama legislators, commented, "This is my first time living in occupied territory." Senator Roland Cooper of Wilcox County replied, "It's one of the silliest things that could happen."

CBS television news correspondent Alex Kendrick told a national audience that the mood of the crowd was subdued, "almost relaxed." The tremor in his voice is apparent as he asks, "What do they do after this? What happens now? Anything could happen. No one knows what the outcome of this day will be. White Montgomery is giving the march the silent treatment. Legendary southern hospitality is certainly lacking here today."[26] Cameras panned the crowd as Kendrick continued, "White Montgomery believes the civil rights movement will not be satisfied with civil rights. They see this march as an invasion of Alabama by outside agitators. Their silent treatment does not denote a lack of concern. It is the silence of injured and wounded pride. Segregation is no longer a local issue. It's being played out on the national scene now. The pace of civil rights may have accelerated, but the pace of acceptance here in Montgomery remains the same."

CBS television newsman Bill Plante was also amazed by the lack of tension in the crowd as people waited for the speeches to begin. Many, he said, just sat on the curbs and waited. "The mood is calm, reflective." Plante commented on the number of black children who marched, noting that it was mid-afternoon on a school day. "White schools in Montgomery are open," he said pointedly. "And the white students will be kept in school until this demonstration is over." Finally, Plante informed the

nation that blacks in the South, especially the older ones, are normally apathetic. He said it was expected many young blacks would be marching,
but he was personally surprised to see so many older people.

By the time Vi reached downtown she had completely recovered from
her panic. She became swept up in the sense of victory and joined the
marchers singing the triumphant "Battle Hymn of the Republic" and
"God Bless America." In the crowd that afternoon a twenty-six-year-old
white Episcopal seminarian was also marching. Jonathan Daniels made
his decision during the march to the capitol to return to Alabama after his
spring semester. Eighteen months later a part-time county sheriff would
murder Daniels as he tried to buy sodas for an integrated group of students and clergy in Lowndes County. In just seven hours Viola Liuzzo
would be assassinated in the same county for driving with a black man in
the front seat of her car.

As the dignitaries gathered on the capitol steps, entertainers Joan Baez,
Harry Belafonte, and Mary Travers (of Peter, Paul, and Mary) led the
crowd in "Go Tell It on the Mountain," "Blowin' in the Wind," and
"You Gotta Move When the Spirit Says Move." Arms crossed, hands
linked, hundreds swayed and sang "We Shall Overcome." It would be the
last major gathering where the verse "black and white together" was sung
over and over again.

"We are not in a struggle of black against white," Rosa Parks told the
crowd, "but rather wrong against right."

Jimmy Breslin, on assignment for the *New York Herald Tribune*, followed U.S. Assistant Attorney General for Civil Rights John Doar. Breslin
reported that a man walked beside Doar commenting compulsively, "It's
all gone, the South is all gone. A whole way of life is going right into
memory." Doar replied, "That's right. That's just what it is."

"You have not lived in this time when everything is changing," Breslin
wrote, "until you see an old black woman with mud on her shoes stand
in the street of a southern city and sing *we are not afraid* and then turn
and look at the face of a cop near her and see the puzzlement and the terrible fear in his eyes. Because he knows and everybody who has ever seen
it knows that it is all over."

Vi stayed to hear Dr. King's speech, which was delivered from the same marble steps where Governor Wallace at his inauguration just two years before had shouted, "Segregation now, segregation tomorrow and segregation forever!"

"Our aim must never be to defeat or humiliate the white man," Dr. King said, "but to win his friendship and understanding. We must come to see that the end we seek is a society at peace with itself, a society that can live with its conscience. That will be a day not of the white man, not of the black man. That will be the day of man as man. I know you are asking today, 'How long will it take?' I come to say to you this afternoon however difficult the moment, however frustrating the hour, it will not be long, because truth pressed to earth will rise again. How long? Not long, because no lie can live forever. How long? Not long, because you still reap what you sow. How long? Not long, because the arm of the moral universe is long, but it bends toward justice. How long? Not long, 'cause mine eyes have seen the glory of the coming of the Lord, trampling out the vintage where the grapes of wrath are stored. He has loosed the fateful lightning of his terrible swift sword. His truth is marching on!"[27]

While Vi worked at St. Jude's, Leroy Moton continued to use her Oldsmobile to ferry marchers back and forth to the Montgomery airport. After the rally Moton picked up five people at the Dexter Avenue Church and drove them back to St. Jude's, where he and Vi had arranged to meet. When they arrived at St. Jude's, Moton slid over and Vi took the wheel. She said she wanted to warm up for the long drive home.

Their passengers included Mrs. Brenton Brown and two teenagers, Liz Steward and Carla Austin. All three were white and from Southampton, Pennsylvania. They were returning to the Carver Homes to pick up their luggage. Bart Coopersmith, a white man from New York going to the airport, and Clarence Smith Jr., a young black man from Selma, were also with them.[28] Moton was returning to Selma to pick up a set of car keys that the transportation committee desperately needed. Vi offered to take him back to Montgomery after she dropped the others off. That way, she said, they could take any last-minute stragglers back to Selma before she picked up her own things at Mrs. Jackson's and headed home. It was about 5:30 P.M. when they left St. Jude's. Vi was full of energy, Moton remembered.

Between the airport and Selma a car full of whites drove up behind them and banged into the bumper of the Oldsmobile several times before passing. Moton recalled that Vi did not seem to be afraid. She told her passengers, "These crazy white people don't have any sense." Jokingly she said she was coming back to Alabama if Governor Wallace didn't have her killed first.

When they stopped for gas, Moton remembered, white bystanders shouted insults at the integrated group. Further along, the driver of another car turned on his high beams and left them shining into Vi's rearview mirror. "Two can play at that game," she said and deliberately slowed up, making the offending car pass her. Finally, when another car pulled up alongside the Oldsmobile while one in front slowed down, Vi had to jam on her brakes. They were boxed in, one of the passengers remembers, but Mrs. Liuzzo seemed to be more annoyed than afraid.

As they drove along Highway 80, Vi began singing freedom songs: "And before I'll be a slave I'll be buried in my grave and go home to my Lord and be free." When they reached Selma, Vi dropped Mrs. Brown and the girls at the Carver Homes, Leroy Moton went to find the badly needed car keys, and Vi went to get dinner. She and Moton met again, as arranged, just after seven o'clock to make the last trip to Montgomery. Moton recalled that when he looked up at the bank clock as they waited at a traffic light on their way out of Selma it was 7:34 P.M.

Reactions

For he who lives more lives than one, more deaths than one must die.
—Oscar Wilde

In July 1965, *Ladies Home Journal* commissioned a national survey of American women. "No matter what your own opinions are on the question of voting rights," the women were asked, "do you think that Mrs. Viola Liuzzo, the Detroit civil rights worker who was killed in the Alabama shooting incident, had a right to leave her five children to risk her life for a social cause or not?" Fifty-five percent of the women polled felt strongly that Viola Liuzzo should have stayed home, 26 percent thought that she had a right to go, and 19 percent had no opinion.

Lyn Tornabene, a *Journal* staff writer, organized a focus group of white middle-class housewives from "a suburb of a medium size city" to discuss the survey results. One woman said, "[Vi] was wrong in leaving her home and going down there and meddling into something. I feel sorry for what happened. It was a shame, but I feel she should have stayed home and minded her own business." Tornabene asked whether Mrs. Liuzzo, or any mother, had the right to fight and perhaps die for a cause beyond home and family. "In her own mind she probably did exactly what she felt was right," another woman responded, "but how could she do it knowing the situation and knowing there was a chance of her not coming back with the children at home?"

All the women in the focus group were involved in local charity, hospital, or community volunteer programs. One told Tornabene, "I don't feel that I have the right to endanger myself and to leave my children motherless. The sorrow they would feel at the loss of a mother is greater than any cause. Their sorrow can turn to resentment. Mrs. Liuzzo may have died in vain if her ideals are not carried on in her children. If they resent her being killed, she hasn't gained a thing." Tornabene commented, "These women lived in a world where their actions were constricted by what was appropriate, what they might be criticized for, and what might open them to resentment or regret."

The group mood took a sudden turn when one of the women reminded the others that when she had been elected president of her volunteer organization she had been sent to a national conference. Technically she, too, had left her family in the care of others and had opened herself up to potential danger by flying to another city. "Mrs. Liuzzo's husband was home, and she did have a capable older daughter." Another asked timidly, "What if we were colored, would we be willing to go out to fight for the right to vote as mothers?" Some of the women began shifting in their chairs or rummaging through their pocketbooks at that point, clearly uncomfortable with the direction the conversation was taking. But those who raised the unpopular issue wouldn't let it go. "I think of that girl in New York City who was killed and no one helped her," one said. Kitty Genovese was murdered on a Queens street in 1964. Thirty-eight of her neighbors witnessed the fatal stabbing from their apartment windows but failed to call the police. "By helping someone you endanger your life, but I certainly hope that someone would help if it was me or my children."

The women who broke with the majority opinion experienced a frightening revelation. One told Tornabene afterward that she was amazed and saddened by how we would fight for the material good of our immediate family but not for an idea. Tornabene was deeply disturbed by what she found. "The overriding belief of the majority of these women," she wrote, "was that civil rights concerns like all major life concerns should be left to men."

Imperial Wizard Shelton quoted extensively from this article during the Wilkins and Thomas trials.

In the white South, reactions to the Liuzzo murder were predictably strong. To white segregationists, consumed by notions of racial purity, a white woman who would drive with a young black man in the front seat of her car was clearly capable of having a sexual relationship with him. White supremacists accepted that a white man might choose to have sex with a black woman for sexual adventure or that a black woman might want to have sex with a white man because of her distaste for the crudeness of black men. These couplings, while disturbing to the social order, were not considered dangerous because they would never lead to intermarriage (thanks to the good judgment of the white man). A white woman's relationship with a black man, however, branded her a sexual deviant. Furthermore, since the black man knew no better, this relationship threatened intermarriage and "the pollution of white blood."

Virginia Durr explained to me that the logic ran something like this: "If you give the blacks the right to vote, then your wife will have a black child." In her autobiography Mrs. Durr wrote that white segregationists, some of whom were lawyers and senators—professional men—believed that "If anything happened to change the Southern system, the white women would just rush to get a black man. We'd have a race of mulattoes. They seemed maniacal on the subject of sex. It used to embarrass me, because I felt it was a terrible reflection on the Southern white man, that he was such a poor lover or husband or impotent or weak that the white Southern women just couldn't wait to get a black man. . . . I also thought it was an awful reflection on Southern white women. These men who claimed to be Southern gentlemen would get up and make vile speeches about white women of the South and how they were protecting them. Every black man wanted to rape a white woman and every white woman apparently wanted to be raped. . . . I really think those fears came from the fact that the white men of the South had had so many sexual affairs with black women. And they just turned it around. It's the only thing I can figure out that made them so crazy on the subject."

Southern women tended to criticize Viola Liuzzo for what they considered her deficiencies as a wife and mother. White southern women of the early 1960s understood that these roles took precedence over everything else in their lives. They had been trained since girlhood to worry about how they appeared to men and were always conscious of the impressions they made. While this was also true of northern women, feminism had made greater inroads in the North by 1965. Northern women were reading and discussing Betty Friedan's *The Feminine Mystique* and questioning, often with anger, the way they had been raised.

Other white Americans who were obsessed by neither sexual behavior nor gender roles felt, for the most part, that white activists were generally misguided, arrogant people. Former president Harry Truman called the Selma march silly. "They can't accomplish a darned thing," he said. "All they want is to attract attention."[29] Four years earlier when asked his opinion about the freedom rides Truman had quipped, "Northerners who go South as Freedom Riders are meddlesome intruders who . . . should stay home and attend to their own business."[30]

White civil rights activism was considered deviant behavior by many whites who said they, too, believed in change—but *gradual* change, "safe" change. Too much change too soon could only cause the type of unrest that the communists would be glad to use to their advantage.

Activists who argued that society was behaving immorally and that the time had come for *total* change were viewed with suspicion and sometimes with hatred.

Journalist Howell Raines remembered a black speaker at an Albany, Georgia, voter registration campaign telling the crowd, "The local white people say these young white people who have come down here to help us are crazy, that they are beatniks and kooks. Whell, sho' they're crazy. Anybody wants to come down here and get beat up and shot at just so's a few American citizens can go and register to vote *is* crazy. I just thank God for such crazy people. I just wish there were more of them in this country."

Older white women often proved to be the most empathetic of the white volunteers in the civil rights movement. Whether they participated as teachers, social workers, nuns, students, lawyers, or independents, like Vi, all had been told at one time or another to accept or adjust or adapt to their traditional roles. Older white women recognized the frustration that was building in the black community, and they could understand some of those feelings.

A majority of white Americans in 1965, however, could not believe that white activists identified with black people. They considered the demonstrators professional agitators who were using black people to gain influence for themselves. Governor Wallace, in a television interview, charged that the Selma march was "not necessarily aimed at voting rights." He said many of the protest leaders wanted employment reorganization and land reform as "part of a plan . . . to immobilize this country." Many of the marchers were communists, he insisted.

"We are witnessing government by law being substituted by government by demonstration," Alabama Senator Lister Hill commented. He railed against the "outsiders" who had come to join the march as "professional agitators and demonstrators, among whom are ministers, college students, beatniks, and other assorted persons who have no legal status in Alabama."

I recalled the irony in Virginia Durr's voice when she said, "They called *me* a radical! [And she *did* have legal status in Alabama.] I had the right to vote without having to earn it. *All* Americans had the right to vote, and black people were Americans. How difficult was that to understand? I was *not* a radical. Those people who opposed letting the blacks register, *they* were the radicals."

In black communities, reactions to Viola Liuzzo's death were mixed. For the blacks of Lowndes, her murder was no surprise. Victimized themselves, they knew the fate that awaited anyone—especially a white outside agitator—who posed a threat to segregation. Others resented that America was stirred, if only temporarily, by the death of a white woman. The death of Jimmy Lee Jackson, a black man killed by an Alabama trooper, was virtually ignored by the national press.

Jackson was a twenty-six-year-old farmer who had been trying to register to vote since he was twenty-one. He lived with his mother, sister, and grandfather in a house with no running water on two acres where they grew corn, timber, and peanuts. Jackson, a deacon in his church, was killed defending his mother and grandfather as they were being beaten by troopers after participating in a voting rights demonstration in Marion, Alabama, on February 18, 1965.

The Selma to Montgomery march was a response to Jimmy Lee Jackson's death. At a memorial service for Jackson, Martin Luther King Jr. told the mourners, "Jimmy Lee Jackson's death says to us that we must work passionately and unrelentingly to make the American dream a reality. His death must prove that unmerited suffering does not go unredeemed. We must not be bitter and we must not harbor ideas of retaliating with violence. We must not lose faith in our white brothers."[31] When the angry mourners threatened to take Jackson's body to the steps of the state capitol and deliver it to Governor Wallace, Rev. James Bevel, Dr. King's associate, suggested instead a march to Montgomery to bring national attention to voting rights abuses. Cager Lee, Jackson's eighty-two-year-old grandfather, would lead the second attempt to march to the capitol a month later on March 21, 1965.

Many blacks felt that Stokely Carmichael, a field director with SNCC's Mississippi Delta Project, spoke for them when he complained that the march to Montgomery, which began as a protest of the death of a black man, attracted major national attention only after the death of a white man—Rev. James Reeb. "Now I'm not saying we shouldn't pay tribute to Rev. Reeb," Carmichael explained. "What I'm saying is that if we're going to pay tribute to one we should also pay tribute to the other. And I think we have to analyze why President Johnson sent flowers to Mrs. Reeb, and not to Mrs. Jackson."[32]

On the Sunday after Viola Liuzzo's murder Dr. Martin Luther King Jr., speaking to a crowd of more than three thousand in San Francisco's Grace Episcopal Cathedral, said of her, "If physical death is the price some must pay to save us and our white brothers from eternal death of the spirit, then no sacrifice could be more redemptive."[33]

On March 27, an integrated crowd of about two hundred protestors, led by Reverend James Orange of SCLC, marched on the Dallas County courthouse in Selma to protest Vi's murder. At the steps they paused for prayer and Rev. James Bevel said, "She gave her life that freedom might be saved throughout this land."

The following week, five hundred demonstrators dressed in black conducted a pilgrimage from White Chapel, near the scene of Vi's murder, to Montgomery to lay ten coffins on the capitol steps—one for each of the ten persons who had been killed fighting for civil rights in Alabama between 1963 and 1965.

On March 28, during an interview with *Meet the Press,* Dr. King called for a boycott of Alabama products and withdrawal of federal support in protest of the murders of Jimmy Lee Jackson, James Reeb, and Viola Liuzzo. "I hope to call on all Americans to refuse to buy Alabama products," he said. "I hope to call on the secretary of the treasury of the United States to withdraw all federal funds that it has on deposit in the Alabama banks. And finally, I think it is necessary to call on all federal agencies in line with the 1964 Civil Rights Bill to withdraw support from a society that has refused to protect life and the right to vote." King later withdrew this request when he realized such an action would make no distinctions and would ultimately cause all Alabamians to suffer.[34]

A grassroots memorial service for Vi was sponsored by the NAACP at the People's Community Church in Detroit on March 29, the night before her funeral. Fifteen hundred people, including Rosa Parks, attended the service, which was conducted by the Reverend Carl Sayers, Episcopal rector of St. Stephen's Church in Birmingham, Michigan. Father Sayers had first met Vi at the hospitality desk in Brown Chapel only a week earlier.

In 1997 I returned to Detroit and drove to Birmingham hoping to find Rev. Sayers. I found that he had died in 1986, but his widow, Janice, spoke with me about him. While in Selma, Sayers had tried to conduct an interracial prayer service for the marchers, but he was refused support by the local Episcopal bishop. At Viola Liuzzo's memorial service Rev. Sayers called for the resignation of the Alabama bishop, an action that infuriated his bishop in Michigan. "Carl saw his ministry as bringing comfort to the afflicted and affliction to the comfortable," Janice Sayers told me. "He was always on the cutting edge of things, and always in trouble." When Rev. Sayers announced he was going to Selma in 1965, many of his affluent parishioners left St. Stephen's.

"He wanted me to go with him," Mrs. Sayers remembered. "But we had three small children. I made the decision Mrs. Liuzzo didn't make. Looking back, I wish I'd gone. There was so much criticism of activists in those days. People do the very same things now and are praised for them." She looked at me and her eyes twinkled, "Perhaps like all prophets Carl and Mrs. Liuzzo were just ahead of their time."

James Leatherer, a young white social worker from Saginaw, Michigan, who had lost a leg and marched the entire fifty-four miles on crutches, also attended the NAACP memorial service. Leatherer's picture had appeared in every major American newspaper; white hecklers had taunted him along Highway 80 by chanting "Left! Left! Left!" as he walked.[35] Leatherer assured the mourners that "Mrs. Liuzzo did not die in vain because thousands of people who've been uncertain of their course on civil rights are realizing you have to get off the fence."

The last speaker at the service was the Reverend Dr. Clarence T. R. Nelson, pastor of the Scott Methodist Church in Detroit, who knew Sarah and Vi from their work with the NAACP. Rev. Nelson said he had received a telephone call from Vi on March 21, four days before her death, informing him that she would be bringing an eighteen-year-old girl from Selma to live in the Liuzzo home. That girl was Frances Jackson, daughter of Mrs. Willie Lee Jackson, with whom Vi had roomed in the Carver Homes.

On March 30, 1965, a high requiem mass was offered for Viola Liuzzo by Father Albert Hutting at the Immaculate Heart of Mary Parish in Detroit. Seven hundred fifty people attended the service, which was televised. As the mahogany casket was wheeled from the church the Reverend Michael O'Hara of Dearborn's Divine Child Church led the mourners in singing "We Shall Overcome." Guests included Teamsters president James Hoffa; Walter Reuther, president of the United Auto Workers; U.S. Attorney Lawrence Gubow, representing President Lyndon Johnson; Lt. Governor William Milliken; City Welfare Superintendent Daniel J. Ryan, representing Mayor Cavanaugh; Damon Keith, co-chair of the Michigan Civil Rights Commission; the Reverend John Donovan, auxiliary bishop of Detroit; and the Reverend C. Kilmer Myers, Episcopal bishop of Michigan. Dr. Martin Luther King Jr. and other black leaders— Roy Wilkins of the NAACP, James Farmer of CORE, and John Lewis of SNCC—also attended. Many blacks were openly critical of some attendees; with the exception of Dr. King, none of the luminaries had made the trip to Marion to bury Jimmy Lee Jackson.

Concurrently a service was held at the Warren Avenue Missionary Baptist Church, and on April 5 a memorial service, sponsored by the Wayne Friends of SNCC, was conducted in the Community Arts Auditorium at Wayne State University.

In 1990 Mary Gadson, a black woman from Birmingham, recalled her community's response. "I never knew more than her name and that she was a freedom rider, but even today she's like part of the family. That's just how much unity there was. During that time I believe she was a part of all black families. She really became kinfolk because she was involved. Her race didn't make a difference. To me she was a human being who was concerned, who had a heart, and who gave her life for what she believed in."[36]

Four years after Vi's murder, Coretta Scott King recalled her reaction to Vi's death in her memoir *My Life with Martin Luther King, Jr.* "When we reached Atlanta," she wrote, "Martin was being paged for the telephone. He received the terrible news that Mrs. Viola Liuzzo, a white woman who was the wife of a Detroit official of the Teamsters union had been shot to death on a Highway 80. . . . Whatever elation we had felt was gone in the sadness of the death of that lovely and brave woman. As a mother, I felt my heart go out to her devoted husband who had been widowed and now had the sole responsibility for the children. Of course, what had obviously inflamed the racists who killed her had been the sight of a white woman in a car with a black man on a dark Alabama road."[37]

The wide range of reactions to Vi's murder mirrored the anger, hope, and frustration in both black and white communities in 1965. The Selma to Montgomery march was the last integrated civil rights effort. Just when the movement seemed to be approaching a new height of unity it suddenly fragmented. Dr. King observed that "the paths of Negro-White unity that had been converging crossed at Selma and like a great X began to diverge."[38]

Five months later, on August 11, 1965, the Watts district of Los Angeles erupted in rioting. When Klonsel Matt Murphy heard about the L.A. riot he said to journalist William Bradford Huie, "Do you remember I told you four months ago that the Klan would elect a president in 1972? I was wrong by four years. We will elect Wallace in 1968. They just went and proved he was right all along."[39]

Back Home

No character, however upright, is a match for constantly reiterated attacks, however false.
—Alexander Hamilton

Back home on Marlowe Street, Jim Liuzzo struggled to keep his grief-stricken family together. Sarah moved in during the week to care for the younger children, and Jim took time off from work to be with them. He tried to protect them—to shield them from the vicious rumors about their mother.

The initial media barrage after Vi's murder had barely subsided when the Wilkins trial began and reporters converged on the family home again. The kids were followed, and Jim and Sarah were hounded by newsmen.

When Sally was jeered as "the nigger lover's baby" Jim pulled her and the boys out of public school and registered them in a Catholic academy. They found little relief there.

Not long after Vi's funeral Mary's marriage broke up, and she temporarily moved back with the family. Tommy, a sensitive thirteen-year-old who had felt especially close to his mother, could not comprehend how people could say such terrible things about her. Dealing with her death was difficult enough, but as the rumors intensified and the kids at school ridiculed him Tommy began to shut down. He withdrew, refusing to go to school, and spent more and more time alone in his room. All Vi's children missed her terribly. Their old neighbor, Gordon Green, remembered that "She was always engaged in interesting projects with her children. The last thing anyone should have accused her of was a lack of motherly love."

Tony, more of a scrapper than Tommy, fought back when the kids taunted him, but both boys' grades dropped, and they began to fail at school—something that never happened while Vi was alive.

Jim worried about Tommy's emotional health and about the physical safety of all his children. Despite hiring armed security guards and installing an alarm system in the house, he couldn't relax. The hate mail, obscene phone calls, and threats were relentless.

Sally remembers days when five or six three-foot-high mail sacks would be delivered. "Sarah would go through them," she said, "and burn the vicious ones in the sink to spare my father. She was my mother's best friend. She shouldn't have had to see all that hateful stuff either."

The only piece that got by Sarah was an article clipped from *Knight Rider*, a Klan magazine, showing a picture of Vi's body hanging out of her car. Somebody mailed it directly to Jim's office. He began to lose his concentration at work, began to miss important meetings, and he refused to travel—a critical part of his job as a union organizer.

Jim had no idea how to nurture his children. He had left that to their mother while he provided for their material comforts. Jim was gruff, impatient; intimacy frightened him. His answer to every problem, Mary remembers, was to write a check. He loved his children, but he didn't know how to express his feelings. Without Sarah's help, life would have been unbearable for the young ones.

"Although their marriage wasn't an easy one, I believe Jim and my mother shared a very deep bond," Mary told me. "In many ways Jim was a tortured soul who needed her love and attention. He always defended her to his family, who didn't approve of her because she'd been divorced and she wasn't Susie Homemaker. Jim supported a lot of the things my mother did—things I don't think many of my friends' fathers would have. They had their battles, but he never once tried to restrict her or abuse her—I can't decide if that was because he wouldn't or because he knew he couldn't!"

More trials, more reporters, more publicity: the assault on the beleaguered family fell into a predictable cycle. Tommy and Tony quit high school, and Jim began drinking heavily. Jim felt guilty, hopeless, lonely, and out of control, and he drank for relief. The more he drank the guiltier he felt and the more out of control he became. As Sarah said, "He just went down like the *Titanic.*"

Finally, Tommy left home to wander aimlessly across the country. For a time he completely lost contact with the family. Sally clung to Sarah for comfort, Penny escaped through an early marriage, and Mary left for California.

In 1968 Jim sold the big house on Marlowe Street and moved to a small apartment with Sally and Tony. In 1972 Vi's mother, Eva Gregg, died, followed by her husband, Heber, two years later. After their deaths Vi's sister Mary (now Mary Sprout), married and with a young family of her own, moved from Detroit and lost touch with the Liuzzo children. In 1975 Jim retired from the Teamsters. He was sixty-one years old, a prematurely aged alcoholic, and in deep financial trouble.

The driving force behind the Liuzzo family was gone. "We didn't know how to help each other," Mary said. "Mom always gave us credit for being more than we were."

Those were terrible years, Tony remembers. He told a reporter for the *Detroit News* that the disintegration of his family was far worse than any abuse they suffered by the public or the press.

7 What Really Happened?

Truth pressed to earth will rise again.
—Martin Luther King Jr.

Historian James Q. Wilson maintains that in the mid-1960s the FBI was not a deviant institution in American society but "a most representative and faithful one." He asserts that "Throughout virtually all of J. Edgar Hoover's administration the mission of the FBI was fully consistent with public expectations, beliefs and values."[1]

Wilson's evaluation is eerily similar to author John Mecklin's assessment of the Klan. In 1924 Mecklin found the "vast majority" of Klansmen to be "conventional Americans, thoroughly human, kind fathers and husbands, hospitable to the stranger, devout in their worship of God, loyal to state and nation and included among the best citizens of the community. . . . If the Klan were utterly un-American," Mecklin concluded, "it could never have succeeded as it did. The Klan is not alien to the American spirit."

Like the FBI, the Klan is a para-military organization whose primary agenda is to preserve the status quo.

In *The Ku Klux Klan,* Mecklin records an address delivered to a group of Atlanta Klansmen by Emperor William Joseph Simmons, who warned them, "My friends, your government can be changed between the rising and the setting of one sun. This great nation with all it provides can be snatched away from you in the space of one day. . . . When the hordes of aliens walk to the ballot box and their votes outnumber yours, then that alien horde has got you by the throat."[2]

In *White Lies, White Power,* researcher Michael Novick goes a step further. He notes that "White-supremacist groups like the Ku Klux Klan have always had a contradictory relationship to the federal governmental system of the U.S. Although these groups are extra-legal by nature, and often carry out illegal acts, they have played a big role in maintaining the political, social and economic order. As a result, they have often been protected by the state apparatus—especially the most racist elements within that apparatus. . . . Organized, violence-prone white supremacists, who make up a small element of society at large, are much better represented in the ranks of law enforcement and the military. This is not an accident. The ideology of law enforcement, the 'us against them' mentality which guides their daily lives and contacts with the public, make the police susceptible to white racist preachings. The police—even if polite, respectful, and individually not personal racists—carry out a commitment to suppress threats to the hierarchy of the state and society which leaves Black people and other people of color on the bottom. Organized white supremacists within the police forces find fertile soil for the argument that democratic and egalitarian values, and concern for human and civil rights, hem them in needlessly. The Klan portrays such procedural safeguards as only so much hypocrisy that interferes with cops' ability to protect themselves and to get tough on crime."[3]

In the 1960s J. Edgar Hoover unilaterally assumed the role of national repressor of threats to the social order. Hoover referred to himself as "the nation's chief law enforcement officer" and believed he had both the right and the responsibility to destroy anything that threatened the collective peace.

Hoover viewed the civil rights movement as a threat to civil order, and he used the same tactics the CIA used against foreign enemies to get information about and discredit civil rights leaders: wiretaps, infiltration, strategically planted rumors, anonymous letters, blackmail, and public accusations of drunkenness, adultery, and theft. Former vice president Walter Mondale commented that Hoover had the power to enforce rules against *ideas*. The authority to investigate "subversives" was granted him by President Franklin Roosevelt, and it was never rescinded.

Hoover's files on American citizens were legendary. He was rumored to have detailed information about the sexual, political, and financial indiscretions of some of the country's most powerful people. Hoover kept his job until he was seventy years old by blackmailing the people who had the authority (and the desire) to remove him.

Hoover's G-men took an oath promising to follow orders exactly as they were given. His goal was to create a lock-step belief system within the bureau. This wasn't difficult given the agency's hiring practices. The FBI was a white organization with middle-class values. Civil rights historian David Garrow asserts that "Not only did the Bureau recruit mostly white men with small-town backgrounds, parochial educations, and strongly conservative political views, but the socialization new agents underwent in the Bureau strongly inculcated or reinforced just such views and orientations."[4]

A deep distrust of all those who were "different" was bred into the bureau's ranks, just as it existed in the larger society. Anything foreign or strange was suspect, and conspiracies orchestrated by "outside agents" (especially communists) were believed to threaten the social order. This conspiracy theory was applied to the civil rights movement. Hoover believed the movement was fueled by outside agitators, not driven by any economic or social injustices.

On March 29, 1965, four days after the Liuzzo murder, Hoover warned law enforcement officials to stand firm against demands by civil rights leaders that the FBI play a more forceful role in securing compliance with the Civil Rights Act of 1964. He insisted the bureau was an investigative not a law enforcement organization. Hoover saw no inconsistency between this stand and his agents making arrests in kidnapping, bank robbery, drug smuggling, and espionage cases. FBI agents (according to the U.S. Administrative Code) had the authority to make arrests without warrants "for any offense against the United States committed in their presence." Still they repeatedly refused to act on their authority in civil rights cases.[5]

The previous summer when three civil rights workers were murdered in Meridian, Mississippi, Hoover was pressured by President Johnson to take more aggressive action against the Klan. Hoover complained bitterly to Justice Department officials that his bureau should not be compelled to investigate murders, lynchings, and assaults in the southern states. "It only stirs up agitation," he said.[6] Johnson had to threaten to turn over some of Hoover's domestic law enforcement power to Allen Dulles and the CIA before Hoover would agree to open a bureau office in Jackson, Mississippi.

On November 19, 1964, an editorial in the *Washington Post* noted that "Over and over the FBI Director emphasized that it is not his agency's business to guard anyone. This, he said, includes protecting the President and 'wet nursing' those 'who go down to reform the South.'"

Professor David Farber observed that "J. Edgar Hoover never saw himself or his bureau as allies of the civil rights movement. Even as he waged war on the KKK, Hoover continued his 'anti-Communist' campaign against Martin Luther King, Jr. His list of subversives, under presidential pressure, had simply grown to include both sides in the fight over racial justice."[7] Coretta Scott King agreed. "The FBI treated the civil rights movement as if it were an alien enemy attack on the United States," she said.[8]

And yet, Garrow insists, the FBI was not the weapon of one disturbed man. It was supported by a majority of American citizens in its charge to maintain order. Garrow's frightening conclusion is that "The Bureau was not a renegade institution secretly operating outside the parameters of American values, but a virtually representative bureaucracy that loyally served to protect the established order against adversary challenges."[9]

COINTELPRO

██████████ If they come for me in the morning, they'll come for you at night.
—Angela Davis

J. Edgar Hoover is surely one of the most tenacious figures of recent American history. With the full endorsement of the federal government he spied on and provoked radicals for almost forty years. In August 1956, even without the authorization of either the attorney general or the president, Hoover decided to concentrate more resources on surveillance of the American Communist Party and other left-wing organizations. By the mid-1960s the Klan, the New Left, the civil rights movement, and the women's liberation movement were added to Hoover's list of national security risks.

Hoover called his intensified intelligence operation the Internal Security Counterintelligence Program or COINTELPRO. It was so secret that two successive attorneys general denied ever having knowledge of it. The stated purpose of COINTELPRO was to "disrupt and neutralize" organizations that threatened the security of the United States.

COINTELPRO was a product of Hoover's frustration over a series of Supreme Court decisions in the 1950s that limited the Justice Department's power to proceed overtly against dissident groups. Hoover gradually shifted the FBI from its role as an investigative organization to an organization that assumed responsibility for controlling and containing radical activists.

COINTELPRO operations abruptly ended in 1970, with a raid on the FBI offices in Media, Pennsylvania. A group that called itself the Citizens Committee to Investigate the FBI stole hundreds of domestic intelligence files and leaked them to the press. Hoover panicked and ordered COINTELPRO dismantled.

In June 1972, a month after Hoover's death, discovery of the Watergate break-in led to further exposure of COINTELPRO's activities. In January 1975 the Senate appointed Senator Frank Church of Idaho chair of a committee assigned to study government operations with respect to intelligence activities, popularly known as the Senate Intelligence Committee or the Church Committee. The investigation turned out to be one of the largest ever conducted by the Senate.

After a fifteen-month investigation, the Church Committee issued a three-volume report. In the section focusing on domestic intelligence, the committee charged that the FBI had knowingly and repeatedly violated the Constitution in its investigation of the political activities of hundreds of thousands of law-abiding citizens. COINTELPRO agents had been authorized to intercept phone calls and first-class mail, plant paid informants, leak derogatory information to the press, and utilize disruptive tactics to interfere with leftist groups and activists. FBI agents had burglarized the New York City offices of the Socialist Workers' Party on ninety-two occasions between 1960 and 1966. Specially trained teams took photos of documents and correspondence relating to all aspects of the party's business, including legal strategies of the members involved in federal proceedings.

An internal memo boasted of the FBI's role in stirring up the dissension that led to the deaths of four Chicago Black Panthers.

The Church Committee reported that Presidents Roosevelt and Johnson had requested that Hoover investigate the personal lives of some of their critics and noted that Hoover kept files on the sex and drinking habits of many public figures. After a series of wiretaps uncovered Dr. King's extramarital affairs, Hoover was determined to get the American press to expose him. David Garrow notes that "One newspaperman approached several times [by Bureau agents] was the *Atlanta Constitution*'s Eugene Patterson. Patterson's visitor encouraged him to send a photographer to a Florida airport at a certain time in order to obtain pictures of King in the company of a woman not his wife. Patterson attempted to explain to the agent that that was not the sort of news the *Constitution* wanted to print. He sent the agent on his way. Several days later the agent returned and the same scenario occurred."[10]

The Church Committee concluded that the FBI's COINTELPRO activities were "indisputably degrading to a free society," and it recommended that court approval be obtained in advance for such activities as wiretapping, the opening of first-class mail, and break-ins by federal agents.

On May 19, 1976, the Senate created a permanent fifteen-member Select Committee on Intelligence with authority to oversee CIA and FBI activities and the power to authorize funds for their operations.

Tommy Rowe was called to testify before the Church Committee in December 1975. Secure in the Witness Protection Program by that time, he admitted he had worked as an FBI informant inside the KKK from 1959 to 1965. Rowe had come to the bureau's attention in the late 1950s when he was accused of impersonating an FBI agent. Barrett Kemp, a

Birmingham bureau agent, then spoke with Rowe at length, and when
Rowe offered to join the Klan and keep the FBI informed of its activities
in the Birmingham area Kemp put him on the payroll.[11]

Rowe's acts of brutality against blacks and civil rights workers during
his tenure with the bureau were systematically exposed by the Church
Committee. But Rowe wasn't going to allow the congressmen to make
him a scapegoat. He testified that in April 1961, not long after the
Congress of Racial Equality (CORE) announced its plans for a Freedom
Ride through Alabama, he attended a meeting in Birmingham with
Imperial Wizard Robert Shelton, Sheriff Bull Connor, and Lieutenant
Tom Cook of the Birmingham police department. Rowe said that Cook
assured Shelton that the police would delay their arrival at the
Birmingham bus depot to meet the Freedom Riders by fifteen minutes.
"You got time to beat them, kick them, burn them, kill them, I don't give
a shit, we just don't care," Rowe recalled Lt. Cook saying. "We don't ever
want to see another nigger ride on the bus into Birmingham again." Cook
promised Shelton there would be no arrests no matter what happened
during those fifteen minutes. Rowe maintained that the FBI was aware
that the Freedom Riders were in grave danger well before violence began
because *he* alerted them, yet the bureau did nothing to prevent it.[12] Rowe
also claimed that the bureau pressured him to deny he had taken part in
the 1961 bus terminal beatings, but he had seen a photo of himself club-
bing one of the demonstrators and was afraid to deny his participation.
Rowe also swore under oath that he had informed his FBI contact that
Klan violence was planned on the night of Viola Liuzzo's murder.

In the summer of 1978, ABC's news magazine show 20/20 produced a
segment about Viola Liuzzo's death in conjunction with its coverage of
the Church Committee hearings. The two surviving convicted Klansmen,
Collie Leroy Wilkins Jr. and Eugene Thomas, agreed to be interviewed for
the show. They had been released from federal prison earlier that year
after serving seven years of their ten-year sentences. On national television they testified that their time in jail had made them reconsider their
Klan-oath-enforced silence, and they charged that Tommy Rowe was the
one who fired the shots that killed Viola Liuzzo. Rowe, also interviewed

for 20/20, maintained as he had before that it was Wilkins who had fired the shots. All three men agreed to take lie detector tests. Wilkins and Thomas passed, but Rowe's results indicted that he was being deceptive.

Jim Liuzzo became very agitated after the show and encouraged his sons, Tom and Tony, to find out just how much information about their mother's murder was buried in the FBI files. The question of why the Lane Report had been written had never been answered to Jim's satisfaction, and he began to suspect that Vi was a victim of some sort of FBI-Klan conspiracy.

In 1974 the Freedom of Information Act—a direct result of the Watergate investigations—was passed by Congress over President Gerald Ford's veto. The FOIA provided expanded public access to government files. It stipulated that secrecy classifications could be challenged in court and had to be justified by federal authorization. Determined to use the Freedom of Information Act to find out what was in the FBI files about their mother, the Liuzzos hired a lawyer.

In February 1978 attorney Dean Robb of the Michigan American Civil Liberties Union (ACLU) filed under the Freedom of Information Act to obtain copies of all FBI documents pertaining to the Liuzzo murder investigation. Nothing happened. The Liuzzos endured months of bureaucratic stalling before the ACLU appealed to Michigan Senator Donald Riegle. Riegle contacted the new FBI director, William Webster, who had succeeded Hoover in 1977, and invited both Tony Liuzzo and Webster to his Washington, D.C., office in October 1978.

Webster, no champion of the Freedom of Information Act, had actively lobbied to get some of the FOIA provisions amended. At the meeting he appeared nervous. It was evident to Tony and Robb that the director had not been informed that Tony would be present. When Tony asked why his family was experiencing so many delays in getting information that they had a right to have, Webster asked Tony why he wanted to see it. It contained allegations, the director said, that his mother had taken drugs and was carrying on an affair with a young black man.

Tony became enraged. He knew from reading the *Detroit News* and *Detroit Free Press* accounts of 1965 that the Alabama state toxicologist testified that there was no evidence of drug use by his mother and that her autopsy clearly revealed no evidence of recent sexual intercourse. But Webster persisted in feeding Tony the old Hoover party line that there had been wrong-doing on his mother's part. Webster also refused to discuss Tommy Rowe's role, and the meeting became very heated.

Webster did, nonetheless, arrange an immediate release of the documents, and Tony left Washington with fifteen hundred pages of heavily censored files containing letters, memorandums, teletypes, and reports of the murder investigation.

From the FBI files the Liuzzo family discovered that the campaign to discredit their mother had been instigated by Hoover himself. They learned of Hoover's insinuations to President Johnson that their mother was a drug addict, that their father was involved with organized crime, and that a sexual relationship existed between Vi and Leroy Moton. On October 27 Howard Simon, director of the Michigan ACLU, told a reporter for the *Detroit Free Press* that Hoover's remarks were "designed to minimize the importance of the crime and then cover up the fact that a paid FBI informant was in a car with three other men when they opened fire on Mrs. Liuzzo." Such reckless slander originating from a top government official both stunned and enraged Vi's sons. Now they understood that their mother's reputation had been *deliberately* sacrificed to protect the FBI's and Hoover's reputations. The same FBI tactics that were employed to discredit leftist organizations had been used to discredit her.

Viola Liuzzo's posthumous experience with the FBI reverberates through the 1996 experience of Richard Jewell, a security guard who worked at Atlanta's Centennial Park during the 1996 Olympics. Jewell was initially hailed as a hero when he moved people away from a mysterious unattended knapsack. The knapsack contained a pipe bomb that detonated, killing two people and injuring more than a hundred. *New York Newsday* reported that "federal officials labeled the bombing an act of terror and vowed that those responsible would be brought to justice."[13]

Gratitude for Richard Jewell's heroism lasted all of three days. A special edition of the *Atlanta Journal-Constitution*, citing a tip from "knowledgeable sources at three federal agencies," named Jewell as the main bombing suspect. Jewell, the sources said, fit the profile of a "lone bomber." Despite the fact that when investigative reporters delved into Jewell's past neither they nor the FBI could find anything to link him directly with the bombing and that Jewell subsequently passed three separate lie detector tests in which he denied involvement, the national media began referring to him as Una-Dufus and Una-Bubba (a play on the nickname of the recently captured Unabomber).

Jewell's lawyer Jack Martin pointed out that through the focus on Jewell the FBI got what it wanted—a suspect—and the press got its story. Nobody dwelled on the possibility that an innocent man might be being railroaded. Jewell's mother appealed to President Clinton to clear her son. Speaking with Mike Wallace on NBC's *60 Minutes,* Jewell complained, "People will be ninety years old that were at the Olympic Games and go, 'do you remember when that bomb went off? Remember that Jewell fellow they accused of that?' It will never end."

A former Olympics security official told *Newsday* that "From the moment of the explosion the FBI was under intense pressure to wrap up the case quickly." On January 8, 1997, *New York Post* reporter Rita Delfiner observed that FBI Director Louis Freeh bungled his agency's probe of Atlanta's Olympic Park bombing.

"Freeh," Delfiner wrote, "whose imperious attitude and micromanagement style won him the nickname 'J. Edgar Hoover with children' within the Bureau, took control soon after the July 27 blast. One of Freeh's first moves was to order the investigation run by Division 5, a former counterintelligence unit, whose strength was intimidation and manipulation rather than the deliberate gathering of evidence." Delfiner reported that Jewell's lawyer Jack Martin said the FBI spent weeks working on the unfounded theory that Richard Jewell was an enraged homosexual cop-hater who had been aided in the bombing by his lover. She then cited Marie Brenner's article in the January 1997 issue of *Vanity Fair* that noted that at the time Jewell was dating a local girl and that the FBI obviously fell for a rumor that was started at Piedmont College, "perhaps invented by several of the students Jewell had turned in for smoking pot" when he worked there as a security guard.

My thoughts drifted back to the words of journalist Ken Fireman who had written for the *Detroit Free Press* a retrospective of the Liuzzo story in 1982, at the time of the renewal of the Voting Rights Act. "The Viola Liuzzo recklessly portrayed in the press," he wrote, "with accusations of emotional instability, drug abuse, adultery, and child abandonment hanging over her head was someone her family, friends and neighbors didn't recognize. She had been created by the FBI because the Birmingham Bureau had failed to prevent her murder from happening."

Had the FBI learned nothing in thirty-one years?

A Second Car

> For murder, though it have no tongue, will speak with most miraculous organ.
> —Shakespeare

Tom and Tony Liuzzo continued their investigation by poring through old newspaper accounts of their mother's murder. They found a disturbing number of contradictions.

The front page of the *Detroit News* of March 26, 1965, for example, described two shots fired from a rifle. The *Alabama Journal*, *Los Angeles Times*, and *Chicago Tribune* mentioned three shots from a high-powered rifle. FBI reports referred to six shots from .38-caliber and .22-caliber handguns. U.S. Assistant Attorney General John Doar, who had been assigned to Selma by the Justice Department to make sure that the federal court order sanctioning the voting march was obeyed, was told that Mrs. Liuzzo had been killed by a rifle. Leroy Moton said the murder weapon was a high-powered rifle and that, since he never heard shots, he assumed a silencer was used. During the Wilkins trial the murder weapon was identified as a .38-caliber pistol. Colonel Al Lingo, Alabama's director of public safety, told a reporter from the *Chicago Tribune* that two shots were fired but that it could not be determined whether they came from another car or from the side of the road.

A handgun recovered on the shoulder of the highway was never dusted for fingerprints. At the time of the murder investigation a state attorney said that it was not dusted because several people had handled the gun and because its handle had rigid plastic grips that wouldn't retain prints. He seemed unaware that the second excuse completely rendered the first meaningless. Whatever the reason, no fingerprints were ever filed in case records by either the local police or by the FBI.[14]

In the March 27 issue of the *Detroit News,* Leroy Moton described a blue Ford used in the first attempt to run him and Vi off the road. FBI records of the murder investigation note that three witnesses also claimed to have seen a 1955 Ford—some described it as green, others light-colored—in the vicinity of Big Swamp. An Alabama state trooper who was providing radar surveillance along Highway 80 on the night of March 25 (he was working with patrolman James Haygood, the officer who had given Gene Thomas a warning notice for speeding earlier that evening) was told about the shooting on the highway and alerted to look for a 1955 gray Ford with out-of-state plates. In his effort to establish reasonable doubt in the October 1965 trial of Collie Leroy Wilkins, defense attorney Arthur Hanes Sr. maintained that the earliest police reports of the Liuzzo murder identified the assassins' car as a red Sprite. (Since Rowe, Thomas, Wilkins, and Eaton were traveling in Thomas's red-and-white Impala, the Ford lead went uninvestigated.)

Leroy Moton said that when he saw Vi slump over he tried to lift her back up, then grabbed the steering wheel and guided the car onto the shoulder of the road. Other cars, filled with marchers, passed him. He honked the horn but nobody stopped.

Then the car came back and Moton, with Vi's blood all over him, pretended to be dead. A light flashed into the front seat and Moton waited, certain he would be killed. After taking a look, however, the men took off. Moton said that when he got out and started to run a late-model red sports car tried to run him down, but he jumped off the road into a ditch and hid. When that car didn't return, he got up and kept running toward Montgomery.

Moton finally waved down a truck full of marchers returning to Selma, driven by the Reverend Leon Riley of the Disciples of Christ Church in Richmond, California. Moton climbed into the truck and hysterically screamed "Everybody down! There's men with guns around here! Let's get out of here. A woman's been killed, hurry, get away or they'll come back!" Then he passed out. The marchers, near hysteria themselves, hid him in the back of the truck, and Riley drove straight to Brown Chapel where he and Reverend Raymond Magee of the United Church of Christ in Lafayette, California, called for an ambulance.

The ministers told a *Los Angeles Times* reporter that Moton described the chase as one car trying to force him and Mrs. Liuzzo off the road shortly after they left Selma and another swerving in front of them on the highway a few miles further on.

Moton was taken to a hospital where he called Hosea Williams, the SCLC's logistics director for the march, who he and Vi knew from the transportation service. Williams counseled Moton to call the Selma police and said that he would alert the National Guard. Rev. Magee had already notified the FBI. Moton was terrified when the Selma police took him into protective custody as a material witness. He was certain they would transfer him to the Lowndes County jail during the night and he would be killed. But Sheriff Clark kept him in Selma.

For most of that night Moton's mother didn't know where he was. She told Stan Koven, a reporter for the *New York Post*, that she feared for her son's life. "We all fear," she said. "We never know what may be coming next. We all are in danger, all my people."

Tony Liuzzo remembered that Vi had been an excellent driver and that she enjoyed driving fast. He believed she would have been able to either outrun or outmaneuver one car. If she had been boxed in by two, however—a Ford *and* the red-and-white Impala—it would have been a different story.

The April 5, 1965, issue of *Newsweek* reported that two cars were involved. "Two cars swept past them and gunfire split the night silence," the article read. "One of the cars came back to check that both victims were dead."

In 1968 Robert Bleiweiss edited a biography of Martin Luther King Jr. titled *Marching to Freedom*, written for use by high school students. Bleiweiss's account of the Liuzzo murder, written less than four years after the event, is as follows:

> After the cheers faded, the marchers began to leave [Montgomery]. The soldiers began the trip back to their armories and bases. And, as

night blackened the Alabama sky, volunteers began driving marchers back to Selma. One of those drivers was Mrs. Viola Liuzzo, a white woman from Michigan.

She had driven a carload of marchers to Selma and was on her way back to Montgomery to pick up another group. A 19 year old Negro volunteer from Selma, Leroy Moton, was riding with her. Out on the lonely two-lane highway, a car drew up behind her and followed tight to her bumper. Then it dropped back a bit and speeded up, smashing into her car's rear end. The sudden impact almost forced her car off the road.

The driver soon tired of playing tag with Mrs. Liuzzo's car. He pulled out, followed by another car, to pass. As the cars rushed by, a blaze of gunfire spit into the Liuzzo car. Mrs. Liuzzo's body slumped to the seat. Her car went off the highway and ripped through a barbed-wire fence. Moton, uninjured, saw one of the cars circle around and head back down the highway. He dropped down on the seat, playing dead, while flashlights lit up the car for a look at the victims. The killers were satisfied. They drove away.

Moton ran down the highway towards Selma. Waving his arms he tried to flag down a car for help. One driver tried to run him over. Finally a truck stopped and gave him a ride.[15]

Who was in the second car?

Tony Liuzzo tried to find Leroy Moton but was unable to. He also called San Francisco, St. Louis, and Chicago attempting to contact the denominational headquarters of the ministers mentioned in the newspaper accounts who had picked Leroy up. Tony finally located Rev. Leon Riley through the Disciples of Christ Headquarters in California.[16]

Rev. Riley told Tony that the marchers had been warned to leave Montgomery as quickly as possible to get away from the racist whites who had also come to the city to watch the procession. Alabama state troopers, under a federal order to protect the same marchers they had beaten in Selma only two weeks earlier, were about to be released from that responsibility, and the organizers of the march were fearful that stray activists would become helpless targets. Colonel Morgan of the Alabama

National Guard had orders to pull his men out of Selma as of 9 P.M. on Thursday. Only a skeleton force would remain to cover between 4 P.M. and 10 P.M. on March 25, 1965. Both state and local police were aware of these orders.

Rev. Riley remembered that on their return trips to Selma cars and trucks carrying marchers had been harassed by state troopers. Many had been issued speeding tickets. Riley's rented truck had been stopped twice. He had been threatened with jail and cursed by uniformed officers. Rev. Riley also told Tony that Highway 80 had been blocked off by the Alabama state troopers sometime around eight o'clock. The flow of traffic was held up, beginning with his truck, until after 8:30. Rev. Riley assumed it was simply harassment, since the highway ahead appeared clear. No headlights came toward them either. Rev. Riley considered it particularly spiteful harassment since people were anxious to get home. The FBI speculated that Viola Liuzzo was killed some time between 8:30 and 8:55 P.M. They were notified of the shooting at 9:30 P.M.

In the FBI report of the Liuzzo murder there is a heavily censored entry that details a call made to the Philadelphia offices of the FBI on March 27, 1965. An individual, whose name has been deleted, called the bureau office to report that he had just returned from participating in the voting rights march and that on the night of March 25, at approximately 9 P.M., he was driving on Highway 80 from Montgomery to Selma when he was stopped for allegedly speeding by three or four Alabama State Police cars. He was stopped about a mile outside Montgomery. His car was filled with other marchers (names also deleted) from Philadelphia.

While the police were questioning this man, something happened—he wasn't sure what—that made them suddenly jump into their cars and speed away, leaving him and his friends alone. The group waited, and in about fifteen minutes one police car returned and escorted them straight through to Selma where the driver paid a fine and was released.

Tony learned that Vi had not been strictly following the civil rights workers' rules of the road as she drove for the transportation service. She had driven fast along Highway 80 and had stopped for gas at the white-owned stations in Lowndes County, as she had been warned not to do.

Her car with Michigan plates was conspicuous. The marchers had been warned not to draw attention to themselves.[17]

J. T. Johnson, an SCLC field organizer, spoke with journalist Howell Raines about meeting Vi that afternoon. "After the march," Johnson recalled, "there were a lot of people who needed transportation back to Selma. She was determined to drive her car. Hosea [Williams] and I sat with her a long time. . . . We really didn't want her to go alone, being a white lady from the North. We appreciated all her participation and support. She had been great. She really had. She was a very nice lady. But she just wouldn't listen . . . she just had to make that trip [back to Selma]."[18]

SCLC headquarters in Montgomery reported receiving an anonymous call on Thursday night sometime after 8 P.M. from a man who said he wanted to warn them that "something funny" was going on along Highway 80. He reported that a 1963 green Oldsmobile with Michigan plates with a white woman driving and a black man in the front seat was being followed very closely by another car. He identified the other car as a 1959 or 1960 two-tone Chevy convertible, "red and some other light color," with Alabama plates. He did not, however, describe a high-speed chase. SCLC workers noted that a Chevy of a similar description had been seen driving around outside the City of St. Jude that afternoon.

Rev. Meryl Ruoss, who assisted Hosea Williams in coordinating the SCLC's Montgomery activities, told me in 1997 that the day they set up operations in the Dexter Avenue Church two men identifying themselves as fire inspectors visited them. They walked through the church and spent what Ruoss and Williams thought was an unusually long time in the belfry. When the men left Ruoss and Williams searched the tower, where they found small, powerful recording devices carefully hidden.

When I asked Rev. Ruoss who he thought was responsible, he said without hesitation, "The FBI. They were very hostile. The Montgomery police and the sheriff's office were antagonistic, but those guys were hostile. Early in the week we wanted to walk around the perimeter of the capitol building to plan our security, but the FBI wouldn't let us near it. They had ordered armed guards to seal it off and wouldn't give us permission to get through."

During his second night in Montgomery, Ruoss was awakened by a phone call at 2 A.M. The caller told him to go back home if he wanted to live. When he reported the call the Montgomery police assigned an officer to the church for the duration of the march.

Ruoss recalls the atmosphere as surreal. None of the officials responsible for public safety could be trusted. He said the only group that tried to be helpful were the officers of the National Guard.

The night Viola Liuzzo was murdered a colonel from the guard came to the church to advise the SCLC that they were in possession of her body. The colonel feared the murderers would try to kidnap the body and asked the SCLC staff for assistance in protecting it. Ruoss made arrangements to have Mrs. Liuzzo taken to White Chapel Funeral Home in Montgomery.

On March 25, 1965, a nine-line story appeared in the *Alabama Journal*, one page before the obituaries. The headline read, "Rumors False" and the story related, "Persistent rumors alleging that a white female civil rights demonstrator had died here or in Selma were quashed late Wednesday when authorities in both Dallas and Montgomery counties reported 'no such death certificates have been issued.'" Could this have been some sort of encoded message? For whom? For what purpose? Was it meant to frighten somebody? Something that *hadn't* happened was hardly news.

After months of investigating, Tony became convinced that his mother's murder was not random. Perhaps she was targeted because she had been careless, or perhaps she had once again used the familiar tactic of calling attention to herself to call attention to an injustice. It is also possible that she was so relieved that her premonition of impending death had not come true that she underestimated the danger of making that final trip back to Montgomery after sunset.

Or was something else going on? Could Vi's murderers have been aided by law enforcement officials? Is it possible that either the Alabama state troopers or the local police had such a bitter taste in their mouths from the events of the previous week that they would not only look the other way (as the Birmingham police had in 1961) but would actually clear a path for an execution? Could someone in authority have ordered Highway 80 closed between 8 and 8:30 P.M. on the night of March 25, knowing what the implications were?

What about the warning citation Gene Thomas received on the highway two hours before the Liuzzo murder? Why did Thomas receive a *warning* when others stopped that afternoon complained about getting tickets? Were the officers who stopped the Klansmen sympathetic to them? Did they make any other special arrangements? Tommy Rowe was, after all, the man who had sat in a room with the imperial wizard, Sheriff Bull Connor, and Lieutenant Tom Cook of the Birmingham police four years earlier, negotiating a delayed police response to a planned attack on a group of unarmed Freedom Riders.[19] Is it merely coincidental that the now *Captain* Tom Cook's name was submitted on the docket of witnesses for the defense in the first Collie Leroy Wilkins trial?[20] Could the Klansmen in Gene Thomas's Impala have been in radio contact with the police that night?

Many Alabama Klansmen had CB radios. Robert Shelton communicated from Tuscaloosa with Klan units in eighteen states via citizens' band. Grady Mars, chief of security for the United Klans of North Carolina, boasted in 1965, "Some of my captains can put a hundred armed Klansmen at a given point within one hour's notice. . . . All our cars are equipped with CB radios and with our Relay Stations, I can talk to any Unit in the state and get a message out to them even when I'm driving along the road."[21]

How difficult would it have been to relay through the local police dispatcher? Why wouldn't the Klansmen call up every resource they had at their disposal to confront the largest northern invasion since the Civil War? March 25, 1965, was, after all, a day that Grand Dragon Creel assured Tommy Rowe he would "never in his life forget."

Journalist Howell Raines's 1977 memoir, *My Soul Is Rested,* records an interview with Nannie Leah Washburn, a sixty-five-year-old white widow from Georgia who came to Selma to march with her daughter and to help with the cooking. She was also staying at the Carver Homes, and she met Vi at Brown Chapel, where they shared lunch one afternoon.

"I understand you met Mrs. Liuzzo," Raines began. "I certainly did . . . and my daughter and her was supposed to be together that night. Anyhow it didn't happen. My daughter got another assignment at the last minute. I told Mrs. Liuzzo, I'm a lot older 'n you and I've had a lot of experience with Jim Crow. . . . I wanna give you a little of my kind of advice. Don't you get in no car with no black man. If you do, they'd a lot ruther kill you than the black man, 'cause I've done been through the experience of it. But she went on anyhow."[22]

Virginia Durr agreed. "It was dangerous for a white woman to be in a car with a black man in those days," she said. "If it was a black woman, it would be all right. I'm surprised that Mrs. Liuzzo did that."

Why did she do it? In 1997 I put that question to the Reverend Meryl Ruoss, the Presbyterian minister who called Jim Liuzzo on the night of Vi's murder. Ruoss had met Vi and Leroy Moton in Selma while he was waiting for an assignment with the SCLC. He recalled that she seemed very protective of the young Leroy Moton—almost motherly. When I told Rev. Ruoss that some people in Selma believed that Moton had gotten Viola Liuzzo killed—by the very act of getting into the front seat of her car—he said that was ridiculous.

"Moton was an intelligent, committed young man," Ruoss told me. "He knew how risky it was to demonstrate for voting rights for blacks, and so did she. Moton was very capably coordinating the transportation service for the SCLC, and he enjoyed working with Mrs. Liuzzo because she was so willing to help wherever she was needed. Everybody in Selma knew Moton. He rode with Mrs. Liuzzo to assure blacks that she was okay, that she could be trusted."

Hosea Williams, the voting march's logistical director, who also spoke with me in 1997, agreed. "Mrs. Liuzzo rode with Moton because he knew his way around Selma," he said. "They got along well because they were both serious—both real hard workers. Leroy was a country boy, a real serious guy who wanted a better life. And Mrs. Liuzzo, she wasn't looking for publicity or even attention. She just wanted to help. That woman wouldn't even accept reimbursement for the gas she used in her car. I remember that," he said. "As field director I knew exactly what was going on. It was my business to know. The scandals they tried to spread after her murder were all lies. These were two dedicated people who got destroyed because they tried to help. They just blew that woman's head off. It made me furious when I heard. I couldn't believe it."

Viola Liuzzo, Leroy Moton, and Hosea Williams were all serious, committed, *and* confrontational. That combination of traits is what the movement needed in 1965. Andrew Young recalled that once Dr. King—refereeing a disagreement between Hosea Williams and another SCLC senior staff member—observed, "We need people [in the SCLC] who are confrontational. Some of us have a tendency to become too comfortable with injustice. Not Hosea. He's going to go out there and start something, and though we don't know what it might lead to, we need people like that."[23]

People who were in Selma during the march and experienced the triumphant procession into Montgomery talk about "fear finally dropping away" in the Black Belt. There was an overwhelming sense of victory. Sheriff Jim Clark's NEVER! button seemed absurd. "Never" had certainly been overcome.

Things were changing. The voting rights march was the first time that whites in large numbers—especially whites from the religious communities—had taken an active role beside blacks. For years white liberals expressed sympathy and contributed financially to the civil rights movement, but now whites and blacks were standing side by side in overwhelming numbers.

Coretta Scott King recalled, "It was a great moment to go back to Montgomery because you see for us it was returning after ten years. I kept thinking about how ten years before there were just black people marching. But in the Selma to Montgomery march there were Catholic priests and nuns, and you had other clergy, and you had a lot of white people. It was a really beautiful thing to pass the Dexter Avenue Church and go toward the capitol marching together."[24]

Author Fred Powledge observed, "What there was *not* on the Selma-To-Montgomery March was the deep, pervading fear that had always infected Negro Southerners. If there was any place for a black person to be afraid in America, it was Black Belt, Alabama. But even there the fear had been beaten, abolished, vanquished. Segregation had been beaten."[25]

It is easy to imagine Vi getting caught up in that heady sense of hope. Certainly Leroy Moton had. He had already lost his job just for passing out voter registration flyers. Certainly he understood it was dangerous for him to be in a car alone with a white woman. Not only was it socially taboo for black men and white women to associate with each other, it was against the law. In 1958 an ordinance had been passed in Montgomery stipulating that it was "unlawful for white and colored persons to play together . . . in any game of cards, dice, dominoes, checkers, pool, billiards, softball, basketball, football, golf, track, and at swimming pools or in any athletic contest." As late as 1965 a black man in Selma could be arrested for "socializing with [talking to] a white woman in private or public surroundings."[26]

But during the week of March 21, 1965, suddenly the ugly tide seemed to be turning. For some it was exhilarating, for others terrifying. A new social order was being born. But sometimes ordinary people die for ideas because other ordinary people are willing to kill for them. A Detroit journalist said that Vi was "struck down by the death throes of a vanishing order. A way of life that will soon be utterly gone with the wind just as the pre–Civil War slave owning days in the south are gone."

An editorial that ran in the *Detroit News* a day after Vi's murder commented, "To note that Mrs. Liuzzo courted death by driving along a U.S. highway in Alabama in a car with Michigan plates—with a Negro by her side to boot—is to note what is wrong with Alabama, not with Mrs. Liuzzo."

Who Was Responsible?

States are as the people are; they grow out of human character.
—Plato

In December 1977 the Liuzzo family filed a two million dollar notice of claim against the federal government for negligence, charging that the FBI knew Tommy Rowe and his fellow Klansmen were planning violence on

March 25, 1965, yet did nothing to prevent it. The government, however, refused to negotiate the claim.

In 1978 a routine state attorney general's audit of the Birmingham, Alabama, city records uncovered literally thousands of stored investigative files from the days of the civil rights movement. These files contained the results of two failed lie detector tests administered in 1963 to Tommy Rowe when he was questioned about his involvement in the Sixteenth Street Baptist Church bombing. (The church had been targeted by the Klan because it was a rallying point for the school desegregation movement.) Rowe's polygraph results also showed that he was "attempting deception" in denying involvement in fire bombing the home of A.G. Gaston that same year.

Far more interesting to the Liuzzos, however, were the incriminating statements Rowe made about their mother's murder to two Birmingham police officers in 1965. On the morning after Vi's assassination, Rowe told officers Lavaughn Coleman and Henry Snow that *he* had been the triggerman!

This was consistent with what Collie Leroy Wilkins and Eugene Thomas had said during their appearance on *20/20* in the summer of 1978. Shortly after the broadcast Wilkins and Thomas were subpoenaed and testified before a grand jury in Lowndes County that Tommy Rowe fired the shot that killed Viola Liuzzo. On the strength of their testimony and the information found in the Birmingham municipal files, Gary Thomas Rowe was indicted for first-degree murder in the death of Viola Liuzzo in September 1978.

The federal government immediately filed a motion to dismiss the murder charge, claiming that Rowe had been granted immunity in 1965 when he agreed to testify against Wilkins, Thomas, and Eaton. An injunction was subsequently issued against the prosecution of Rowe based on his immunity as a government informant. The federal courts permanently enjoined the State of Alabama from trying Rowe for the Liuzzo murder "for reasons not bearing on his guilt or innocence."

Despite this ruling, Senator Ted Kennedy, then chair of the Senate Judiciary Committee, asked the Justice Department to conduct an independent investigation. Kennedy wanted to know if Rowe had been involved in violent crimes while employed by the FBI and, if so, whether the Birmingham bureau agents had helped to hide it. A formal inquiry was ordered by Deputy Attorney General Benjamin Civiletti in 1978 and completed in February 1980. In a 302-page report the Justice Department confirmed that the FBI knew about and covered up Rowe's involvement in violent attacks on blacks, civil rights activists, and journalists. It further determined that Rowe was not merely a paid informant but a high-ranking decisionmaker in the Eastview Klavern 13 while he was on the FBI payroll. Rowe had veto power over any violent activity contemplated by the Eastview Klavern 13. Still, the independent investigation produced no credible evidence to substantiate the allegations that Rowe fired the shot that killed Viola Liuzzo.[27]

The Justice Department investigators said they believed Rowe was innocent because he had been a reliable informer throughout his career and because he had reported the shooting to the bureau immediately after it happened.

The Ann Arbor Trial

Who thinks the Law has anything to do with Justice? It's what we have because we can't have justice.
—William McIlvanney

Gary Thomas Rowe would never stand trial for Viola Liuzzo's murder, and the federal government refused to negotiate the Liuzzos' 1977 negligence claim. Ultimately, the family filed a formal suit against the government in July 1979. They were represented by attorney Dean Robb, with the assistance of attorney Jack Novik of the Michigan ACLU. "The lawsuit was filed," Robb said, "so the government would treat the claim we filed in a more serious manner. We have no illusions that this is not a difficult case. The family lives with this every day. If we can do something to put this to rest properly, we should."

The case came to trial early in 1983. Howard Simon, executive director of the Michigan ACLU, commenting on the actions of the FBI in

1965, noted, "They had a monster working for them [Tommy Rowe]. They took no effort to keep him on a leash. The FBI had a direct choice between preventing a crime and keeping him as an informant. They kept him as an informant."

Jack Novik requested that the full text of Senator Kennedy's Justice Department report be released to the family. Once again the federal bureaucracy went into stall. Tony had less patience this time and removed Jack Novik from the case. As a result, the Michigan ACLU reduced its role in the Liuzzo matter. That may have been a fatal mistake.

On March 21, 1983, eighteen years after her murder, the civil trial charging the FBI with responsibility for the death of Viola Liuzzo at the hands of the Klan opened in Ann Arbor, Michigan. The case was presented to federal judge Charles W. Joiner, without benefit of a jury. Dean Robb charged that Gary Thomas Rowe was in fact the murderer of Mrs. Liuzzo and that the FBI had been negligent in recruiting, training, and supervising him—that their negligence had resulted in her death.

Ann Robertson, the government's attorney, argued that the statute of limitations in a charge of negligence had expired (an argument that was rejected) and that the testimonies of witnesses Collie Leroy Wilkins and Eugene Thomas were tainted because of their desire for revenge on Rowe, whose testimony had sent them to prison.

New York Times reporter Iver Peterson wrote that the Liuzzo case was constitutionally significant because it represented the first test of the FBI's obligation to protect citizens it knew to be in danger.

On March 21, Wilkins and Thomas testified that they were present in the car on the night Viola Liuzzo was murdered and that it had been Tommy Rowe who shot her. Thomas said he had loaned his gun, which was the identified murder weapon, to Tommy Rowe earlier on the day of the murder. Thomas insisted that Wilkins was unarmed. "After the shooting I looked in the rearview mirror," Thomas said, "and saw her [Liuzzo's] car veering off to the side of the road. And Rowe said, 'Well, I got 'em. Damn good shooting.'"[28]

Under cross examination Thomas admitted he had frequently lied as a Klansman, but he said he had become a born-again Christian in prison and didn't lie anymore. Both men agreed to take lie detector tests. A polygraph expert testified that Wilkins and Thomas were telling the truth when they said that Rowe shot Mrs. Liuzzo.[29]

On March 23, Attorney General Ramsay Clark testified for the plaintiffs. He maintained that southern FBI agents at the time of the Liuzzo murder often regarded civil rights activists as agitators. They shared those sentiments with both southern police officials and members of the Klan. In 1965 Clark had been in charge of the federal forces assigned to protect the marchers. He said the Justice Department received numerous reports that violence-prone individuals were flocking to the area "like moths drawn to a candle." Clark's testimony gave weight to the charge that the FBI both knew and accepted the fact that Rowe was a violent man.

At the end of the first week Judge Joiner was shown the videotaped testimonies of two Birmingham police officers—Lavaughn Coleman, who was retired, and Henry Snow. Coleman testified that he and Snow went to Rowe's apartment the morning after the Liuzzo murder, before any arrests were made. Coleman maintained that Rowe admitted to him and to Officer Snow that he had killed Mrs. Liuzzo. Snow's testimony substantiated Coleman's.

Government attorney Ann Robertson argued that Snow and Coleman were part of a Klan effort to take revenge on Rowe. Then, the following week, she produced a surprise witness—Flossie Louise Creel of Springville, Alabama. Mrs. Creel was the ex-wife of Eugene Thomas Creel; the couple divorced in 1970. She testified that Thomas told her two or three weeks after the murder that it was Wilkins, not Rowe, who fired the shots. Mrs. Creel was not on the original witness list. She said she had decided to end eighteen years of silence after hearing news reports of her ex-husband's testimony that Rowe killed Mrs. Liuzzo.[30]

On the last day of the trial FBI Director William Webster appeared at the Ann Arbor courthouse. Tony recognized him from their meeting in Washington five years earlier. The following day, May 27, 1983, federal district judge Charles W. Joiner rejected the Liuzzos' suit. He said the plaintiffs failed to show that the FBI had been negligent in directing its agent, Gary Thomas Rowe, in his undercover actions as a Klansman. In a fourteen-page opinion Judge Joiner held that "Rowe did not kill, nor did he do or say things causing others to kill. He was there to provide information, and his failure to take steps to stop the planned violence by uncovering himself and aborting his mission cannot place liability on the government."[31]

The family was stunned. Tony, wearing a white cardigan sweater that once belonged to his father, burst into tears.

Throughout the trial Judge Joiner had repeatedly rebuffed the government's attempts to dismiss the case. Dean Robb was so confident of prevailing that he had prepared a press release proclaiming "victory for the children of Viola Liuzzo."

Robb told the *Detroit Free Press*, "I'm never comfortable in suing the government. Down the hall from the courthouse is the FBI office . . . and the U.S. attorney's office. They are all drawing the same pension, and they all have the same buddies. . . . We had courageous clients and a wonderful staff," Robb said in a trembling voice. "If there is a possible case to hold the FBI liable for its misdeeds, this is it." He said he believed a jury trial would have rendered a different verdict and that Judge Joiner's opinion illustrated the need for amending the Federal Tort Claims Act to allow jury trials in such cases. Co-counsel Jeff Long protested that the ruling ignored the question of what restrictions the government is obligated to place on its informants.

Michigan ACLU Director Howard Simon charged that Judge Joiner missed the point of federal negligence. Simon insisted that the FBI was clearly responsible for failing to prevent violence since Rowe, by his own admission, had alerted his FBI superiors that violence was being planned the night of the murder.[32]

The *Washington Post* declared the decision, "a complete victory for the government" and ran a photo of a slim, dark-haired woman leaning her head against a marble wall, weeping. The image was of twenty-four-year-old Sally Liuzzo.

The *Los Angeles Times* of May 28 reported that Tony Liuzzo called the decision "not just a defeat for our family, but a defeat for America. I'm disappointed when our government can hide things and never be called into account." Tony called Rowe a "demented maniac" who had been let loose by the FBI to conduct a "reign of terror."

Free Press reporter Helen Fogel summarized the situation succinctly. "For nearly a decade," she wrote, "Tony Liuzzo lived and worked for the day when the word of a federal judge would show the world what manner of men his mother's killers were, and make her heroism clear: even to doubters. . . . Anthony Liuzzo, Sr. died in 1978 still troubled, according to his children, by gossip that his wife was unfaithful to him during her civil rights work."[33]

The Liuzzo family suit was the first of three brought against the federal government in the early 1980s as a result of the Freedom of Information Act, the Church Committee hearings, and Senator Kennedy's Justice Department investigation.

On January 23, 1983, James Peck, a white Freedom Rider, sued in New York Federal Court over injuries he had received in beatings during a freedom ride in Alabama on Mother's Day 1961. (Peck had also marched in Selma in 1965, representing CORE.) He was among fourteen Freedom Riders who had divided into two integrated groups in 1961 to travel from Washington, D.C., to New Orleans. From Atlanta to Birmingham their only scheduled stop was Anniston, Alabama. Peck was in the second bus with his friend Walter Bergman and Bergman's wife, Frances. Bergman was a sixty-one-year-old retired psychology professor from Wayne State University. Ironically, he had worked for the Detroit Board of Education a few years before Vi's 1963 protest and was an active Unitarian Universalist. While it is entirely possible that their paths crossed on either the Wayne State campus or at the First UUC on Cass Street, there is no way to know if Viola Liuzzo and Walter Bergman ever met.

When the first bus entered the Anniston station a white mob attacked it, broke all the windows, and slashed the tires.[34] The bus sped away but had to stop six miles out of town when the tires went flat. The mob, which had pursued the bus, surrounded the vehicle and forced the passengers off by tossing a firebomb into one of the broken windows. They beat the Freedom Riders as they fled, and the bus burst into flames while the Anniston police watched.

Peck's bus was an hour behind the other. When it pulled into Anniston the driver said he wouldn't go on to Birmingham unless the group segregated itself. The mob entered the newly arrived bus and began to beat the blacks who were sitting in the front seats. Peck was knocked to the floor, and Bergman was hit on the skull and thrown to the back of the vehicle. He suffered a stroke four months later and was confined to a wheelchair for the rest of his life.

When Peck's bus reached Birmingham another mob was waiting. As passengers got off and entered the "white" waiting room they were attacked with iron bars. Peck was dragged into an alley where six men beat him. Fifty-seven stitches were required to close the wounds on his head. Dr. Bergman was beaten into unconsciousness a second time.

The Birmingham police did not respond to the attack for nearly half an hour. Sheriff Bull Connor explained that few cops were on duty because it was Mother's Day.

At a press conference after the beatings, Alabama Governor John Patterson, who had filed suit to outlaw the NAACP in Alabama during his term as state attorney general, told reporters that he had no sympathy for the Freedom Riders. "When you go somewhere looking for trouble," the governor said, "you usually find it."[35]

Peck charged that the federal government knew there was a conspiracy among Klan members to attack the Freedom Riders when they got to Alabama, that the government did nothing to prevent the violence, and that, therefore, the government was liable for the injuries that the riders sustained. On December 10, 1983, federal district court judge Charles E. Steward awarded Peck $25,000 in damages.

Eighty-four-year-old Dr. Walter Bergman brought his suit in Michigan the same year.

At his 1978 extradition hearing in Savannah, Georgia, where Tommy Rowe was living under an assumed name, Detroit ACLU attorney William Goldman, representing Walter Bergman, saw Rowe swear that the Alabama Highway Patrol and the Birmingham Police Department planned the Klan attack on Bergman's bus. Goldman said Rowe maintained that Birmingham police officials met with Klan leaders and urged them to attack the Freedom Riders. Rowe testified that Al Lingo, then director of the Alabama Highway Patrol (and in 1965 Alabama's director of public safety), followed the second bus and radioed the Birmingham police detailed information about its route. Rowe testified that the FBI gave hourly reports of the bus's progress to Lt. Thomas Cook, despite the fact that Rowe told the FBI that Cook was a Klansman.

On February 8, 1984, federal district judge Richard A. Enslen ruled that the federal government was liable for failing to prevent the attack on Bergman. The judge ruled that the bureau's responsibility did not end with alerting local police, especially when the bureau knew that the Birmingham police leadership was sympathetic to the Klan. The FBI was ordered to pay $35,000 to Bergman and $15,000 to the estate of his wife, Frances. Bergman commented to the press, "We have a better America in 1983 than we had in 1961."[36]

The Liuzzos, however, were ordered to pay the government's court costs of $80,000 in addition to their own legal fees which amounted to more than $60,000. Tony told reporters, "I will never pay a penny to the United States Government for bringing action to find out what happened to my mother. They'll have to drag me to jail."[37]

In August the *Detroit Free Press* observed that "The principle that the loser in a lawsuit may be assessed costs is a reasonable one, meant to deter frivolous litigation. Indiscriminately applied, especially in lawsuits against the government, it can have a chilling effect on the ability of injured persons to seek reform and redress."

On September 22, 1983, 20/20 aired a follow-up segment to the 1978 show, updating viewers on the outcome of the Liuzzo trial and expressing outrage that the family had been ordered to pay the Justice Department's court costs. In November, U.S. Senators Carl Levin and Charles Percy proposed a resolution for the Justice Department to drop its request for court costs. Shortly thereafter, Tony got a call from Dean Robb informing him that the Justice Department had dropped its claim and the family would not be responsible for any costs.

In attempting to explain the different outcomes of the three cases, a *Washington Post* editorial noted that the Bergman and Peck suits were able to point to a clear plan for violence of which the FBI was aware but chose to ignore. The Liuzzo case, the writer noted, was less strong because the FBI informant merely alerted the bureau to vague plans for violence on the night of March 25 without any specific reference to a time and a place where an intervention could have been expected.[38]

Tommy Rowe slipped back into the Federal Witness Protection Program. He, unlike the Liuzzos, was financially secure. Rowe was working as a private investigator and managing a security firm in Savannah. During the 1975 Church Committee hearings Rowe had performed so well as a "domestic intelligence informant" that he was offered a contract for $25,000 from Bantam Books for his life story. Within a year he produced *My Undercover Years with the KKK*, a rambling fantasy that cast him as a tough, courageous, hard-living, hard-drinking sex machine. In the book Rowe claimed he had been instructed by his FBI contacts to disrupt, discredit, and disorganize the Klan as much as possible. He said he was encouraged to cause dissension by informing Klansman that their wives were sleeping with other men. He was also told to sleep with as many Klan wives as he could, because it was believed that was the best way to gather sensitive information.[39] Rowe appeared on a number of talk shows (with a bag over his head) to promote his book. Columbia Pictures gave him another $25,000 for the rights to film his life for NBC television. In 1978, tall, handsome actor Don Meredith portrayed the squat, overweight, ruddy-faced Rowe as a rough but well-meaning champion of justice in a made-for-TV movie called *The Freedom Riders*.[40] The movie had to be updated with a voice-over epilogue after Rowe was indicted for the murder of Viola Liuzzo. It was subsequently re-released as *Undercover with the KKK*.

A representative from Walt Disney Productions approached the Liuzzo family and purchased the rights to their mother's story. A treatment called "A Rose in the Snow" was developed by playwright Jim McGinn. His title was based on something Vi had written a month before she died. In February 1965 a heavy snowstorm hit the city of Detroit. The snow in the Liuzzo backyard was over two feet high, but for some reason a rose pushed its way through and bloomed. Vi took a picture of the rose and when the print was developed she wrote on back of it "this is typical of the love in the Liuzzo house."

A Rose in the Snow was never produced, however. Studio executives decided there wouldn't be enough commercial interest in Vi's story to make it marketable. The main character, they felt, was too scattered—female viewers would have a difficult time identifying with her.

Collie Leroy Wilkins died in Birmingham, Alabama, on December 23, 1994. He was fifty-one years old. The *Birmingham News* mentioned only that he was a member of the Fairfield First Baptist Church and that he was survived by his mother, daughter, and two brothers. No mention was made of his Klan activities or of the Liuzzo murder.

On the day after Wilkins was buried, the *News* covered a memorial service at Greenwood's Woodlawn Cemetery for Carol Robertson, one of the four teens killed in the Sixteenth Street Baptist Church bombing. Carol Robertson would have been forty-three years old.

In 1987 Morris Dees and his Southern Poverty Law Center legal team won a $7 million judgment against the United Klans of America for the 1981 lynching death of Michael Donald, a black college student in Mobile, Alabama. It was the first time a Klan organization had been sued for the acts of one of its members. The historic decision bankrupted the Eastview Klavern 13—Rowe's Klan, the group believed to have been responsible for beating the Freedom Riders, bombing the Sixteenth Street Baptist Church, and the night rider murders of Lt. Colonel Lemuel Penn and Viola Liuzzo.

8 Coda

Let God do it all, someone will say; but if man folds his arms God will
go to sleep.
—Miguel DeUnamuno Y Jugo

Jim Liuzzo, one of twelve children born into an immigrant Italian coal
mining family, had grown up in Carbondale, Pennsylvania. Tough, outgoing, intelligent—he was always a hard worker and a good provider. Jim
was, in many ways, a traditional man who had been both delighted and
exasperated by his young, non-traditional wife. After Vi's death Jim was
publicly accused of not being able to control her. This was a humiliating
blow to his Latin ego. Jim knew all about a man's home being his castle,
but he had worked hard during his marriage not to be a tyrant. Vi had always been after him to be easier with the kids—not to be such a bear—
and he had tried. Was that a mistake? Would things have been different if
he had kept tighter control?

In 1965 people were asking what kind of man would allow his wife to
run wild with black men? It made Jim sick. He exhausted himself, but he
couldn't protect Vi's reputation because the attacks on her were too many
and too widespread. In 1965 he didn't realize who was orchestrating
them. He couldn't explain fast enough, couldn't demand enough retrac-
tions, to get ahead of the ugly, baseless rumors.

Jim suffered through the Hayneville trials with Klonsel Murphy referring to his wife as white trash, a white nigger, and a whore. He bore the
indignities of the Lane Report. It twisted him—made him go inside himself. In the end Jim felt he had let everybody down.

Jim lived to hear the Church Committee's findings but not long enough to see the bitter outcome of the family's suit against the federal government. Sadly, he realized that the country he had been so proud of defending in the Second World War had permitted its "chief crime fighter" the power to personally authorize blackening a murder victim's reputation to cover up his agency's incompetency. Vi had been expendable.

The wife and mother who had meant so much to her family, who had loved them, was dragged through the mud just to keep a bunch of bureaucrats in their jobs. How could that be? That lively, feisty presence who had encouraged them, pushed them, taught them that life was an adventure and that other people counted, was gunned down on a road like an animal and tossed aside as if her life meant nothing. And worse, there was no evidence of remorse. Not from those who murdered her, not from those who slandered her. For them it was just something that happened a long time ago—something that didn't need to be stirred up again.

In October 1978, a month after Tommy Rowe was indicted for Vi's murder, Jim suffered a massive stroke. He was taken to a rehabilitation center near his family home in Carbondale where two months later he had a second stroke and died. Shortly before the first stroke Jim had pleaded guilty in Recorder's Court to involvement in an arson-for-profit ring. In financial straits, he had turned to his old gambling friends for help and was caught trying to burn down a Detroit grocery store for the insurance money. When he died he was serving five years' probation. Jim Liuzzo was sixty-four years old. His youngest child was still a teenager.[1]

In 1965, Jim had laid his wife to rest in an expensive mausoleum in Holy Sepulchre Cemetery in Southfield, Michigan. When he died thirteen years later there was not enough money for him to be buried next to her. The money had gone into security guards, private schools, attorneys' fees, and medical bills.

In the summer of 1997 I drove to Southfield and through the iron gates of Holy Sepulchre to West Chapel. Inside there is a simple marker: Viola Gregg Liuzzo 1925–1965. The inscription is set in raised black letters against a gray marble wall. A small gold crucifix is fixed above Vi's name. Viola Liuzzo is surrounded by strangers.

I left the chapel sick at heart, but before I got halfway down the gravel path I spotted a granite marker. The section of the cemetery containing the mausoleum was rededicated in 1994 and is now named Holy Innocents in memory of abortion victims. The words on the marker lifted my spirits: "I will never forget you. Behold, I have inscribed you on the palm of my hand." The quoted passage is taken from the forty-ninth chapter of Isaiah, verses 15–18: "Does a woman forget her baby at the breast, or fail to cherish the son of her womb? Yet even if these forget, I will never forget you. Behold, I have inscribed you on the palm of my hand, your ramparts are always under my eye. Your rebuilders make haste, and your destroyers and despoilers depart. Look round about you, look, all are assembling, coming to you." Why did I assume she was among strangers? Viola Liuzzo never let anyone stay a stranger for long.

After Tommy Rowe was indicted by the Alabama grand jury in 1978, Tommy Liuzzo went to Lowndes to wait for the trial he was convinced would begin shortly. He was there when his father died and stayed for nearly a year, running through his savings. Tommy had worked as a truck driver in Michigan and made a good living, but the only jobs available in Lowndes paid minimum wage. He bounced from one job to another restlessly.

The black community tried to help Tommy—they remembered Vi—but as he repeatedly abandoned the work they provided they lost patience with him. Lowndes whites avoided him. Some, thinking he was back to avenge his mother's murder, speculated about what he might be planning to do. Tommy *looked* wild—he was big and burly like his father, with shoulder-length dark hair. He talked obsessively about the contract he believed the FBI had on his life because of what he knew.

Tommy insisted Rowe's trial would expose the FBI's plot to murder Viola Liuzzo to keep her from uniting southern blacks and northern labor unions. When he complained of receiving death threats from the government, even those closest to him believed he was coming apart. Tommy insisted that the federal government was delaying the trial because it wanted to kill him first to prevent his testimony about its plot to murder his mother. "The word's out over there in Selma that somebody's trying to kill me," he told journalist Johnny Green. "There's an elitist group of powerful people that create changes at a whim."[2]

Less than a year after moving to Lowndes, Tommy Liuzzo was no longer competent to work on the negligence suit, and Tony was forced to shoulder the family's legal battles for the next four years. Ultimately, Tommy shot up his cabin in Lowndes, swearing that the government had finally made its move. Then he packed up and went back to Detroit. In 1980 Tony filed a formal complaint against his brother, and after a hearing in Michigan, Tommy Liuzzo was committed to a state mental institution. He had completely lost touch with reality by the time he was twenty-six years old.

Tony's reaction to opening the old wounds was very different from Tommy's. The research he did in preparation for the family's lawsuit gave him new respect for his mother's courage and a deeper understanding of the cause that had meant so much to her.

In 1982 the federal Voting Rights Act that Vi had marched in support of was in danger of being repealed by Congress. The Act had demolished the southern system of officially sanctioned discrimination against blacks at the polls. It outlawed state-sanctioned literacy tests and poll and property taxes, and it empowered federal examiners to supervise voter registration if state officials failed to register citizens who were entitled to vote. Black voter registration soared from two million in 1965 to nine million in 1982.

In 1981 the Senate recommended extending the Act's provisions to continue federal review of election procedures in the twenty-two states that had been cited in 1965 for another twenty-five years. The cited twenty-two states still had a history of discrimination or low minority turnout at the polls. Without a formal extension, the Voting Rights Act's oversight provisions would cease to exist on August 6, 1982.

The House passed a renewal bill, but President Reagan argued that the original Voting Rights Act violated the constitutional provision that states should regulate their own elections. This was consistent with his New Federalism philosophy.

Tom Wicker, retired *New York Times* political columnist, wrote, "Reagan claimed with his accustomed brand of sincerity that he was 'in complete sympathy with the goals and purposes' of the voting rights legislation. What patriotic American could not be? He nevertheless professed to see in it 'flaws and faults' that he said were dangerous enough to cause him to oppose renewal altogether. He even suggested that the bill 'humiliated the south,' without reference to the humiliations for so long suffered by southern blacks turned away from the voting booth."[3]

There was real concern that the Act might not be renewed. In February 1982 Leon Hall of the Southern Christian Leadership Conference called Tony Liuzzo and informed him that a march was being organized to support renewal of the Voting Rights Act. Part would run from Selma to Montgomery along the same route as the 1965 march. Hall asked Tony if he would be willing to participate.

Tony arrived in Selma on February 14, 1982, and met the marchers at Brown Chapel just as his mother had done seventeen years earlier. More than one hundred people, many of whom had marched in 1965, crossed the Pettus Bridge and walked along Highway 80 for two days. On February 16, when they reached the spot called Big Swamp before the swamps were drained—the spot where Vi had been murdered— they stopped to lay a wreath. Tony said he could feel his mother's presence. "Her spirit was moving me," he said. "I thought I could feel her with me."[4]

The Reverend Joseph Lowrey, president of the SCLC, told the crowd: "Seventeen years ago a brave, gallant woman defied the traditions and chains of segregation and discrimination. She defied those who said white people ought not to get involved. She knew that injustice anywhere was fatal to justice everywhere. Our presence here testifies that her light still shines." When he finished the marchers sang "We Shall Overcome," and an old black man murmured, "Not in vain, not in vain."[5]

On June 18, 1982, the U.S. Congress adopted a bill extending for another twenty-five years the section of the Voting Rights Act of 1965 that required twenty-two states to submit changes in election procedures for federal approval. Several amendments expanding access to the ballot were also approved, including one that gave many non-English-speaking citizens the right to have ballots printed in their native languages.

A Legacy

The pattern of your essential self is woven by the threads of all that you have desired and loved, of all that you have done, believed, thought, felt, and willed.
—Dr. Elisabeth Kubler-Ross

Viola Liuzzo's murder provoked a popular wave of revulsion for the Klan that moved President Johnson to declare all-out war against it. On March 30, 1965, the day of Vi's funeral, the House Un-American Activities Committee voted unanimously to make a "full and formal investigation of the Ku Klux Klan organizations." Citing delivery of the Lane Report into the hands of the imperial wizard, Rep. Charles Longstreet Weltner, congressman from Georgia and a member of HUAC, declared, "One of the expressed purposes of this inquiry is to determine what connection or liaison there is between law enforcement agencies and the Klan organization. . . . The appearance of this dossier on Mrs. Liuzzo under these circumstances is most assuredly a matter that will be of deep interest to the Committee."

HUAC subpoenaed Imperial Wizard Robert Shelton in October 1965. He took the stand with a NEVER! button pinned to his lapel and claimed protection under the Fifth Amendment 158 times. He even took the Fifth when asked if he was ashamed of being a Klan member.

On February 2, 1966, the House voted to cite seven Klan leaders, including Shelton, for contempt of Congress after they refused to produce subpoenaed records. All were indicted by a federal grand jury and subsequently found guilty.

HUAC's Klan investigation increased the Justice Department's pressure on Congress to impose stricter penalties for civil rights murder under the Federal Conspiracy Act of 1870. President Johnson presented a bill to Congress shortly after Vi's death that expanded the Act to make civil rights murder a federal crime. Congress voted the bill into law after the murder of Dr. Martin Luther King Jr.

The circumstances of Viola Liuzzo's death also increased congressional support for passage of the Voting Rights Bill. Congressman David Mays of Virginia labeled it "a war measure aimed at the South," Howard

Calloway of Georgia insisted that there was "no moral or constitutional basis" for it, and Judge Leander Perez of Louisiana predicted it would be "but one step in a Communist plan for Negro domination of the South"; despite these protestations, the Voting Right Act of 1965 was passed.

The Act changed the course of southern politics. Following the arrival of a federal examiner in Selma, the percentage of voting-age blacks registered rose from less than 10 percent to more than 60 percent in just two months. By 1966 more than nine thousand blacks were registered in Dallas County.

If Viola Liuzzo's death became the catalyst for so much important change, why has she been forgotten? Though J. Edgar Hoover could be blamed for molding her tarnished public image, that does not explain why the American people only too willingly accepted it.

Viola Liuzzo was consistently a frame out of sync in her own time. Even before her reputation was ruined by the FBI she was virtually useless as a symbol for the civil rights movement. Her circumstances, background, class, and education were all unexceptional.

During the summer of 1964 James Chaney, Michael Schwerner, and Andrew Goodman became, like Vi Liuzzo, caught up in the maelstrom of history. Like Vi, to Mississippi segregationists the young men symbolized all the white northern agitators pouring into the Magnolia State to inflame an "otherwise docile" black population. Unlike Vi, however, these men were also embraced as powerful symbols by the civil rights movement.

Goodman, Schwerner, and Chaney were all young men of promise. A white activist college student, a selfless white social worker, and a black community worker determined to fight for the freedom of his people— these men elicited positive images. Viola Liuzzo, on the other hand, was too old, too pushy, too independent, and she trampled on too many social norms.

Vi had ventured beyond the role of wife and mother to demonstrate on behalf of a social movement that a majority of white Americans felt was already moving too fast. Her activism couldn't be chalked up to youthful idealism. Hers threatened the family, the protected status of women, and the precarious balance of race relations. Americans, especially white American women, could not afford to make her a hero. To do so would be to invite questions about their own lives, values, and priorities. Everyone understood that female independence threatened the very heart of American society: the family.

Image is critical in American political life. Consider Rosa Parks, the mother of the civil rights movement, who refused to give up her seat to a white man and thus ignited the Montgomery Bus Boycott. Mrs. Parks wasn't the first black woman to take such an action; she was, however, the *right* black woman. Responsible, articulate, a past secretary of the NAACP who had been married a long time, Mrs. Parks was someone the segregationists could investigate forever without uncovering a hint of scandal. Claudette Colvin, the fifteen-year-old high school student who had refused to give up her seat on a city bus a few weeks before Mrs. Parks's arrest, is not so well remembered. Though Claudette's courage was never questioned, when it was discovered that she was pregnant and unmarried the NAACP's legal defense fund rejected her as a test candidate for a suit that was bound to generate extensive publicity. Claudette Colvin's image was all wrong.[6]

Schwerner, Chaney, and Goodman were young, bright, and committed. Their deaths were emblematic of wasted potential, brutally crushed courage, and interracial solidarity. Their images would inspire more students, faculty, and middle-class professionals to go south in 1964 and more northern sympathizers to write checks. Viola Liuzzo was thirty-nine (considered middle-aged in 1965) and expected to stay home. Her death opened her motives, stability, and judgment to speculation. The circumstances of her death raised more questions than spirits.

The Goodman, Schwerner, and Chaney families worked hard to ensure that these young men would not be forgotten. Dr. Carolyn Goodman, Andrew's mother, gave interviews to the press and on television, wrote about him for *Good Housekeeping,* and appeared at the dedication of memorials to all three young men, as did Rita Schwerner, widow of Michael. Mrs. Fannie Lee Chaney, James's mother, and his younger brother Ben continued to demonstrate for voting rights in Meridian, Mississippi. All three families supported the young men's involvement in civil rights causes.

Jim Liuzzo, on the other hand, had always been ambivalent about his wife's involvement. After Vi's murder, Jim found himself continually defending her reputation, refuting vicious rumors, and trying to protect his children. He had little time, energy, or opportunity to worry about her immortality. Viola Liuzzo's children were taunted by their classmates, shunned by their neighbors, and shamed by the cloud of suspicion that hung over their mother's activism.

Vi's outwardly conventional blue-collar lifestyle rendered her uninteresting even to the feminists, who never acknowledged her. Yet, ironically, Vi was murdered precisely *because* she afforded such a clear symbol to the segregationists; the image of a white female outside agitator driving after dark with a local black activist resonated for them. The Klansmen chose her precisely because she would make a good example and send a clear message that northern whites and southern blacks would understand. Viola Liuzzo fell through nearly every conceivable crack in our image-conscious culture, and within a year of her brutal murder she dropped out of memory.

Vi's struggles with the people she loved were as critical to her quest to understand herself and her world as the intellectual and spiritual growth she achieved on the Wayne State campus. It was all one piece. She absorbed every experience—even those that threatened to destroy her—and grew because of them. My effort to understand her forced me to grow as well. Like her, I have come to accept that sometimes there are no good solutions and to believe that for good or ill human beings are inescapably interconnected.

Viola Liuzzo's critics were right when they said she was unpredictable but wrong when they called her irresponsible. Who of us hasn't had trouble with our spouse? Our children? Who hasn't known a co-worker out to get us? Who hasn't been overwhelmed? Who hasn't dreamed of a richer life? Who hasn't made bad choices? alienated family and friends? And who of us hasn't ached to make things right again?

Throughout her short life Viola Liuzzo retained a resilience that enabled her to learn from painful experience and to recoup. She never let the complexities of life paralyze her. She wasn't afraid to make decisions or to act on them.

Vi Liuzzo's tragedy was that white society, even in death, wished she would just go away. Her murder was an embarrassment to the federal government, an inconvenience to the Alabama state prosecutor's office, and frustrating to the media who could not get a handle on who this woman was: the amoral adventuress described by the FBI and the Selma police or the woman her family, friends, and neighbors back in Detroit called "good hearted."

Like many older white female civil rights activists, Vi became energized by the possibility that life could be lived differently. Participation in the movement made her aware of what organization and solidarity could accomplish. Some of her contemporaries went on to apply those lessons to the women's movement. The National Organization for Women held its first meeting in 1966. In 1970 Betty Friedan wrote, "we are a revolution for all, not for an exceptional few . . . we do not speak for every woman in America, but we speak for the *right* of every woman in America to become all she is capable of becoming."[7]

It is hard to imagine Vi Liuzzo not wanting to get involved in something like that. When I asked Sarah Evans what she thought Vi might have done if she had lived, she thought for a minute. "Well, she would have finished her degree—that's for sure—and I think maybe she would have become a teacher or a journalist after that. Maybe she would even have gone into politics. Vi always wanted to be involved. She wanted to be part of the civil rights movement—and she was. She did that. Even though people turned what she did inside out and we couldn't even get a street named after her here in Detroit, it hardly matters now. She was part of the movement. People boast all their lives that they marched at Selma. Well, she did that. She was there."

As I talked to people in the North, Southeast, and Midwest, what seemed most consistent to me was that black people over forty remember Viola Liuzzo and white people over forty—for the most part—don't know who she is. To those blacks she is unquestionably a positive figure. They don't weigh what she thought or the choices she made or how she reacted to life's difficulties. They don't really care about those things. What they remember is that she *did something*. She went south when Dr. King asked for help, she rolled up her sleeves and went to work. Her life *meant* something. That is exactly the way I think she would like to be remembered.

All of mid-century America's ambivalence about dissenters, protesters, and "cranks" is reflected in the experience of Viola Gregg Liuzzo. Like Dr. Martin Luther King Jr. she believed in the power of confrontation. Making injustice dramatically visible was her avenue of social protest. It took a few attempts to focus her activism, but in the end she got it right.

Viola Liuzzo made mistakes, of course, but through her struggles and searching one glimpses the sincerity of 1960s white activism at its best. She expressed her social concerns through direct action and her caring through individual acts of support and love. This, I believe, was the spiritual dimension that Rev. Malcolm Boyd recognized in her.

I believe her life *became* heroic, and that has very little to do with the circumstances surrounding her death. As Rev. Boyd told his students at Wayne State more than thirty years ago, there are no born heroes. We are what we *do*, not what we think or what we say. Sarah, Tyrone, Penny, Mary, and Sally told me over and over again, Vi was *real*, she was *genuine*, she really cared.

History may be ambivalent about Viola Liuzzo's legacy, but for me the question is settled. I've fallen (maybe jumped) into the biographer's trap. Somewhere along my journey I came to love my subject, and I lost all my objectivity.

In 1965 when I read about her tragic death it was her personal courage that I admired. I wanted to know somebody like her—a woman who wasn't afraid. My early image of Viola Liuzzo was of someone who refused to be trapped, smothered, or suffocated—all the things I was terrified of. As it turns out, I wasn't too far off the mark.

Many years passed before I came to respect Viola Liuzzo's dedication to social justice. I responded to her death with the hope that if one woman with a husband and family was able to muster the courage to travel thousands of miles to take an independent action separate from the life of her husband and children then maybe I could too.

Vi gave me the hope that maybe my life wouldn't have to be constricted by the boundaries of appropriateness, acceptability, and inoffensiveness.

Maybe I could find a partner to *share* my life. Maybe I could find a purpose that went beyond the kitchen and would last after my youngest child left home. Maybe I could live a life that would cause my children to admire me. Viola Liuzzo made me aware that other women—older than I and more settled—were longing for some of these same things.

Before reading about her I never believed any of that was possible. I had certainly never seen it in Queens. I could say, with Betty Friedan, "I never knew a woman, when I was growing up, who used her mind, played her own part in the world, and also loved, and had children."[8] What resonated for me was Viola Liuzzo's determination to make her life mean something. I tried not to think too hard about what that determination had cost her.

Viola Liuzzo possessed deep sensibilities, a short temper, abiding warmth, painful restlessness, and a strong moral compass. Once upon a time she did something extraordinary for civil rights, for social justice, and for a frightened young woman from Queens.

It wasn't easy knowing you, or even hearing you. I felt in fact, that you were often strong-willed, uncharitable, and impolite. But I saw you pouring out your life. I resented that too, as I safely clutched my own. But I did see you, though sometimes I didn't want you to know it.

Yes, I heard the criticism—and I joined in. At times I thought I hated you, because what you said and did cut so painfully against my mask, my security, my being.

I miss you very much. Thank you—for who you were and whose you were. You wouldn't want me to wish you "peace," and I could never think of you in any misalliance with a false truce or easy compromise.

But I do, with all my heart, wish you peace with deep restlessness, a cock crowing at down to announce battle, and love to heal all the necessary wounds.
—Rev. Malcolm Boyd, "To a Prophet Dying Young"

Epilogue

Viola Liuzzo's five children are spread out across the country. Mary, Penny, and Sally have settled on the West Coast, Tommy has returned to Alabama, and Tony has remained in Michigan.

At a time when many Baby Boomers are trying to finesse early retirement, Penny has plans to open her own catering business. Mary is a successful executive whose responsibilities keep her traveling most of the time. Sally is working as a regional manager for a cable company while completing her bachelor's degree.

Vi's oldest grandchildren are in their twenties now (one is married); the youngest are in elementary school. Nearly ten years ago, on March 25 Sally gave birth to twin daughters. None of the sisters believes the date was coincidental. "Mom didn't want us to remember March 25th with sorrow," Mary said. "I don't know how, but she arranged for those two little girls to arrive on the same date she was murdered." Sally named one baby Christina and the other Sarah, after her mother's closest friend—the friend who kept her promise and raised Vi's youngest child.

In 1995 Tony Liuzzo, once a long-haul truck driver, became vice president of Ithemba Productions, a company that conducts diversity training workshops for corporations and schools. He and a colleague recently taught a course on the civil rights movement at Battle Creek's Kellogg Community College. Tony continues to struggle with the Detroit City Council to get a street named after his mother. He offered to donate his copy of the FBI report of his mother's murder and all the news articles he compiled during his research for the family's civil suit against the federal government to the Wayne State University Archives. As of this writing they are not interested. Tony is angry and disappointed, but he perseveres. He is planning to write his own book about Viola Liuzzo.

When I asked Sarah's grandson, Tyrone, why he thought Tommy went back to Alabama, he said Tommy recently told him that people in Alabama treat him like a human being. "Tom said they were kinder than the people of Detroit had ever been," Tyrone shrugged. "Who would believe it?"

In 1996 the U.S. Congress designated the Selma-to-Montgomery National Historic Trail along Highway 80 in Alabama. The Federal Highway Administration authorized almost three million dollars for the project. It will ultimately include a historical center and markers for twelve sites along the route. Viola Liuzzo's memorial marker sits right in the middle of the trail. She is back in the heart of the action. Representative John Lewis of Georgia, who was chairman of the Student Non-Violent Coordinating Committee in 1965, who was beaten on the Pettus Bridge on Bloody Sunday, and who marched beside Dr. King into Montgomery, proposed the designation of the trail. "People have got to have a feeling that they're walking on precious ground, holy soil in a sense," Rep. Lewis said. "This is where people suffered, this is where people bled, this is where a woman gave her life—died—in the cause of the right to vote."

In 1997 the Liuzzo marker was defaced once again. Someone painted the flag of the Confederacy across the front of it. But it is still standing. The SCLC has decided not to remove the paint this time. They want to leave it as a reminder that the struggle isn't over.

Notes

Chapter One. The Black Belt

1. Stephen B. Oates, *Let the Trumpet Sound: The Life of Martin Luther King, Jr.* (New York: Harper and Row, 1982), 67.

2. *Detroit Free Press*, November 5, 1989.

3. *Washington Post*, November 5, 1989.

4. Ibid.

5. Senator James Eastland subpoenaed Cliff and Virginia Durr to appear before his Senate Investigating Committee hearings in New Orleans in March 1954. It was Eastland's attempt to become the Senator Joe McCarthy of the South. The hearings yielded nothing, but the "red taint" stuck to the Durrs.

6. Interview with Virginia Durr, April 12, 1994.

7. Charles W. Eagles, *Outside Agitator: Jon Daniels and the Civil Rights Movement in Alabama* (Chapel Hill: University of North Carolina Press, 1993), 112. For an excellent history of Lowndes County see chapter 4 of Eagles's book.

8. Ibid., 113.

9. Robert Penn Warren, *Who Speaks for the Negro?* (New York: Random House, 1965), 121.

10. Stetson Kennedy, *Jim Crow Guide: The Way It Was* (Boca Raton: Florida Atlantic University Press, 1992), 97.

11. Ibid., 98.

12. Stephen L. Longenecker, *Selma's Peacemaker: Ralph Smeltzer and Civil Rights Mediation* (Philadelphia: Temple University Press, 1987), 37.

13. *New York Times*, March 10, 1965.

14. Interview with Joanne Bland, tour director, National Voting Rights Museum and Institute, April 13, 1994.

15. Sheyann Webb and Rachel West Nelson, *Selma, Lord, Selma: Girlhood Memories of the Civil Rights Days* (Tuscaloosa: University of Alabama Press, 1980), 100–102.

16. *Detroit Free Press*, March 4, 1990.

17. *New York Times*, August 2, 1994.

Chapter Two. The Story

1. *New York Herald Tribune*, April 7, 1965.

2. *Chicago Tribune*, April 5, 1965.

3. Morris Dees, *A Season for Justice* (New York: Charles Scribner's Sons, 1991), 322.

4. Ralph David Abernathy, *And the Walls Came Tumbling Down* (New York: Harper and Row, 1989), 358.

5. Jack Mendelsohn, *The Martyrs: Sixteen Who Gave Their Lives for Racial Justice* (New York: Harper and Row, 1966), 169.

6. *New York Times*, April 23, 1965.

7. Mendelsohn, *The Martyrs*, 191.

8. Bill Stanton, *Klanwatch: Bringing the Ku Klux Klan to Justice* (New York: Weidenfeld, 1991), 244.

9. Dees, *A Season for Justice*, 324.

10. Stanton, *Klanwatch*, 225.

11. Dees, *A Season for Justice*, 323.

12. *The FBI File on the KKK Murder of Viola Liuzzo*, microfilm released by Scholarly Resources, Inc., New York, 1990. This file contains the detailed FBI investigation of the Liuzzo murder, newspaper clippings, background information on the Liuzzo family, and memos from FBI officials interpreting the information and directing the case. This file has provided much of the background information about the investigation, trials, and campaign to slander Mrs. Liuzzo.

13. Dees, *A Season for Justice*, 322.

14. *Detroit News*, March 28, 1965.

15. *New York Journal American*, March 28, 1965.

16. *Washington Post*, March 21, 1983.

17. *Detroit News*, March 28, 1965.

Chapter Three. Unlocking the Past

1. *Detroit Free Press*, March 26, 1965.

2. *Detroit Free Press*, May 12, 1965.

3. *The FBI File on the KKK Murder of Viola Liuzzo.*

4. James Tracy, *Direct Action: Radical Pacifism from the Union Eight to the Chicago Seven* (Chicago: University of Chicago Press, 1996), 110–11.

5. *Detroit News*, March 31, 1965.

6. Anthony Ripley, "The Enigma of Mrs. Liuzzo," *Detroit News*, May 23, 1965.

7. Mendelsohn, *The Martyrs*, 178.

8. Ibid., 179.

9. Interview with Penny Liuzzo, August 11, 1995.

10. Garry Wills, *The Second Civil War: Arming for Armageddon* (New York: New American Library, 1968), 52–53.

11. B. J. Widick, *Detroit: City of Race and Class Violence* (Detroit: Wayne State University Press, 1989), 184.

12. *Wayne State University Daily Collegian*, April 7, 1965.

13. Interview with Sarah Evans and Tyrone Green, September 18, 1995.

Chapter Four. Outside Agitator

1. The only published accounts of Viola Liuzzo's life are Beatrice Siegel's *Murder on the Highway: The Viola Liuzzo Story* (New York: Four Winds Press, 1993), written for young-adult readers; a chapter in Mendelsohn's *The Martyrs* titled "Only a Housewife"; and an entry in Sara Bullard's *Free at Last: A History of the Civil Rights Movement and Those Who Died in the Struggle* (New York: Oxford University Press, 1993), 80–81. I have drawn extensively on these sources and background articles that appeared in the *Detroit Times* and *Detroit Free Press* at the time of her murder for the biographical material about Mrs. Liuzzo. Where I speculate about her motives, her thoughts, and her insights, I do so based on these resources and on the discussions I had with Sarah Evans, Tyrone Green, Penny Liuzzo Herrington, Mary Liuzzo Ashley, and Sally Liuzzo Prado.

2. Kennedy, *Jim Crow Guide*, 58–71.

3. Robert H. Mast, ed., *Detroit Lives* (Philadelphia: Temple University Press, 1994), 198–99.

4. Widick, *Detroit*, 103.

5. Background information about the Lane Report is taken from Walter Rugaber's articles in the *Detroit Free Press* from May 12 through May 28, 1965, and from *The FBI File on the KKK Murder of Viola Liuzzo.*

6. Wills, *The Second Civil War*, 47–48.

7. Stephan Lesher, *George Wallace: American Populist* (New York: Addison-Wesley, 1994), 339.

8. William Bradford Huie, *Three Lives for Mississippi* (New York: Signet Books, 1964), 127.

9. Mast, *Detroit Lives*, 319.

10. Alphonso Pinckney, *The Committed: White Activists in the Civil Rights Movement* (New Haven, Conn.: College and University Press, 1968), 51.

11. Mendelsohn, *The Martyrs*, 181.

12. *Detroit News*, March 26, 1965.

13. Mendelsohn, *The Martyrs*, 181.

14. Phyllis Chesler, *Women and Madness* (New York: Doubleday, 1972), 167.

15. Hendrik M. Ruitenbeek, ed., *Going Crazy: The Radical Therapy of R. D. Laing and Others* (New York: Bantam Books, 1972), 234.

16. Ibid., 237.

17. Ibid., 245–46.

18. Ken Fireman, "Babe, I'm Going to Alabama," *Detroit Free Press*, March 28, 1982.

19. Betty Friedan, *The Feminine Mystique* (New York: W. W. Norton, 1963), 15–32.

20. Ripley, "The Enigma of Mrs. Liuzzo."

Chapter Five. Never!

1. *New York Times*, May 4, 1965.

2. *New York Times*, March 28, 1965.

3. Murray Kempton, "Trial of a Klansman," *New Republic*, May 22, 1965, 10–13.

4. *Time*, May 14, 1965.

5. *Selma Times Journal*, September 15, 1965.

6. Michael Novick, *White Lies, White Power: The Fight against White Supremacy and Reactionary Violence* (Monroe, Maine: Common Courage Press, 1995), 45.

7. *New York Times*, May 6, 1965.

8. Dees, *A Season for Justice*, 260.

9. Seth Cagin and Philip Dray, *We Are Not Afraid: The Story of Goodman, Schwerner and Chaney and the Civil Rights Campaign for Mississippi* (New York: Macmillan, 1988), 442.

10. Richard K. Tucker, *The Dragon and the Cross: The Rise and Fall of the Ku Klux Klan in Middle America* (Hamden, Conn.: Archon Books, 1991), 189–90.

11. "The Informer," *Time*, April 30, 1965.

12. Kempton, "Trial of a Klansman," 10–13.

13. This was a reference to the NEVER! button Sheriff Clark wore on his uniform. The button was popular among segregationists, making very clear their response to the *Brown vs. Board of Education* decision.

14. *Newsweek*, May 17, 1965.

15. *New York Herald Tribune*, May 9, 1965.

16. *Time*, May 14, 1965.

17. *New York Times*, May 9, 1965.

18. CBS Reports, "The KKK: The Invisible Empire," September 21, 1965.

19. William H. McIlhany, *Klandestine* (New Rochelle, N.Y.: Arlington House, 1975), 163.

20. Mendelsohn, *The Martyrs*, 194.

21. Stokely Carmichael and Charles V. Hamilton, *Black Power* (New York: Random House, 1967), 91–100.

22. Clayborne Carson, *In Struggle: SNCC and the Black Awakening of the 1960s* (Cambridge, Mass.: Harvard University Press, 1981), 165.

23. Fred Powledge, *Free at Last? The Civil Rights Movement and the People Who Made It* (Boston: Little Brown, 1991), 635.

24. Carson, *In Struggle*, 166.

25. *Los Angeles Times*, August 12, 1965.

26. Powledge, *Free at Last?* 481–82, 489–90, 494.

27. Eagles, *Outside Agitator*, 245.

28. *Newsweek*, November 1, 1965.

29. *The FBI File on the KKK Murder of Viola Liuzzo*.

30. Powledge, *Free at Last?* 289–90.

31. Lesher, *George Wallace*, 343–44.

32. *New York Times*, December 4, 1965.

33. *The FBI File on the KKK Murder of Viola Liuzzo*.

34. Ibid.

35. Mendelsohn, *The Martyrs*, 195.

36. *Detroit News*, March 27, 1965.

37. James Washington, ed., *I Have a Dream: Writings and Speeches That Changed the World* (San Francisco: Harper, 1986), 85.

38. Jack Mendelsohn, *Why I Am a Unitarian Universalist* (New York: Thomas Nelson and Sons, 1964), 18.

39. Duncan Howlett, *No Greater Love: The James Reeb Story* (New York: Harper and Row, 1966), 51.

40. Background information on Malcolm Boyd is taken from the *Detroit Free Press*, June 25, 1961, September 12, 1961, January 17, 1963.

41. Malcolm Boyd, *The Hunger, the Thirst* (New York: Morehouse-Barlow, 1964).

42. *Wayne State University Daily Collegian*, March 12, 1965.

43. Ibid., March 15, 1965.

44. *The FBI File on the KKK Murder of Viola Liuzzo*.

45. Siegel, *Murder on the Highway: The Viola Liuzzo Story* (New York: Four Winds Press, 1993), 54.

46. G. B. Leonard, "Journey of Conscience: Midnight Plane to Alabama," *Nation*, May 10, 1965.

47. *Detroit Free Press*, March 27, 1965.

48. *Montgomery Advertiser*, March 23, 1965.

49. *New York Times*, March 30, 1965.

50. Ibid.

51. Peter Wyden, *Bay of Pigs: The Untold Story* (New York, 1979), 59–64.

52. *Time*, May 5, 1965.

53. Howell Raines, *My Soul Is Rested: Movement Days in the Deep South Remembered* (New York: Penguin Books, 1977), 218–19.

54. Everett Tilson, *Segregation and the Bible* (New York: Abingdon Press, 1958), 35.

55. Eddy L. Harris, *South of Haunted Dreams* (New York: Simon and Schuster, 1993), 244–45.

56. James Silver, *Mississippi: The Closed Society* (New York: Harcourt, Brace and World, 1963), 67.

57. Calvin C. Hernton, *Sex and Racism in America* (New York: Anchor Books, 1965), 113.

58. Allison Davis, Burleigh Gardner, and Mary Gardner, *Deep South* (Chicago: University of Chicago Press, 1941), 122.

59. Arnold Rose, *The Negro in America* (Boston: Beacon Press, 1944), 137.

60. Peter Levy, *Let Freedom Ring: A Documentary History of the Modern Civil Rights Movement* (New York: Praeger, 1992), 214–15.

Chapter Six. The Great March

1. *The FBI File on the KKK Murder of Viola Liuzzo.*

2. *Detroit News,* May 23, 1965.

3. Amelia Boynton Robinson, *Bridge across Jordan* (Washington, D.C.: Schiller Institute Press, 1991), 271.

4. Mendelsohn, *The Martyrs,* 183.

5. Oates, *Let the Trumpet Sound,* 346.

6. Charles King Jr., *Fire in My Bones* (Grand Rapids, Mich.: William B. Eerdmens, 1983), 57.

7. *Selma Times Journal,* March 22, 1965.

8. Longenecker, *Selma's Peacemaker,* 36.

9. *Saturday Evening Post,* May 22, 1965.

10. *The FBI File on the KKK Murder of Viola Liuzzo.*

11. CBS Reports, "Who Speaks for Birmingham?" May 15, 1961.

12. Juan Williams, *Eyes on the Prize: America's Civil Rights Years: 1954–1965* (New York: Penguin Books, 1987), 282.

13. *New York Journal American,* March 22, 1965.

14. Boynton Robinson, *Bridge across Jordan,* 266.

15. Renata Adler, "Letter from Selma," *New Yorker,* April 10, 1965.

16. *Montgomery Advertiser,* March 26, 1965.

17. Adler, "Letter from Selma."

18. Abernathy, *And the Walls Came Tumbling Down,* 349.

19. *New York Times,* March 25, 1965.

20. Andrew Young, *An Easy Burden: The Civil Rights Movement and the Transformation of America* (New York: Harper Collins, 1996), 366.

21. *New York Times,* March 25, 1965.

22. *Detroit News,* March 31, 1965.

23. Abernathy, *And the Walls Came Tumbling Down,* 491–92.

24. Young, *An Easy Burden,* 366–67.

25. Boynton Robinson, *Bridge across Jordan,* 267.

26. CBS News Special Report, "March on Montgomery," March 25, 1965.

27. Oates, *Let the Trumpet Sound,* 353–54.

28. *The FBI File on the KKK Murder of Viola Liuzzo.*

29. *Alabama Journal,* March 22, 1965.

30. James Peck, *Freedom Ride* (New York: Simon and Schuster, 1962), 154–55.

31. Bullard, *Free at Last,* 77.

32. Carson, *In Struggle*, 161.

33. David L. Lewis, *King: A Biography* (Urbana: University of Illinois Press, 1978), 292–93.

34. David Garrow, *Bearing the Cross* (New York: Vintage Books, 1986), 414–20.

35. Raines, *My Soul Is Rested*, 219.

36. Ellen Levine, *Freedom's Children: Young Civil Rights Activists Tell Their Own Stories* (New York: G. P. Putnam's Sons, 1993), 121.

37. Coretta Scott King, *My Life with Martin Luther King, Jr.*, rev. ed. (New York: Puffin Books, 1993), 250.

38. Martin Luther King Jr., *Where Do We Go from Here? Chaos or Community* (New York: Harper and Row, 1967), 5.

39. *New York Herald Tribune*, August 22, 1965.

Chapter Seven. What Really Happened?

1. James Q. Wilson, *The Investigators: Managing FBI and Narcotics Agents* (New York: Basic Books, 1978), 179.

2. John Moffatt Mecklin, *The Ku Klux Klan: A Study of the American Mind* (New York: Harcourt Brace, 1924), 47–49.

3. Novick, *White Lies, White Power*, 60–65.

4. David Garrow, *The FBI and Martin Luther King, Jr.* (New York: Penguin Books, 1981), 225.

5. Howard Zinn, *SNCC: The New Abolitionists* (Boston: Beacon Press, 1964), 195.

6. *Chicago Tribune*, March 29, 1965.

7. David Farber, *The Age of Great Dreams: America in the 1960s* (New York: Farrar, Straus and Giroux, 1994), 98.

8. Garrow, *The FBI and Martin Luther King, Jr.*, 212–13.

9. Ibid., 225.

10. Ibid., 135–36.

11. Powledge, *Free at Last?* 272.

12. Stanton, *Klanwatch*, 222.

13. *New York Newsday*, September 22, 1996.

14. *Time*, May 14, 1965.

15. Robert M. Bleiweiss, *Marching to Freedom: The Life of Martin Luther King, Jr.* (New York: Signet Books, 1968), 136.

16. For the story of Tony Liuzzo's research and his theories about his mother's murder see Johnny Green, "Did the FBI Kill Viola Liuzzo?" *Playboy,* October 1980, 162, 164.

17. Charles E. Fager, *Selma, 1965: The March That Changed the South* (Boston: Beacon Press, 1974), 159.

18. Raines, *My Soul Is Rested,* 220.

19. Powledge, *Free at Last?* 273.

20. *The FBI File on the KKK Murder of Viola Liuzzo.*

21. Gerold Frank, *An American Death* (New York: Doubleday, 1972), 165n.

22. Raines, *My Soul Is Rested,* 405.

23. Young, *An Easy Burden,* 281.

24. Williams, *Eyes on the Prize,* 283.

25. Powledge, *Free at Last?* 627.

26. Hernton, *Sex and Racism in America,* 69–71.

27. *New York Times,* December 16, 1980.

28. *Detroit Free Press,* March 22, 1983.

29. *New York Times,* March 27, 1983.

30. Ibid., March 31, 1983.

31. *Washington Post,* May 28, 1983. .

32. *New York Times,* May 28, 1983.

33. *Detroit Free Press,* May 28, 1983.

34. For eyewitness accounts of the violence against the Freedom Riders in Anniston and Birmingham see Peck, *Freedom Ride,* 114–32, and Dorothy B. Kaufman, *The First Freedom Ride: The Walter Bergman Story* (Detroit: ACLU Fund Press, 1989), 1–9, 146–202.

35. Eyes on the Prize Video Series, *Ain't Scared of Your Jails, 1960–1961.*

36. *Washington Post,* February 9, 1984.

37. Siegel, *Murder on the Highway,* 115.

38. *Washington Post,* June 5, 1983.

39. Kaufman, *The First Freedom Ride,* 100.

40. David Chalmers, *Hooded Americanism: The History of the Ku Klux Klan* (Durham, N.C.: Duke University Press, 1987), 400.

Chapter Eight. Coda

1. *Detroit News,* December 11, 1978.

2. Green, "Did the FBI Kill Viola Liuzzo?" 185.

3. Tom Wicker, *Tragic Failure: Racial Integration in America* (New York: William Morrow, 1996), 57.

4. Fireman, "Babe, I'm Going to Alabama."

5. Ibid.

6. Garrow, *Bearing the Cross*, 15–16.

7. Betty Friedan, "Our Revolution Is Unique," in *Voices of the New Feminism*, edited by Mary Lou Thompson (Boston: Beacon Press, 1970).

8. Friedan, *The Feminine Mystique*, 75.

Bibliography

Abernathy, Ralph David. *And the Walls Came Tumbling Down.* New York: Harper and Row, 1989.

Adler, Renata. "Letter from Selma." *The New Yorker,* April 10, 1965.

Albert, Peter, and Ronald Hoffman, eds. *We Shall Overcome: MLK and the Black Freedom Struggle.* New York: Pantheon Books, 1990.

Bell, Derrick. *And We Are Not Saved: The Illusive Quest for Racial Justice.* New York: Basic Books, 1987.

Blackstock, Nelson. *COINTELPRO: The FBI's Secret War on Political Freedom.* New York: Random House, 1976.

Bleiweiss, Robert, ed. *Marching to Freedom: The Life of Martin Luther King, Jr.* New York: Signet Books, 1968.

Bloom, Jack. *Class Race and the Civil Rights Movement.* Bloomington: Indiana University Press, 1987.

Blumberg, Rhoda Lois. *Civil Rights: The 1960's Freedom Struggle.* Boston: Twayne Publishers, 1991.

Boyd, Malcolm. *The Hunger, the Thirst.* New York: Morehouse-Barlow, 1964.

Branch, Taylor. *Parting the Waters: America in the King Years, 1954–1963.* New York: Simon and Schuster, 1988.

Breslin, Jimmy. *The World of Jimmy Breslin.* New York: Viking Press, 1967.

Brink, William, and Louis Harris. *The Negro Revolution in America.* New York: Simon and Schuster, 1964.

Brooks, Thomas. *Walls Come Tumbling Down: A History of the Civil Rights Movement, 1940–1970.* New York: Prentice Hall, 1974.

Bullard, Sara. *Free at Last: A History of the Civil Rights Movement and Those Who Died in the Struggle.* New York: Oxford University Press, 1993.

———, ed. *The Ku Klux Klan: A History of Racism and Violence.* Montgomery: Klanwatch, 1991.

Cagin, Seth, and Philip Dray. *We Are Not Afraid: The Story of Goodman,*

Schwerner and Chaney and the Civil Rights Campaign for Mississippi. New York: Macmillan, 1988.

Califano, Joseph A., Jr. *The Triumph and Tragedy of Lyndon Johnson: The White House Years*. New York: Simon and Schuster, 1991.

Capeci, Dominic J., Jr., and Martha Wilkerson. *Layered Violence: The Detroit Rioters of 1943*. Jackson: University Press of Mississippi, 1991.

Carmichael, Stokely, and Charles V. Hamilton. *Black Power*. New York: Random House, 1967.

Carson, Clayborne. *In Struggle: SNCC and the Black Awakening of the 1960s*. Cambridge, Mass.: Harvard University Press, 1981.

Carson, Clayborne, et al., eds. *The Eyes on the Prize Civil Rights Reader*. New York: Penguin Books, 1991.

CBS News Special Report. "March on Montgomery." March 25, 1965.

CBS Reports. "The KKK: The Invisible Empire." September 21, 1965.

———. "Who Speaks for Birmingham?" May 15, 1961.

Chalmers, David M. *And the Crooked Places Made Straight: The Struggle for Social Change in the 1960s*. Baltimore: Johns Hopkins University Press, 1991

———. *Hooded Americanism: The History of the Ku Klux Klan*. 3d ed. Durham, N.C.: Duke University Press, 1987.

Chesler, Phyllis. *Women and Madness*. New York: Doubleday, 1972.

Chestnut, J. L., and Julia Cass. *Black in Selma*. New York: Anchor Books, 1990.

Cobbs, Elizabeth H., and Petric J. Smith. *Long Time Coming: An Insider's Story of the Birmingham Church Bombing That Rocked the World*. Birmingham, Ala.: Crane Hill, 1994.

Coffin, William Sloane, Jr. *Once to Every Man: A Memoir*. New York: Atheneum, 1977.

Crawford, Vicki L., Jacqueline A. Rouse, and Barbara Woods, eds. *Women in the Civil Rights Movement, 1941–1965*. Bloomington: Indiana University Press, 1993.

Davis, Allison, Burleigh Gardner, and Mary Gardner. *Deep South*. Chicago: University of Chicago Press, 1941.

Dees, Morris. *A Season for Justice*. New York: Charles Scribner's Sons, 1991.

Demerath, N. J., III, Gerald Marwell, and Michael T. Aiken. *Dynamics of Idealism: White Activists in a Black Movement*. San Francisco: Jossey Bass, 1971.

De Toledano, Ralph. *J. Edgar Hoover: The Man in His Time*. New Rochelle, N.Y.: Arlington House, 1973.

Dollard, John. *Caste and Class in a Southern Town*. New York: Harper and Brothers, 1949.

Dorman, Michael. *We Shall Overcome*. New York: Dell, 1964.

Durr, Virginia Foster. *Outside the Magic Circle*. Tuscaloosa: University of Alabama Press, 1985.

Eagles, Charles W. *Outside Agitator: Jon Daniels and the Civil Rights Movement in Alabama*. Chapel Hill: University of North Carolina Press, 1993.

Evans, Sara. *Personal Politics: The Roots of Women's Liberation in the Civil Rights Movement and the New Left*. New York: Vintage Books, 1980.

Eyes on the Prize Video Series. Blackside Productions, Boston.

Fager, Charles E. *Selma, 1965: The March That Changed the South*. Boston: Beacon Press, 1974.

————. *White Reflections on Black Power*. Grand Rapids, Mich.: William B. Eerdmans, 1967.

Farber, David. *The Age of Great Dreams: America in the 1960s*. New York: Farrar, Straus and Giroux, 1994.

Farmer, James. *Lay Bare the Heart: An Autobiography of the Civil Rights Movement*. New York: Arbor House, 1985.

The FBI File on the KKK Murder of Viola Liuzzo. Microfilm. New York: Scholarly Resources, 1990.

Fireman, Ken. "Babe, I'm Going to Alabama." *Detroit Free Press*, March 28, 1982.

Frank, Gerold. *An American Death*. New York: Doubleday, 1972.

Freeman, Jo. *The Politics of Women's Liberation*. New York: Longman Press, 1975.

Friedan, Betty. *The Feminine Mystique*. New York: W. W. Norton, 1963.

Friendly, Michael, and David Gallen. *MLK and the FBI File*. New York: Carroll and Graf, 1993.

Furman, J. "The Origins of the Woman's Liberation Movement." *American Journal of Sociology* 78, no. 4.

Garrow, David J. *Bearing the Cross*. New York: Vintage Books, 1986.

————. *The FBI and Martin Luther King, Jr.* New York: Penguin Books, 1981.

————. *Protest at Selma*. New Haven: Yale University Press, 1978.

Gentry, Curt. *J. Edgar Hoover: The Man and the Secrets*. New York: Penguin Books, 1991.

Giddings, Paula. *When and Where I Enter: The Impact of Black Women on Race and Sex in America*. New York: Bantam Books, 1984.

Green, Johnny. "Did the FBI Kill Viola Liuzzo?" *Playboy*, October 1980.

————. "Return to Selma." *New Republic*, April 25, 1981.

Grier, William H., and Price M. Cobbs. *The Politics of Protest*. New York: Ballantine Books, 1969.

Hampton, Henry, and Steve Fayer. *Voices of Freedom: An Oral History of the Civil Rights Movement from the 1950s through the 1980s*. New York: Bantam Books, 1990.

Handlin, Oscar. *Fire Bell in the Night: The Crisis in Civil Rights*. Boston: Little, Brown., 1964.

Harris, Eddy L. *South of Haunted Dreams*. New York: Simon and Schuster, 1993.

Hernton, Calvin C. *Sex and Racism in America*. New York: Anchor Books, 1965.

Herron, Jerry. *Afterculture: Detroit and the Humiliation of History*. Detroit: Wayne State University Press, 1993.

Hole, Judith, and Ellen Levine. *Rebirth of Feminism*. New York: Quadrangle Books, 1971.

Howlett, Duncan. *No Greater Love: The James Reeb Story*. New York: Harper and Row, 1966.

Huie, William Bradford. *Three Lives for Mississippi*. New York: Signet Books, 1964.

Jamison, Kay Redfield. *Touched with Fire: Manic-Depressive Illness and the Artistic Temperament*. New York: Free Press, 1993.

Kasher, Steven. *The Civil Rights Movement: A Photographic History, 1954–68*. New York: Abbeville Press, 1997.

Kaufman, Dorothy B. *The First Freedom Ride: The Walter Bergman Story*. Detroit: American Civil Liberties Union Fund Press, 1989.

Kaufman, Jonathan. *Broken Alliance: The Turbulent Times between Blacks and Jews in America*. New York: New American Library, 1988.

Kempton, Murray. "Trial of a Klansman." *The New Republic*, May 22, 1965.

Kennedy, Stetson. *Jim Crow Guide: The Way It Was*. Boca Raton: Florida Atlantic University Press, 1992.

Killian, Lewis, and Charles Grigg. *Racial Crisis in America*. Englewood Cliffs, N.J.: Prentice Hall, 1964.

King, Charles, Jr. *Fire in My Bones*. Grand Rapids, Mich.: William B. Eerdmens, 1983.

King, Coretta Scott. *My Life with Martin Luther King, Jr*. Rev. ed. New York: Puffin Books, 1993.

King, Martin Luther, Jr. *Stride toward Freedom: The Montgomery Story*. San Francisco: Harper Collins, 1958.

———. *Where Do We Go from Here? Chaos or Community?* New York: Harper and Row, 1967.

————. *Why We Can't Wait.* New York: Mentor Books, 1964.

King, Mary. *Freedom Song: A Personal History of the Civil Rights Movement.* New York: William Morrow, 1987.

Leonard, G. B. "Journey of Conscience: Midnight Plane to Alabama." *The Nation,* May 10, 1965.

Lerner Gerda, ed. *Black Women in White America.* New York: Pantheon Books, 1972.

Lesher, Stephan. *George Wallace: American Populist.* New York: Addison-Wesley, 1994.

Levine, Ellen. *Freedom's Children: Young Civil Rights Activists Tell Their Own Stories.* New York: G. P. Putnam's Sons, 1993.

Levy, Peter, ed. *Let Freedom Ring: A Documentary History of the Modern Civil Rights Movement.* New York: Praeger, 1992.

Lewis, David L. *King: A Biography.* Urbana: University of Illinois Press, 1978.

Longenecker, Stephen L. *Selma's Peacemaker: Ralph Smeltzer and Civil Rights Mediation.* Philadelphia: Temple University Press, 1987.

Lyon, Danny. *Memories of the Southern Civil Rights Movement.* Chapel Hill: University of North Carolina Press, 1992.

McIlhany, William H. *Klandestine.* New Rochelle, N.Y.: Arlington House, 1975.

Mast, Robert H., ed. *Detroit Lives.* Philadelphia: Temple University Press, 1994.

Mecklin, John Moffatt. *The Ku Klux Klan: A Study of the American Mind.* New York: Harcourt Brace, 1924.

Mendelsohn, Jack. *The Martyrs: Sixteen Who Gave Their Lives for Racial Justice.* New York: Harper and Row, 1966.

————. *Why I Am a Unitarian Universalist.* New York: Thomas Nelson and Sons, 1964.

Metzger, Milton. *The Truth about the Ku Klux Klan.* New York: Franklin Watts, 1982.

Miller, Merle. *Lyndon: An Oral Biography.* New York: Ballantine Books, 1980.

Millet, Kate. *Sexual Politics.* Garden City, N.Y.: Doubleday, 1970.

Newfield, Jack. *Prophetic Minority.* New York: New American Library, 1966.

Novick, Michael. *White Lies, White Power: The Fight against White Supremacy and Reactionary Violence.* Monroe, Maine: Common Courage Press, 1995.

Oates, Stephen B. *Let the Trumpet Sound: The Life of Martin Luther King, Jr.* New York: Harper and Row, 1982.

Peck, James. *Freedom Ride.* New York: Simon and Schuster, 1962.

Persons, Albert. *The True Selma Story: Sex and Civil Rights.* Birmingham: Esco, 1965.

Pinckney, Alphonso. *The Committed: White Activists in the Civil Rights Movement.* New Haven, Conn.: College and University Press, 1968.

Poussaint, Alvin. "The Stresses of the White Female Worker in the Civil Rights Movement in the South," *American Journal of Psychiatry* 118.

Powers, Richard. *Secrecy and Power: The Life of J. Edgar Hoover.* New York: Free Press, 1987.

Powledge, Fred. *Free at Last? The Civil Rights Movement and the People Who Made It.* Boston: Little, Brown, 1991.

Raines, Howell. *My Soul Is Rested: Movement Days in the Deep South Remembered.* New York: Penguin Books, 1977.

Riley, David. "Who Is Jimmy Lee Jackson?" *The New Republic*, April 3, 1965.

Ripley, Anthony. "The Enigma of Mrs. Liuzzo." *Detroit News*, May 23, 1965.

Robinson, Amelia Boynton. *Bridge across Jordan.* Washington, D.C.: Schiller Institute Press, 1991.

Rose, Arnold. *The Negro in America.* Boston: Beacon Press, 1944.

Roszak, Betty, and Theodore Roszak, eds. *Masculine/Feminine: Readings in Sexual Mythology and the Liberation of Women.* New York: Harper, 1969.

Rothschild, Mary Aickin. *A Case of Black and White: Northern Volunteers and the Southern Freedom Summers, 1964–1965.* Westport, Conn.: Greenwood Press, 1982.

Rowan, Carl T. *The Coming Race War in America: A Wake-Up Call.* New York: Little, Brown, 1996.

Ruitenbeek, Hendrik M., ed. *Going Crazy: The Radical Therapy of R.D. Laing and Others.* New York: Bantam Books, 1972.

Sellers, Cleveland, with Robert Terrell. *The River of No Return.* New York: William Morrow, 1973.

Siegel, Beatrice. *Murder on the Highway: The Viola Liuzzo Story.* New York: Four Winds Press, 1993.

Silberman, Charles E. *Crisis in Black and White.* New York: Random House, 1964.

Silver, James. *Mississippi: The Closed Society.* New York: Harcourt, Brace and World, 1963.

Sitkoff, Harvard. *The Struggle for Black Equality, 1954–1980.* New York: Hill and Wang, 1981.

Smith, Kenneth, and Ira G. Zepp Jr. *Search for the Beloved Community: The Thinking of Martin Luther King, Jr.* Valley Forge, Pa.: Judson Press, 1974.

Spike, Robert W. *The Freedom Revolution and the Churches.* New York: Association Press, 1965.

Stanton, Bill. *Klanwatch: Bringing the Ku Klux Klan to Justice.* New York: Weidenfeld, 1991.

Theoharis, Athen G., and John Stuart Cox. *The Boss: J. Edgar Hoover and the Great American Inquisition.* Philadelphia: Temple University Press, 1988.

Thompson, Mary Lou, ed. *Voices of the New Feminism.* Boston: Beacon Press, 1970.

Tilson, Everett. *Segregation and the Bible.* New York: Abingdon Press, 1958.

Tornabene, Lyn. "Murder in Alabama." *Ladies Home Journal,* July 1965.

Tracy, James. *Direct Action: Radical Pacifism from the Union Eight to the Chicago Seven.* Chicago: University of Chicago Press, 1996.

Tucker, Richard K. *The Dragon and the Cross: The Rise and Fall of the Ku Klux Klan in Middle America.* Hamden, Conn.: Archon Books, 1991.

Wade, Wyn Craig. *The Fiery Cross.* New York: Simon and Schuster, 1987.

Ware, Vron. *Beyond the Pale: White Women, Racism and History.* London: Verso Press, 1992.

Warren, Robert Penn. *Segregation: The Inner Conflict in the South.* New York: Random House, 1956.

———. *Who Speaks for the Negro?* New York: Random House, 1965.

Washington, James M., ed. *I Have a Dream: Writings and Speeches That Changed the World.* San Francisco: Harper, 1986.

Watters, Pat. *Down to Now.* New York: Pantheon Books, 1971.

Watters, Pat, and Reese Cleghorn. *Climbing Jacob's Ladder: The Arrival of Negroes in Southern Politics.* New York: Harcourt, Brace and World, 1967.

Webb, Sheyann, and Rachel West Nelson. *Selma, Lord, Selma: Girlhood Memories of the Civil Rights Days.* Tuscaloosa: University of Alabama Press, 1980.

Weeks, David, and Jaime James. *Eccentrics.* New York: Villard, 1995.

Weisbrot, Robert. *Freedom Bound: A History of America's Civil Rights Movement.* New York: Penguin Books, 1990.

West, Guida, and Rhoda Lois Blumberg. *Women and Social Protest.* New York: Oxford University Press, 1990.

Whitehead, Don. *Attack on Terror: The FBI against the KKK.* New York: Funk and Wagnalls, 1970.

Wicker, Tom. *Tragic Failure: Racial Integration in America.* New York: William Morrow, 1996.

Widick, B. J. *Detroit: City of Race and Class Violence.* Rev. ed. Detroit: Wayne State University Press, 1989.

Williams, Juan. *Eyes on the Prize: America's Civil Rights Years: 1954–1965.* New York: Penguin Books, 1987.

Wills, Garry. *The Second Civil War: Arming for Armageddon*. New York: New American Library, 1968.

Wilson, James Q. *The Investigators: Managing FBI and Narcotics Agents*. New York: Basic Books, 1978.

Woodford, Frank B., and Arthur Woodford. *All Our Yesterdays: A Brief History of Detroit*. Detroit: Wayne State University Press, 1969.

Woodward, C. Vann. *The Strange Career of Jim Crow*. 3d rev. ed. New York: Oxford University Press, 1974.

Yarborough, Tinsely. *Judge Frank Johnson and Human Rights in Alabama*. Tuscaloosa: University of Alabama Press, 1981.

Yates, Gayle Graham. *What Women Want: The Ideas of the Movement*. Cambridge, Mass.: Harvard University Press, 1975.

Young, Andrew. *An Easy Burden: The Civil Rights Movement and the Transformation of America*. New York: Harper Collins, 1996.

Zinn, Howard. *SNCC: The New Abolitionists*. Boston: Beacon Press, 1964.

———. *The Southern Mystique*. New York: Simon and Schuster, 1959.

Zinsser, William. "I Realized Her Tears Were Becoming Part of the Memorial. . . ." *Smithsonian*, September 1991.

Index

Walker's Cafe (Selma), 47
Wallace, George C., 5, 28, 31, 123,
    125, 129, 163, 164, 166, 167, 169,
    170, 174, 175, 179
Watts riot (Los Angeles 1965),
    125–28, 179
Wayne State University, 73–74. *See
    also* Liuzzo, Viola, education
Webster, William, 189–90, 206
white activists, 102, 105–6, 143,
    173–75, 201
White Citizens' Council, 32, 33, 35,
    123, 127, 129, 153, 166
white privilege. *See* Southern Way of
    Life
white supremacy, 33, 48, 117, 121–
    22, 125, 127, 149–51, 153, 158

white women (1965), 33, 97, 107–9,
    117, 140–43, 147, 152–53,
    172–73
Wilkins, Collie Leroy, Jr., 44–46,
    49–51, 111, 112, 116–22, 128,
    130, 153, 188, 192, 193, 199, 203,
    205, 206; death of, 212; trials,
    111–22, 126–30
Williams, Hosea, 37, 58, 194, 197,
    200–201
Witness Protection Program. *See*
    Federal Witness Protection
    Program

Young, Andrew, 37, 163, 165, 201